The Gallup Poll

Public Opinion 1992

Other Gallup Poll Publications Available from Scholarly Resources

The Gallup Poll: Public Opinion Annual Series

1991 (ISBN 0-8420-2397-6)
1990 (ISBN 0-8420-2368-2)
1989 (ISBN 0-8420-2344-5)
1988 (ISBN 0-8420-2330-5)
1987 (ISBN 0-8420-2292-9)
1986 (ISBN 0-8420-2274-0)
1985 (ISBN 0-8420-2249-X)
1984 (ISBN 0-8420-2234-1)
1983 (ISBN 0-8420-2220-1)
1982 (ISBN 0-8420-2214-7)
1981 (ISBN 0-8420-2200-7)
1980 (ISBN 0-8420-2181-7)
1979 (ISBN 0-8420-2170-1)
1978 (ISBN 0-8420-2159-0)
1972–77 (ISBN 0-8420-2129-9, 2 vols.)
1935–71 (ISBN 0-394-47270-5, 3 vols.)

International Polls

The International Gallup Polls: Public Opinion, 1979
ISBN 0-8420-2180-9 (1981)

The International Gallup Polls: Public Opinion, 1978
ISBN 0-8420-2162-0 (1980)

The Gallup International Public Opinion Polls: France, 1939, 1944–1975
2 volumes ISBN 0-394-40998-1 (1976)

The Gallup International Public Opinion Polls: Great Britain, 1937–1975
2 volumes ISBN 0-394-40992-2 (1976)

The Gallup Poll

Public Opinion 1992

George Gallup, Jr.

Scholarly Resources Inc.
Wilmington, Delaware

ACKNOWLEDGMENTS

The preparation of this volume has involved the staff of both the Gallup Poll and Scholarly Resources Inc., and their contributions are gratefully acknowledged. I also wish to thank Professor Fred L. Israel of the City College of New York, who was the principal coordinator.

G.G., Jr.

The paper used in this publication meets the minimum requirements of the American National Standard for permanence of paper for printed library materials, Z39.48, 1984.

First published 1993
Printed in the United States of America

Scholarly Resources Inc.
104 Greenhill Avenue
Wilmington, DE 19805-1897

Library of Congress Catalog Card Number: 79-56557
International Standard Serial Number: 0195-962X
International Standard Book Number: 0-8420-2463-8

CONTENTS

DESIGN OF THE SAMPLE

The Gallup Poll gathers information both in personal interviews and in interviews conducted by telephone. Although the method for selecting households in which to conduct interviews is different, the goal is the same: to provide representative samples of adults living in the United States. In either case the standard size for Gallup Polls is 1000 interviews. More interviews are conducted in specific instances where greater survey accuracy is desired.

Design of the Sample for Personal Surveys

The design of the sample for personal (face-to-face) surveys is that of a replicated area probability sample down to the block level in the case of urban areas and to segments of townships in the case of rural areas.

After stratifying the nation geographically and by size of community according to information derived from the most recent census, over 350 different sampling locations are selected on a mathematically random basis from within cities, towns, and counties that, in turn, have been selected on a mathematically random basis.

The interviewers are given no leeway in selecting the areas in which they are to conduct their interviews. Each interviewer is given a map on which a specific starting point is marked and is instructed to contact households according to a predetermined travel pattern. At each occupied dwelling unit, the interviewer selects respondents by following a systematic procedure that is repeated until the assigned number of interviews has been completed.

Design of the Sample for Telephone Surveys

The samples of telephone numbers used in telephone interview surveys are based on a random digit stratified probability design. The sampling procedure involves selecting listed "seed" numbers, deleting the last two digits, and randomly generating two digits to replace them. This procedure provides telephone samples that are geographically representative. The random digit aspect, since it allows for the inclusion of unlisted and unpublished numbers, protects the samples from "listing bias"—the unrepresentativeness of telephone samples that can occur if the distinctive households whose telephone numbers are unlisted or unpublished are excluded from the sample.

Weighting Procedures

After the survey data have been collected and processed, each respondent is assigned a weight so that the demographic characteristics of the total weighted sample of respondents match the latest estimates of the demographic characteristics of the adult population available from the U.S. Census Bureau. Telephone surveys are weighted to match the characteristics of the adult population living in households with access to a telephone. The weighting of personal interview data includes a factor to improve the representation of the kind of people who are less likely to be found at home.

The procedures described above are designed to produce samples approximating the adult civilian population (18 and older) living in private households (that is, excluding those in prisons, hospitals, hotels, religious and educational institutions, and those living on reservations or military bases)—and in the case of telephone surveys, households with access to a telephone. Survey percentages may be applied to census estimates of the size of these populations to project percentages into numbers of people. The manner in which the sample is drawn also produces a sample that approximates the distribution of private households in the United States. Therefore, survey results also can be projected to numbers of households.

Sampling Tolerances

In interpreting survey results, it should be borne in mind that all sample surveys are subject to sampling error—that is, the extent to which the results may differ from what would be obtained if the whole population surveyed had been interviewed. The size of such sampling errors depends largely on the number of interviews.

The following tables may be used in estimating the sampling error of any percentage. The computed allowances have taken into account the effect of the sample design upon sampling error. They may be interpreted as indicating the range (plus or minus the figure shown) within which the results of repeated samplings in the same time period could be expected to vary, 95 percent of the time, assuming the same sampling procedure, the same interviewers, and the same questionnaire.

Table A shows how much allowance should be made for the sampling error of a percentage. Let us say a reported percentage is 33 for a group that includes 1000 respondents. First, we go to the row headed "percentages near 30" and then go across to the column headed "1000." The number here is 4, which means that the 33 percent obtained in the sample is subject to a sampling error of plus or minus 4 points. Another way of saying it is that very probably (95 chances out of 100) the average of repeated samplings would be somewhere between 29 and 37, with the most likely figure being the 33 obtained.

In comparing survey results in two samples, such as for men and women, the question arises as to how large must a difference between them be before one can be reasonably sure that it reflects a real difference. In Tables B and C, the number of points that must be allowed for in such comparisons is indicated. Table B is for percentages near 20 or 80, and Table C is for percentages near 50. For percentages in between, the error to be allowed for is between those shown in the two tables.

TABLE A

Recommended Allowance for Sampling Error of a Percentage

	In Percentage Points (at 95 in 100 confidence level)* Sample Size					
	1000	750	600	400	200	100
Percentages near 10	2	3	3	4	5	7
Percentages near 20	3	4	4	5	7	9
Percentages near 30	4	4	4	6	8	10
Percentages near 40	4	4	5	6	8	11
Percentages near 50	4	4	5	6	8	11
Percentages near 60	4	4	5	6	8	11
Percentages near 70	4	4	4	6	8	10
Percentages near 80	3	4	4	5	7	9
Percentages near 90	2	3	3	4	5	7

*The chances are 95 in 100 that the sampling error is not larger than the figures shown.

TABLE B

Recommended Allowance for Sampling Error of the Difference

	In Percentage Points (at 95 in 100 confidence level)* Percentages near 20 or percentages near 80			
	750	600	400	200
Size of sample				
750	5			
600	5	6		
400	6	6	7	
200	8	8	8	10

TABLE C

	Percentages near 50			
	750	600	400	200
Size of sample				
750	6			
600	7	7		
400	7	8	8	
200	10	10	10	12

*The chances are 95 in 100 that the sampling error is not larger than the figures shown.

Here is an example of how the tables would be used: Let us say that 50 percent of men respond a certain way and 40 percent of women also respond that way, for a difference of 10 percentage points between them. Can we say with any assurance that the 10-point difference reflects a real difference between men and women on the question? The sample contains approximately 600 men and 600 women.

Since the percentages are near 50, we consult Table C, and since the two samples are about 600 persons each, we look for the number in the column headed "600" that is also in the row designated "600." We find the number 7 here. This means that the allowance for error should be 7 points, and that in concluding that the percentage among men is somewhere between 3 and 17 points higher than the percentage among women, we should be wrong only about 5 percent of the time. In other words, we can conclude with considerable confidence that a difference exists in the direction observed and that it amounts to at least 3 percentage points.

If, in another case, men's responses amount to 22 percent and women's 24 percent, we consult Table B because these percentages are near 20. We look in the column headed "600" that is also in the row headed "600" and see that the number is 6. Obviously, then, the 2-point difference is inconclusive.

RECORD OF GALLUP POLL ACCURACY

Year	Gallup Final Survey*		Election Result*		Deviation
1992**	49.0%	Clinton	43.2%	Clinton	+5.8
1990	54.0	Democratic	54.1	Democratic	-0.1
1988	56.0	Bush	53.9	Bush	+2.1
1984	59.0	Reagan	59.2	Reagan	-0.2
1982	55.0	Democratic	56.1	Democratic	-1.1
1980	47.0	Reagan	50.8	Reagan	-3.8
1978	55.0	Democratic	54.6	Democratic	+0.4
1976	48.0	Carter	50.0	Carter	-2.0
1974	60.0	Democratic	58.9	Democratic	+1.1
1972	62.0	Nixon	61.8	Nixon	+0.2
1970	53.0	Democratic	54.3	Democratic	-1.3
1968	43.0	Nixon	43.5	Nixon	-0.5
1966	52.5	Democratic	51.9	Democratic	+0.6
1964	64.0	Johnson	61.3	Johnson	+2.7
1962	55.5	Democratic	52.7	Democratic	+2.8
1960	51.0	Kennedy	50.1	Kennedy	+0.9
1958	57.0	Democratic	56.5	Democratic	+0.5
1956	59.5	Eisenhower	57.8	Eisenhower	+1.7
1954	51.5	Democratic	52.7	Democratic	-1.2
1952	51.0	Eisenhower	55.4	Eisenhower	-4.4
1950	51.0	Democratic	50.3	Democratic	+0.7
1948	44.5	Truman	49.9	Truman	-5.4
1946	58.0	Republican	54.3	Republican	+3.7
1944	51.5	Roosevelt	53.3	Roosevelt	-1.8
1942	52.0	Democratic	48.0	Democratic	+4.0
1940	52.0	Roosevelt	55.0	Roosevelt	-3.0

1938	54.0	Democratic	50.8	Democratic	+3.2
1936	55.7	Roosevelt	62.5	Roosevelt	-6.8

NOTE: No congressional poll was taken in 1986.
*The figure shown is the winner's percentage of the Democratic-Republican vote except in the elections of 1948, 1968, and 1976. Because the Thurmond and Wallace voters in 1948 were largely split-offs from the normally Democratic vote, they were made a part of the final Gallup Poll preelection estimate of the division of the vote. In 1968, Wallace's candidacy was supported by such a large minority that he was clearly a major candidate, and the 1968 percentages are based on the total Nixon-Humphrey-Wallace vote. In 1976, because of interest in McCarthy's candidacy and its potential effect on the Carter vote, the final Gallup Poll estimate included Carter, Ford, McCarthy, and all other candidates as a group.
**The Ross Perot candidacy created an additional source of error in estimating the 1992 presidential vote. There was no historical precedent for Perot, an independent candidate who was accorded equal status to the major party nominees in the presidential debates and had a record advertising budget. Gallup's decision to allocate none of the undecided vote to Perot, based on past performances of third-party and independent candidates, resulted in the overestimation of votes for Bill Clinton.

Trend in Deviation

Elections	*Average Error*
1952–1992	1.6
1936–1950	3.6

Average Deviation for 28
National Elections.................................... 2.2 percentage points

CHRONOLOGY

This chronology is provided to enable the reader to relate poll results to specific events, or series of events, that may have influenced public opinion.

1991

	The Gulf War (Operation Desert Storm) dominates the news for the first half of the year.
	Throughout 1991 state governments across the nation face increased financial shortfalls, with the alternative being either deep cuts in spending or increases in taxes. Nationally, economic news remains dismal as the country slips further into a recession.

1992

January 1–10	George Bush tours Australia and Asia. At a state dinner in Tokyo on January 9, the president collapses.
January 3	Among the Democratic candidates for president, Arkansas Governor Bill Clinton raised the most money in 1991.
January 8	Governor Douglas Wilder of Virginia withdraws from the race for the 1992 Democratic presidential nomination.

January 10	The Labor Department reports the unemployment rate at the end of 1991 at 7.1%, a five-and-one-half-year high.
January 15	The European Community recognizes the independence of Croatia and Slovenia, thus signaling the end of Yugoslavia's seventy-five-year-old federation.
January 17	The media report allegations that Democratic candidate Clinton has had an extramarital affair. Radio and television stations play tape recordings of telephone conversations purporting to be between Clinton and his mistress.
January 19	Five Democratic presidential candidates debate in New Hampshire: Clinton, former California Governor Jerry Brown, Senator Tom Harkin of Iowa, Senator Bob Kerrey of Nebraska, and former Massachusetts Senator Paul Tsongas.
January 22	The Commerce Department reports that 1991 new housing starts dropped to their lowest level in forty-six years.
January 23	Secretary of State James Baker announces that U.S. military planes will begin an emergency airlift of food and medicine to the Commonwealth of Independent States (the former Soviet Union).
January 27	Macy's, one of the nation's largest retailers, files for bankruptcy protection.
January 29	President Bush sends Congress a $1.52-trillion budget for fiscal year 1993.

January 31	The Commerce Department reports that 1991 was the worst year since 1982 for sales of new houses.
February 6	The *Wall Street Journal* publishes an article alleging that Governor Clinton avoided military service during the Vietnam War by misleading his draft board.
February 9	Former President Ronald Reagan endorses President Bush's reelection bid.
February 12	President Bush announces his candidacy for reelection.
February 18	In the New Hampshire Republican primary, Pat Buchanan makes a strong showing, with 37% of the vote compared to President Bush's 53%. In the Democratic primary, Tsongas leads with 33%. A write-in vote for New York Governor Mario Cuomo barely reaches 4%.
February 21	The United Nations Security Council unanimously approves sending 14,000 peace-keeping troops to Croatia to protect the ethnic Serb minority.
February 24	General Motors, the world's largest industrial corporation, reports for 1991 a $4.45-billion loss, the highest ever for an American company.
February 25	Senator Kerrey wins the South Dakota Democratic primary. President Bush wins the state's republican primary, but one third of GOP voters chose "uncommitted."
March 2	The American Bankruptcy Institute states that individual and corporate bankruptcies set a record high in 1991.

March 3	In seven Democratic presidential primaries, Clinton and Tsongas each win states seen as crucial to their campaigns. In three GOP primaries, President Bush wins, but Buchanan continues to draw about one third of the Republican votes.
March 6	The unemployment rate rose to 7.3% in February.
March 10	Governor Clinton sweeps six southern Democratic primaries. Both Clinton and President Bush move to a commanding lead in delegates to their respective national party conventions.
March 19	Tsongas withdraws from the Democratic presidential race.
April 7	Clinton wins 51% of the vote in New York's Democratic primary.
	The European Community and the United States recognize the independence of Bosnia-Herzegovina. The United States also recognizes Croatia and Slovenia. Ethnic fighting engulfs Bosnia.
April 9	The Conservative party of British Prime Minister John Major is reelected.
April 13	Officials of the AFL-CIO endorse Clinton for president.
April 17	The Federal Reserve Board reports that the economy grew at a 2% annual rate in the first quarter of 1992.

April 21	H. Ross Perot announces that he is considering a bid as an independent presidential candidate. He continues to receive an increasing amount of media attention as national polls show him gaining on Bush and Clinton.
April 28	Both President Bush and Governor Clinton win primaries in Pennsylvania.
	The Commerce Department reports that the sale of new houses dropped sharply in March, the steepest decline since October 1982.
April 29–May 3	Riots erupt in Los Angeles after a jury acquits white police officers in the beating of a black motorist, which was filmed on videotape. The violence is the worst since the August 1965 Watts riots in the same city. Forty-eight people are killed, and property damage is estimated at $1 billion. The governor declares a state of emergency in Los Angeles. A dusk-to-dawn curfew imposed on April 30 is lifted on May 4.
May 7–16	The U.S. space shuttle *Endeavour* carries out a dramatic mission in which its crew captures a wayward communications satellite and places it in the proper orbit.
May 19	President Bush and Governor Clinton easily win primaries in Oregon and Washington.
	Housing starts continued to plunge during April.
May 26	After primaries in Kentucky and Arkansas, Clinton is only 300 delegates short of the 2,145 needed to win the Democratic presidential nomination.

May 30	The UN Security Council votes sweeping international sanctions against Yugoslavia as a means of ending the bloodshed in Bosnia-Herzegovina.
June 2	Governor Clinton wins primaries in six states and gains enough delegates to assure him the Democratic presidential nomination at his party's national convention.
June 3	Perot reveals that he has hired Hamilton Jordan and Ed Rollins as political consultants, thus virtually announcing his independent candidacy for president.
June 3–14	The Earth Summit is held in Rio de Janeiro, Brazil. Delegates from 178 nations (including President Bush) agree on several landmark pacts intended to reconcile global economic development with environmental protection.
June 5	Unemployment jumped to 7.5% in May, the highest since August 1984.
June 9	Vice President Dan Quayle attacks the so-called cultural elite who, he says, ignore family values, religion, and patriotism. Three weeks earlier Quayle had criticized the television series "Murphy Brown" for portraying the title character as having a child out of wedlock.
June 16–17	President Bush and Russian President Boris Yeltsin hold the first Russian-American summit in Washington, DC.
June 18	Prompted by the Los Angeles riots, Congress passes emergency aid to cities. President Bush will sign the billion-dollar urban aid bill on June 22.

June 20	Czech and Slovak leaders agree to dissolve Czechoslovakia on January 1, 1993.
July 2	The Federal Reserve Board cuts its key interest rates in an attempt to boost economic recovery. This action comes after government statistics show that the unemployment rate rose to 7.8% in June.
July 16	Governor Clinton accepts the Democratic presidential nomination at the party's national convention in New York. He chooses Senator Al Gore of Tennessee as his running mate.
	Perot declares an end to his efforts to seek the presidency as an independent candidate.
July 17–22	Buoyed by a surge in public-opinion polls, Clinton and Gore lead a campaign bus tour from New York to St. Louis.
July 19–24	The Eighth International Conference on AIDS is held in Amsterdam.
July 26	The employment-rights provisions of a 1990 federal law banning discrimination against disabled people becomes effective.
August 2	The *Orange County Register*, a conservative Southern California newspaper, calls for President Bush to abandon his reelection effort.
August 6	President Bush asks the UN Security Council to authorize the use of force to protect deliveries of food and medicine to war-torn Sarajevo.
August 7	The unemployment rate declined slightly in July to 7.7%.

August 12	The United States, Canada, and Mexico draft the North American Free-Trade Agreement, which would eliminate tariff restrictions among the three nations over the next fifteen years.
August 13	Secretary of State Baker resigns to oversee President Bush's reelection campaign.
August 20	President Bush and Vice President Quayle are renominated by the Republican national convention meeting in Houston.
August 24–26	Hurricane Andrew ravages southern Florida and Louisiana.
August 26	The United States and its allies order the Iraqi government to halt all aircraft flights over southern Iraq in order to protect Shiite Moslems in the region from attack.
September 4	The August unemployment rate fell to 7.6%.
September 22	President Bush vetoes legislation that would require large corporations to grant unpaid family and medical leaves to their employees. Congress upholds the veto.
October 1	Perot reenters the presidential race as an independent candidate.
October 2	The unemployment rate dropped to 7.5% in September.
October 11	The first in a series of televised presidential debates is held between President Bush, Clinton, and Perot.

October 13	Quayle, Gore, and independent candidate James Stockdale take part in the televised vice presidential debate.
October 15	The second televised presidential debate between President Bush, Clinton, and Perot takes place.
October 19	The third and final televised presidential debate is held between President Bush, Clinton, and Perot.
October 28	The federal budget deficit for fiscal year 1992, which ended on September 30, was $290 billion, the highest government deficit ever.
November 3	Arkansas Governor Bill Clinton is elected president of the United States, thus ending twelve consecutive years of Republican control of the White House. He and his running mate, Al Gore, win thirty-two states in all regions of the country. Clinton, born in 1946, will become the first president born after the end of World War II.
November 6	President-elect Clinton names the leaders of his transition team.
	The unemployment rate in October dropped to 7.4%.
November 16	The UN Security Council authorizes a naval blockade against Yugoslavia.
December 3	The Security Council votes to send a U.S.-led military force to Somalia to safeguard the delivery of food to thousands of starving people.

December 9	U.S. Marines arrive in the Somali capital of Mogadishu.
December 14–15	President-elect Clinton hosts an economic conference in Little Rock, Arkansas, attended by more than three hundred economists and business and labor leaders.
December 15	IBM announces plans to eliminate 25,000 jobs in 1993.

GALLUP REGIONS

Sections 1 and 2 = East
Sections 3 and 4 = Midwest
Sections 5 and 6 = South
Sections 7 and 8 = West

Section 1 New England
Maine
New Hampshire
Vermont
Massachusetts
Rhode Island
Connecticut

Section 2 Middle Atlantic
New York
New Jersey
Pennsylvania
Maryland
Delaware
West Virginia
District of Columbia

Section 3 East Central
Ohio
Michigan
Indiana
Illinois

Section 4 West Central
Wisconsin
Minnesota
Iowa
Missouri
North Dakota
South Dakota
Nebraska
Kansas

Section 5 Southeast
Virginia
North Carolina
South Carolina
Georgia
Florida
Kentucky
Tennessee
Alabama
Mississippi

Section 6 Southwest
Arkansas
Louisiana
Oklahoma
Texas

Section 7 Rocky Mountain
Montana
Arizona
Colorado
Idaho
Wyoming
Utah
Nevada
New Mexico

Section 8 Pacific
California
Oregon
Washington
Hawaii
Alaska

Johnson (1963)	**	74	–
Eisenhower (1955)	78†	75	77

*Carter approval inflated due to seizure of U.S. hostages in Iran
**Took office in November 1963 to complete unexpired term of John F. Kennedy
†Based on November approval

JANUARY 12
PRESIDENT BUSH—AN ANALYSIS

Interviewing Date: 12/12–15/91
Survey #GO 222028

Presidential Approval Ratings
(Average First-term Ratings of Postwar Presidents Who Ran for Reelection)

	First year	*Second year*	*Third year*	*Fourth year*
Bush	64%	68%	71%	–
Reagan	58	44	44	56
Carter	62	46	37	39
Ford	*	54	43	48
Nixon	61	57	50	57
Johnson	**	–	–	74
Eisenhower	68	66	71	73

*Completed unexpired term of Richard Nixon
**Completed unexpired term of John F. Kennedy

Presidential Approval Ratings
(In Fourth Quarter Prior to Reelection Year)

	October	*December*	*Average*
Bush (1991)	65%	50%	57%
Reagan (1983)	45	54	51
Carter (1979)	29	54*	39
Ford (1975)	47	39	43
Nixon (1971)	52	50	50

Bush's Decline from His Post-Gulf War Approval Rating

	Approval	*Point change from previous quarter*
End of 4th Quarter (late Dec. 1991)	50%	-16
End of 3d Quarter (late Sept. 1991)	66	-6
End of 2d Quarter (late June 1991)	72	-10
End of 1st Quarter (late March 1991)	82	+19
Gulf War Victory (Feb. 28–March 3)	89	–
End of 4th Quarter (late Dec. 1990)	63	–

Note: Eight months after he scored the highest public approval rating on record, George Bush's reelection seems far from certain. An analysis of Gallup Poll presidential approval figures shows that while his ratings overall compare favorably with those of his predecessors, the recent decline in approval puts him into the danger zone in terms of his reelection prospects. After scoring an all-time high of 89% at the end of the Gulf War last March—the highest approval rating ever received by any president in Gallup's annals—Bush finished the year 1991 with his lowest approval rating ever: 50% in a mid-December Gallup Poll.

When compared with those of his postwar predecessors, President Bush's approval ratings for his first three years in office are very impressive. In fact, Bush is the first president since Dwight Eisenhower whose average approval rating for his third year surpassed his first-year average. Bush scored

64% in 1989, his initial year in office. His average rating improved to 68% in 1990 and rose further to 71% in 1991. Ronald Reagan, Jimmy Carter, and Richard Nixon all saw their yearly averages decline over a similar period. Eisenhower's average rating for his third year in office (71%) equaled Bush's 1991 average. Eisenhower then went on to defeat Adlai Stevenson in 1956 by a wide margin.

Unfortunately for President Bush, the spectacular ratings he received during the Gulf War do not seem relevant today. Having fallen to 50% in December, Bush must find a way to reverse the downward trend or risk defeat next November. Achieving an approval rating of at least 50% during an election year has proved critical to electoral success. Reagan, Nixon, and Eisenhower all scored average approval ratings above 50% in their fourth year in office, when each easily won reelection. Similarly, Lyndon Johnson, who had only recently filled John F. Kennedy's shoes, had an average approval of 74% during 1964. In contrast, both Carter and Gerald Ford, who ran unsuccessfully, had approval ratings that averaged below 50% during their reelection campaign year (39% and 48%, respectively).

The president's political fortunes changed rather abruptly over the past few months. During the last quarter of 1991, Bush approval dropped from 65% in October to 50% in December. This is the sharpest decline during a three-month period since November 1986, when Reagan's image was damaged by news of the Iran-*contra* scandal. Reagan's approval dropped from 63% to 47% in the last quarter of 1986.

No recent president has gone into an election year with such a sharp drop in ratings. The last president to lose significant approval at a comparable point in the election cycle is Ford, whose approval fell by 8 percentage points during the last quarter of 1975. Despite regaining some popularity, he went on to lose his bid for reelection to Carter the following year.

Carter's ratings during a comparable time frame did not reflect his true prospects for reelection. His ratings had been consistently low over the years but shot up 25 percentage points during December 1979 as the public rallied around the president during the U.S. hostage crisis in Iran. Approval dropped below 40% during the following year, and Reagan won the election.

Bush's all-time low presidential approval rating was recorded in the last Gallup survey of 1991, when it dropped 16 percentage points and reached the critical 50% mark. The current economic climate is at least partially responsible for this decrease. A Gallup Poll conducted in early December found that only 22% of Americans approve of the way that Bush is handling economic conditions. Barring a war or international crisis, the most accurate barometer of his reelection prospects is likely to be the state of the economy over the next nine months.

JANUARY 18
ABORTION

Interviewing Date: 12/12–15/91
Survey #GO 222028

In its 1973 Roe v. Wade *decision, the Supreme Court ruled that states cannot place restrictions on a woman's right to an abortion during the first three months of pregnancy. Would you like to see this ruling overturned, or not?*

Yes	30%
No	64
No opinion	6

	Yes	*No*	*No opinion*
By Sex			
Male	30%	65%	5%
Female	30	63	7
By Ethnic Background			
White	31	63	6
Nonwhite	24	71	5
Black	25	71	4
By Education			
College Graduate	20	78	2
College Incomplete	25	72	3

High-School Graduate	33	58	9
Less Than High-School Graduate	39	50	11
By Region			
East	28	66	6
Midwest	30	61	9
South	31	64	5
West	30	65	5
By Age			
18–29 Years	24	74	2
30–49 Years	31	65	4
50 Years and Over	33	55	12
By Household Income			
$50,000 and Over	24	74	2
$30,000–$49,999	28	66	6
$20,000–$29,999	30	65	5
Under $20,000	36	57	7
By Politics			
Republicans	32	62	6
Democrats	28	65	7
Independents	30	66	4
By Religion			
Protestants	34	60	6
Catholics	27	68	5
By Political Ideology			
Liberal	26	69	5
Moderate	17	80	3
Conservative	38	57	5
By Bush Approval			
Approve	31	63	6
Disapprove	28	66	6

Selected National Trend

	Yes	*No*	*No opinion*
1991			
September	36%	57%	7%
July	37	56	7
May	42	52	6
1989			
July	34	58	8
April	39	51	10
1988			
December	37	58	5

Do you favor or oppose a law requiring a pregnant woman to notify her husband if she decides to have an abortion?

Favor	63%
Oppose	34
No opinion	3

	Favor	*Oppose*	*No opinion*
By Sex			
Male	69%	28%	3%
Female	57	39	4
By Ethnic Background			
White	63	34	3
Nonwhite	63	32	5
Black	70	25	5
By Education			
College Graduate	51	47	2
College Incomplete	52	45	3
High-School Graduate	69	26	5
Less Than High-School Graduate	79	20	1
By Region			
East	61	35	4
Midwest	69	29	2
South	68	30	2
West	50	43	7
By Age			
18–29 Years	59	39	2
30–49 Years	60	38	2
50 Years and Over	70	25	5
By Household Income			
$50,000 and Over	51	47	2
$30,000–$49,999	64	33	3
$20,000–$29,999	62	32	6
Under $20,000	69	27	4
By Politics			
Republicans	69	29	2
Democrats	55	40	5
Independents	64	33	3

By Religion			
Protestants	67	30	3
Catholics	63	32	5
By Political Ideology			
Liberal	53	44	3
Moderate	39	53	8
Conservative	71	28	1
By Bush Approval			
Approve	72	27	1
Disapprove	54	41	5

Note: The Supreme Court and public opinion appear to be moving in different directions on the abortion issue. A recent Gallup Poll finds that public support for maintaining the legal status quo on abortion is at its highest level in three years: nearly two thirds (64%) of Americans oppose an overturn of *Roe v. Wade*, the 1973 Supreme Court decision establishing a legal right to abortion. Only three in ten (30%) would like to see the current Court reverse that decision.

In six Gallup surveys taken since December 1988, the percentage of respondents opposing *Roe*'s reversal did not reach 60%. Last September, 57% said that they opposed a reversal, while 36% took the opposite view.

Since its 1989 *Webster v. Reproductive Services* decision, which permitted states further to restrict abortion, the Rehnquist Court has chipped away at earlier Courts' protection of abortion rights. The recent addition of another conservative justice, Clarence Thomas, increases the chances that *Roe v. Wade* soon will be completely overturned. The Supreme Court may announce in January whether it will review a Pennsylvania law restricting abortion, written after the *Webster* decision. That would give the Court its first opportunity in this presidential year to reverse *Roe*.

Although abortion is often seen as a women's issue, similar majorities of men (65%) and women (63%) oppose reversing *Roe*. The largest differences in opinion on this issue are seen by education and ideology. Only one half (50%) of those who did not finish high school oppose a reversal, compared with three quarters (78%) of college graduates. Less than six in ten (57%) political conservatives oppose changing the legal status quo on abortion, compared with seven in ten (69%) political liberals.

Despite their expressions of support for keeping *Roe v. Wade* in place, surveys have found high levels of public support for certain types of restrictions on abortion. One restriction included in the Pennsylvania law is spousal notification—the requirement that a woman's husband be told that she is planning to have an abortion. The public favors such a law by a 63%-to-34% margin. Not surprisingly, a higher proportion of men (69%) than women (57%) favors it.

JANUARY 19
PRESIDENT BUSH/PRESIDENTIAL CANDIDATES

Interviewing Date: 1/3–6/92*
Survey #GO 222034

Do you approve or disapprove of the way George Bush is handling his job as president?

Approve	46%
Disapprove	47
No opinion	7

	Approve	*Dis-approve*	*No opinion*
By Sex			
Male	47%	46%	7%
Female	45	47	8
By Ethnic Background			
White	49	44	7
Nonwhite	26	64	10
Black	20	70	10
By Education			
College Graduate	50	45	5
College Incomplete	48	45	7
High-School Graduate	46	46	8
Less Than High-School Graduate	38	54	8

*Gallup survey for CNN/*USA Today*

By Region			
East	41	52	7
Midwest	51	42	7
South	46	46	8
West	46	48	6
By Age			
18–29 Years	56	39	5
30–49 Years	47	45	8
50–64 Years	40	55	5
65 Years and Over	36	53	11
By Household Income			
$50,000 and Over	56	39	5
$30,000–$49,999	53	42	5
$20,000–$29,999	43	51	6
Under $20,000	38	52	10
By Politics			
Republicans	79	17	4
Democrats	20	74	6
Independents	43	47	10
By Religion			
Protestants	49	43	8
Catholics	45	50	5
By Political Ideology			
Liberal	35	59	6
Moderate	46	47	7
Conservative	54	40	6

Selected National Trend

	Approve	*Dis-approve*	*No opinion*
1991			
December 5–8	52%	42%	6%
November 21–24	52	39	9
November 14–17	56	36	8
November 7–10	56	36	8
October 31–November 3	59	33	8
October 24–27	62	29	9
October 17–20	66	26	8
October 10–13	66	28	6
October 3–6	65	27	8

Please tell me whether you approve or disapprove of the way George Bush is handling each of the following issues and problems:

Foreign affairs?

Approve..........64%
Disapprove..........31
No opinion..........5

Race relations?

Approve..........55%
Disapprove..........32
No opinion..........13

Drug abuse?

Approve..........54%
Disapprove..........40
No opinion..........6

Environment?

Approve..........49%
Disapprove..........41
No opinion..........10

Foreign trade?

Approve..........46%
Disapprove..........46
No opinion..........8

Education?

Approve..........46%
Disapprove..........49
No opinion..........5

Taxes?

Approve..........32%
Disapprove..........63
No opinion..........5

Unemployment?

Approve..........27%
Disapprove..........68
No opinion..........5

Health care?

Approve	26%
Disapprove	66
No opinion	8

Poverty and homelessness?

Approve	26%
Disapprove	68
No opinion	6

Federal budget deficit?

Approve	25%
Disapprove	68
No opinion	7

Economy?

Approve	24%
Disapprove	73
No opinion	3

Asked of registered voters: If George Bush runs for reelection this year, in general are you more likely to vote for Bush or for the Democratic party's candidate for president? [Those who were undecided were asked: As of today, do you lean more to Bush or to the Democratic party's candidate for president?]

Bush	47%
Democratic candidate	45
Undecided; other	8

Selected National Trend

	Bush	*Democratic candidate*	*Undecided; other*
1991			
December 5–8	52%	38%	10%
November 21–24	53	40	7

Asked of registered Democrats and those who lean Democratic: I will read off the names of six Democratic candidates for president. After I read all six names, please tell me which one you would like to see nominated as the Democratic party's candidate for president. [Those who were undecided were asked: As of today, to which Democratic candidate do you lean most?]

Jerry Brown	21%
Bill Clinton	17
Bob Kerrey	11
Tom Harkin	9
Douglas Wilder*	9
Paul Tsongas	6
Undecided; other	27

*Wilder withdrew from the Democratic race after the January survey had begun.

Asked of registered Republicans and those who lean Republican: I will read off the names of three Republican candidates for president. After I read all three names, please tell me which one you would like to see nominated as the Republican party's candidate for president. [Those who were undecided were asked: As of today, to which Republican candidate do you lean most?]

George Bush	85%
Pat Buchanan	10
David Duke	3
Undecided; other	2

Note: As the election year begins, George Bush's approval rating has dipped below 50% in the Gallup Poll for the first time in his presidency. This continues a downward trend from last spring that accelerated in the final months of 1991. Americans are now closely divided in their evaluations of the president's performance: 46% approve, while 47% disapprove. As recently as last October, two thirds (66%) gave Bush positive marks.

The historical record does not suggest, however, that a single approval rating below 50% is a strong predictor of defeat for an incumbent president. In January 1972, Richard Nixon, at 49%, also fell below the halfway mark, but he was able to improve his ratings over the next few months and went on to win reelection in a landslide.

Of greater importance than Bush's current rating is the fact that he is the first president in forty years of polling to go into an election with declining approval ratings. To win in November, history suggests that Bush must find a way to move his approval figures back up to the 50% level. The last two incumbent presidents to be rejected by the voters—Jimmy Carter and Gerald Ford—both averaged below 50% in approval during their election years.

One year ago the Persian Gulf crisis sent Bush's approval ratings on an upward course that culminated in a record 89% last March. Since that time, the political environment has changed dramatically. Now, Bush receives very negative approval ratings for his handling of four of the five issues seen as most important by the public. These include unemployment (27%), health care (26%), the economy (24%), and the federal budget deficit (25%). He rates significantly better on education but fails to win the majority (46% versus 49%). The president continues to score his highest ratings in the area of foreign affairs: 64% approve, while 31% disapprove.

As Bush's popularity has slumped, the Democrats' hopes for recapturing the White House have revived. The Gallup Poll now finds about as many voters saying that they favor or lean toward a Democrat for president (45%) as say that they expect to reelect Bush next November (47%).

Although many voters are ready to support a Democratic candidate, the current field of Democratic presidential hopefuls remains unknown to large segments of the electorate. Of the five major candidates, only former California Governor Jerry Brown is recognized by more than one half of the voters.

Arkansas Governor Bill Clinton has begun to emerge as a front-runner from this relatively obscure field, no doubt benefiting from the recent spate of favorable news coverage. Support for Clinton among registered Democrats and independents who lean Democratic has doubled, from 9% to 17%, since November. Brown, the leader in name recognition, continues to top the list with 21%. Support for other candidates has not changed by more than one point since November: Nebraska Senator Bob Kerrey now receives 11%, followed by Iowa Senator Tom Harkin with 9% and former Massachusetts Senator Paul Tsongas with 6%.

Virginia Governor Douglas Wilder, who announced his withdrawal from the race toward the end of the survey's interviewing period, receives 9% support. Poll analysis suggests that none of the remaining five candidates has a particular advantage at this time in winning over Wilder's former supporters.

Dissatisfaction with President Bush's performance has increased in recent months among Republicans as well as Democrats. Few Republican voters polled, however, say that they would support either Pat Buchanan, the conservative television commentator who opposes Bush in the New Hampshire primary, or former Ku Klux Klansman David Duke for the GOP presidential nomination. Fully 85% of registered Republicans and independents who lean Republican now say that they prefer Bush over Buchanan and Duke. Ten percent currently favor Buchanan, up from 5% in November, while only 3% support David Duke, down from 6% in November.

JANUARY 22
ABORTION

Interviewing Date: 1/16–19/92
Survey #GO 222035

I have some questions about abortion. Do you think abortions should be legal under any circumstances, legal only under certain circumstances, or illegal in all circumstances?

Legal, any circumstances	31%
Legal, certain circumstances	53
Illegal, all circumstances	14
No opinion	2

	Legal, any	*Legal, certain*	*Illegal, all**
By Sex			
Male	28%	55%	13%
Female	33	51	15
By Ethnic Background			
White	31	53	13
Nonwhite	27	49	22
Black	21	52	26

By Education			
College Graduate	42	47	10
College Incomplete	39	45	14
High-School Graduate	29	57	11
Less Than High-School Graduate	12	56	25
By Region			
East	34	49	15
Midwest	27	55	14
South	27	58	13
West	36	47	14
By Age			
18–29 Years	34	48	15
30–49 Years	33	55	12
50 Years and Over	27	53	15
By Household Income			
$50,000 and Over	43	45	12
$30,000–$49,999	33	51	15
$20,000–$29,999	26	61	10
Under $20,000	25	54	17
By Politics			
Republicans	27	56	12
Democrats	31	52	16
Independents	35	51	13
By Religion			
Protestants	28	54	15
Catholics	28	57	13
By Political Ideology			
Liberal	47	40	13
Moderate	29	57	11
Conservative	27	54	17
By Bush Approval			
Approve	27	54	15
Disapprove	35	51	12

*"No opinion" is omitted.

Selected National Trend

	Legal, any	*Legal, certain*	*Illegal, all**
September 1991	33%	49%	14%
May 1991	32	50	17
1990	31	53	12
July 1989	29	51	17
April 1989	27	50	18
1988	24	57	17
1983	23	58	16
1981	23	52	21
1980	25	53	18
1979	22	54	19
1977	22	55	19
1975	21	54	22

*"No opinion" is omitted.

Do you favor or oppose each of the following:

A law requiring doctors to inform patients about alternatives to abortion before performing the procedure?

Favor	86%
Oppose	12
No opinion	2

A law requiring women seeking abortions to wait twenty-four hours before having the procedure done?

Favor	73%
Oppose	23
No opinion	4

A law requiring women under age 18 to get parental consent for any abortion?

Favor	70%
Oppose	27
No opinion	3

A law requiring that the husband of a married woman be notified if she decides to have an abortion?

Favor	73%
Oppose	25
No opinion	2

Do you think it is important for the Supreme Court to decide on the constitutionality of abortion rights before the November presidential election, or does the timing not matter much to you?

Before election 27%
Timing does not matter 67
After election (volunteered).....................3
No opinion..3

Asked of registered voters: In its 1973 Roe v. Wade *decision, the Supreme Court ruled that states cannot place restrictions on a woman's right to an abortion during the first three months of pregnancy. If the current Supreme Court overturns the* Roe v. Wade *decision, would you be more likely to vote for George Bush's reelection in November, less likely, or would it not make much difference?*

More likely...9%
Less likely...19
Not much difference.............................70
No opinion..2

Note: On the eve of the nineteenth anniversary of the Supreme Court's 1973 *Roe v. Wade* decision, a recent Gallup Poll confirms past findings that most Americans seek the middle ground on abortion law. While 31% favor access to abortion under all circumstances, a 53% majority says that abortion should be legal only under certain circumstances. Only 14% favor an outright ban.

More respondents now take a pro-choice position—that all abortions should be legal—than did so three years ago. Prior to 1989 the size of the pro-choice and right-to-life groups, as measured by this Gallup Poll question, has differed only slightly. But beginning with a July 1989 survey, taken soon after the Court's *Webster v. Reproductive Services* decision gave the states new authority to restrict abortion, roughly twice as many Americans have favored making all abortions legal as have favored the abolition of abortion.

The *Webster* decision set the stage for a legal challenge to *Roe v. Wade* that could come as early as this year if the Court decides to accept a case involving a 1989 Pennsylvania statute governing abortion. The Pennsylvania law, which has been challenged by Planned Parenthood, requires parental consent for minors, notification to husbands, a twenty-four-hour waiting period, and the restriction that doctors inform women about alternatives before an abortion can be performed.

In Gallup Polls taken soon after the *Webster* decision, a majority of respondents expressed disapproval of that ruling. When asked about specific elements of the Pennsylvania law in the current poll, however, the public overwhelmingly supports provisions that regulate access to abortion in that state. More than eight in ten (86%) support the concept of informed consent where doctors must inform their patients about alternatives to abortion before performing the procedure. Nearly three quarters (73%) support a requirement that husbands be notified if a woman decides to have an abortion. An identical proportion (73%) supports an aspect of the law that requires women seeking abortions to wait twenty-four hours before having the procedure done. And finally, seven in ten (70%) support a requirement that women under age 18 must have parental consent.

With a major new Supreme Court decision on the issue pending, abortion is shaping up as an election-year hot potato. If the Court takes action which is perceived as hostile to women's rights or mobilizes pro- and anti-abortion forces, there could be an election backlash. Now, however, relatively few Americans believe that it is urgent for the Court to settle the issue of *Roe v. Wade.* Asked whether it is important for the Court to decide on the constitutionality of abortion rights before the election, only 27% say that it is important, while 67% say that the timing does not matter much to them.

Asked specifically whether a reversal of *Roe v. Wade* before the election would affect their vote for or against President George Bush, 70% of registered voters say that it would not. However, while only 9% reply that such a decision would make them more likely to vote for Bush, 19% would be less likely to support him.

JANUARY 22
PRESIDENT BUSH/VICE PRESIDENT QUAYLE

Interviewing Date: 1/16–19/92
Survey #GO 222035

Do you approve or disapprove of the way George Bush is handling his job as president?

Approve	46%
Disapprove	47
No opinion	7

Selected National Trend

	Approve	Dis-approve	No opinion
Jan. 3–6, 1992	46%	47%	7%
Dec. 5–8, 1991	52	42	6

From what you may have heard or read about President Bush's recent trip to Japan, would you say it was a success or a failure?

Success	23%
Failure	57
Both (volunteered)	8
No opinion	12

Based on what you know about Vice President Dan Quayle, do you think he is qualified to serve as president if it becomes necessary, or not?

Yes	37%
No	54
No opinion	9

Selected National Trend

	Yes	No	No opinion
1991			
November	37%	53%	10%
August	40	54	6
May	38	53	9
1990			
November	33	59	8
March	31	54	15
1989			
May	34	52	14
1988			
October	46	42	12
September	34	47	19
August	41	40	19

Note: President George Bush's recent trip to Japan, although far from a public relations success, may not have been as damaging to his image as some of his critics have suggested. In a recent Gallup Poll, a majority (57%) of Americans characterizes the trip as a failure, while only about one in four (23%) calls it a success. But the president's overall approval rating is unchanged: 46% now approve of the way that he is handling his job. He received the same rating two weeks ago in a poll taken before a flu-stricken Bush collapsed in Tokyo.

The president's recent illness focused public attention on Vice President Dan Quayle and his fitness to serve as president should it ever become necessary. A majority (54%) continues to believe that Quayle is not qualified to fill Bush's shoes, despite the positive publicity generated from the *Washington Post*'s recent in-depth investigative series on the vice president. About four in ten (37%) now say that Quayle is qualified to be president. Current results are statistically identical to those of Gallup's last three polls on Quayle taken between May and November 1991.

JANUARY 26 KEY CAMPAIGN ISSUES/ABORTION

Interviewing Date: 1/3–6/92
Survey #GO 222034

We'd like to know which issues you think are important for the presidential candidates to discuss and debate in the 1992 campaign. As I read a list of issues, please rate each as very important, somewhat important, not too important, or not at all important:

	Very important
Economy	93%
Education	87
Unemployment	84
Health care	80
Federal budget deficit	79
Crime	77
Drugs; drug abuse	77

Poverty; homelessness	76
Taxes	70
AIDS	67
Environment	60
Foreign trade	53
Race relations	48
National defense	43
Abortion	38
Foreign affairs	37

Asked of registered voters: Would you be more likely or less likely to vote for a presidential candidate who favored making abortion illegal, except in cases of rape, incest, and when the woman's life is in danger, or would it not make much difference?

More likely	44%
Less likely	46
Not much difference	8
No opinion	2

Note: A key event affecting the presidential race may have occurred on January 21, when national attention was refocused on the abortion issue. The Supreme Court's decision to review a restrictive Pennsylvania abortion law later this year sets up the possibility that *Roe v. Wade*, the Court's 1973 ruling establishing a constitutional right to abortion, might be overturned before the November election.

Such an outcome might prove damaging to President George Bush's reelection prospects. In the event that *Roe* is reversed, twice as many voters in a recent Gallup survey say that they would be less likely to support Bush as say they would be more inclined to vote for him (19% versus 9%). The president's potential for losing votes on the abortion issue is highest among some groups that have reliably supported him in the past, including young voters, suburbanites, the better educated, and the more affluent.

Abortion did not seem very likely to heat up as a presidential campaign issue before this week's announcement by the Court. When voters were recently asked by Gallup to rate the importance of sixteen issues in this year's presidential campaign, abortion finished at the bottom, tied for last place with foreign affairs. While nearly all voters (93%) rate the economy—the dominant campaign issue so far—as very important, fewer than four in ten (38%) so rate abortion.

If the Court's action on abortion had been postponed until after the election, the issue would have been much less worrisome for the Bush campaign. By itself, the president's personal position on abortion—that it should be legal only in cases of rape, incest, and when a woman's life is in danger—would not leave him especially vulnerable. About as many voters say that they would be more likely to vote for a candidate who holds Bush's views as say they would be less inclined to support such a candidate (44% versus 46%).

Nineteen years after *Roe* liberalized abortion law in this country, most Americans do not want a sweeping change in the legal status quo. (Opponents and supporters of legal abortion marked the anniversary of *Roe* on January 22 with rallies and demonstrations.) A Gallup Poll in December found close to two thirds (64%) opposed to a reversal of *Roe*.

If the Court strikes down the constitutional protection of abortion rights, however, the pro-choice activists are likely to be mobilized. Since President Bush has personally appointed two justices—David Souter and Clarence Thomas—the public without doubt will make a connection between Bush and the actions of the Court. If Souter and Thomas vote with the majority to undercut *Roe*, then Bush's opponents are likely to have a big issue to use against him in the fall.

JANUARY 28
STATE OF THE UNION

Interviewing Date: 1/16–19/92
Survey #GO 222035

Are you planning to watch President Bush's State of the Union address on television next Tuesday evening, January 28?

Yes	69%
No	25
No opinion	6

Do you think it would be a good idea or a bad idea for President Bush to include each of the following in his State of the Union address:

A plan to reform the nation's health-care system?

Good idea....................93%
Bad idea....................5
No opinion....................2

New ideas for solving the country's economic problems?

Good idea....................92%
Bad idea....................6
No opinion....................2

Stories of people who have achieved something in their lives as models for the country?

Good idea....................49%
Bad idea....................45
No opinion....................6

The platform for his reelection campaign?

Good idea....................44%
Bad idea....................49
No opinion....................7

In his State of the Union address, would you rather see President Bush offer to compromise with Congress on economic policy or present an economic program and challenge Congress to pass it?

Offer to compromise....................43%
Challenge Congress....................50
No opinion....................7

Do you expect the president to address the issues that concern you most, or not?

Yes....................53%
No....................41
No opinion....................6

Note: As election-year politics shift into high gear, over two thirds (69%) of Americans say that they will tune in to President George Bush's State of the Union address on January 28. Whether or not they will be turned on depends upon Bush's ability to address the issues that concern people most—and whether he gains their confidence in his ability to handle these issues during difficult times.

An overwhelming majority (92%) believes that it would be a good idea for the president to include in his address new ideas for solving the country's economic problems. One half (50%) wants Bush to develop his own economic program and challenge Congress to pass it, while 43% say that he should work with Congress and come to a compromise.

Also of high interest to Bush's audience will be health care: 93% say that it would be a good idea for the president to present his plan to reform the nation's health-care system during the State of the Union address. This sentiment extends to members of both political parties and across all age groups, showing that health care is no longer an issue only for liberals and the elderly but has become part of the mantra of politics.

The public is far less receptive to hearing Bush's campaign platform spelled out (44%) or to stories presented as examples of personal achievement (49%). These are viewed more as politicking rather than the substantive responses that the public now is demanding from public officials. Indeed, despite the high level of interest in the speech, only slightly more than one half (53%) say that they expect to hear the president address the issues that concern them most.

FEBRUARY 2
PERSONAL FINANCES/RECESSION

Interviewing Date: 1/16–19/92
Survey #GO 222035

We are interested in how people's financial situation may have changed. Would you say that you are financially better off now than you were a year ago, or are you financially worse off now?

Better....................30%
Worse....................43

Same (volunteered)..............................26
No opinion.. 1

	Better	Worse	Same	No opinion
By Sex				
Male	30%	42%	27%	1%
Female	30	44	25	1
By Ethnic Background				
White	31	40	28	1
Nonwhite	27	57	15	1
Black	26	60	14	*
By Education				
College Graduate	43	31	24	2
College Incomplete	35	41	24	*
High-School Graduate	26	47	27	*
Less Than High-School Graduate	23	48	29	*
By Region				
East	28	50	21	1
Midwest	28	42	29	1
South	35	39	26	*
West	30	40	28	2
By Age				
18–29 Years	42	38	19	1
30–49 Years	31	48	20	1
50 Years and Over	23	39	37	1
By Household Income				
$50,000 and Over	43	32	24	1
$30,000–$49,999	33	43	24	*
$20,000–$29,999	29	44	27	*
Under $20,000	22	51	26	1

*Less than 1%

Selected National Trend

	Better	Worse	Same	No opinion
1991				
October	35%	42%	22%	1%
September	34	28	37	1
April	29	33	37	1
February–March	37	28	34	1
January	27	33	39	1

Looking ahead, do you expect that at this time next year you will be financially better off than now or worse off than now?

Better..51%
Worse..28
Same (volunteered)..............................15
No opinion.. 6

Selected National Trend

	Better	Worse	Same	No opinion
1991				
October	55%	23%	16%	6%
September	53	19	22	6
April	56	17	18	9
February–March	64	9	20	7
January	41	25	21	13

Interviewing Date: 1/3–6/92
Survey #GO 222034

Please tell me whether you are worried or not worried about each of the following happening in the next twelve months:

That you or your husband (wife) will lose a job?

Worried..36%
Not worried.......................................62
No opinion.. 2

That you will not be able to maintain your standard of living?

Worried..48%
Not worried.......................................52
No opinion.. *

*Less than 1%

That you will not be able to pay medical or health-care costs?

Worried....................................48%
Not worried...............................52
No opinion.................................*

*Less than 1%

Now, here are two questions about whether you are satisfied or dissatisfied with various things about America today. Are you satisfied or dissatisfied with:

The opportunity for the next generation of Americans to live better than their parents?

Satisfied..................................36%
Dissatisfied...............................61
No opinion.................................3

The opportunity for a poor person in this country to get ahead by working hard?

Satisfied..................................40%
Dissatisfied...............................58
No opinion.................................2

How would you rate economic conditions in this country today—excellent, good, only fair, or poor?

Excellent..................................*
Good.......................................12
Fair.......................................46
Poor.......................................41
No opinion.................................1

*Less than 1%

Right now, do you think that economic conditions in the country as a whole are getting better or getting worse?

Better.....................................22%
Worse......................................71
Same (volunteered).........................6
No opinion.................................1

Selected National Trend

	Better	*Worse*	*Same*	*No opinion*
1991				
December	19%	69%	9%	3%
October	25	64	8	3
September	27	60	10	3
July	34	51	9	6

Do you think the U.S. economy is now in a recession, or not?

Yes..84%
No...14
No opinion.................................2

Which of the following statements best describes your opinion of the U.S. economy:

The economy is fundamentally sound.........3%
The economy is fundamentally sound
but needs minor changes....................41
The economy needs a complete overhaul......55
No opinion.................................1

Note: In his State of the Union address on January 28, President George Bush sought to restore public confidence that the country can rebound economically. That is not an easy task. Since the fall, Gallup's consumer confidence barometers show people becoming increasingly unhappy with their personal financial situation. In addition, greater numbers of Americans fear for their economic future: one half (48%) of the adult population are worried about being unable to maintain their standard of living over the next twelve months. Similarly, 48% worry about not being able to pay medical bills during the next twelve months, and more than one third (36%), up from 31% in November, are worried about personally losing their job in the next twelve months or seeing their spouse become unemployed.

The stalled economy of the past two years may even be affecting this country's image as the land of opportunity. Upward mobility, a key element in the so-called American Dream, no longer seems to be taken for granted. Six in ten (61%) say that they are dissatisfied with the next generation's opportunity to live better than their parents, while a similar proportion (58%) is unhappy with a poor person's opportunity to get ahead by working hard.

Since the mid-1970s, Gallup has monitored Americans' attitudes toward their personal financial situation. When asked about their current state of affairs, more today say that they are worse off relative to one year ago (43%) than say that they are better off (30%). Response to this question began to tilt negatively last October, apparently signaling an end to a period in which international events, including the Gulf War victory and political change in the former Soviet Union, helped lessen the effects of the recession on the public mood.

In the latest Gallup Poll, the percentage of those who see their financial situation improving in the next year has fallen to 51%. This is down from 64% last March, after victory in the Persian Gulf. Nearly three in ten (28%) now expect to be financially worse off next year. With the exception of a poll taken in October 1990, when the budget stalemate in Washington drew a harshly negative public reaction, this is the highest level of economic pessimism in a Gallup survey since 1982, during the more severe Reagan recession.

President Bush's decision to accept the proposition that the national economy is in recession—and stop arguing about whether it fits the textbook definition—was politically necessary. Fully 84% believe that the economy is in recession, while only 14% take the contrary view. At this point, relatively few profess to see light at the end of the tunnel; only 22% think that the economy is getting better, while 71% say that it is getting worse.

There is some divergence of opinion on the seriousness of our economic problems, but few believe that things are going well. Only 12% characterize economic conditions in a clearly positive manner as good, while four in ten (41%) go so far as to say conditions are poor. Another 46% describe the state of the economy as only fair. Similarly, a 55% majority says that the economy needs a complete overhaul, while 41% find it fundamentally sound but needing minor changes. Only 3% say without qualification that the economy is fundamentally sound.

FEBRUARY 5
PRESIDENT BUSH/PRESIDENTIAL CANDIDATES

Interviewing Date: 1/31–2/2/92*
Survey #GO 222037

Do you approve or disapprove of the way George Bush is handling his job as president?

Approve	47%
Disapprove	48
No opinion	5

Selected National Trend

	Approve	Dis-approve	No opinion
1992			
January 16–19	46%	47%	7%
January 3–6	46	47	7

Asked of registered voters: If George Bush runs for reelection this year, in general are you more likely to vote for Bush or for the Democratic party's candidate for president? [Those who were undecided were asked: As of today, do you lean more to Bush or to the Democratic party's candidate for president?]

Bush	52%
Democratic candidate	43
Undecided; other	5

Selected National Trend

	Bush	Demo-cratic candidate	Undecided; other
1992			
January 3–6	47%	45%	8%
1991			
December 5–8	52	38	10
November 21–24	53	40	7

*Gallup survey for CNN/*USA Today*

Asked of registered Democrats and those who lean Democratic: I will read off the names of six Democratic candidates for president. After I read all six names, please tell me which one you would like to see nominated as the Democratic party's candidate for president. [Those who were undecided were asked: As of today, to which Democratic candidate do you lean most?]

Bill Clinton	42%
Jerry Brown	16
Bob Kerrey	10
Tom Harkin	9
Paul Tsongas	9
Douglas Wilder*	–
Undecided; other	14

Selected National Trend

	Jan. 3–6, 1992	*Oct. 31–Nov. 3, 1991*
Bill Clinton	17%	9%
Jerry Brown	21	21
Bob Kerrey	11	10
Tom Harkin	9	10
Paul Tsongas	6	7
Douglas Wilder*	9	12
Undecided; other	27	31

*Wilder withdrew from the Democratic race after the January survey had begun.

Asked of registered Republicans and those who lean Republican: I will read off the names of three Republican candidates for president. After I read all three names, please tell me which one you would like to see nominated as the Republican party's candidate for president. [Those who were undecided were asked: As of today, to which Republican candidate do you lean most?]

George Bush	84%
Pat Buchanan	11
David Duke	4
Undecided; other	1

Selected National Trend

	Jan. 3–6, 1992	*Dec. 5–8, 1991*
George Bush	85%	86%
Pat Buchanan	10	5
David Duke	3	6
Undecided; other	2	3

I will read off the names of some people in politics. As I read each name, tell me if you have a favorable or unfavorable opinion of this person, or if you have never heard of him:

George Bush?

Favorable	56%
Unfavorable	41
Heard of; no opinion	2
Total heard of	99

Bill Clinton?

Favorable	39%
Unfavorable	32
Heard of; no opinion	15
Total heard of	86

Clinton's Ratings among Registered Democrats and Those Who Lean Democratic

	Favorable	*Unfavorable*	*Heard of; no opinion*	*Total heard of*
1992				
January 31–February 2	51%	24%	14%	89%
January 3–6	28	11	16	55

Do the allegations about Bill Clinton's personal conduct and his handling of them make you more likely or less likely to vote for him, or will they not have much effect on your vote?

	Total	*Republicans; those who lean Republican*	*Democrats; those who lean Democratic*
More likely	3%	3%	5%

Less likely	23	27	19
Not much effect	71	67	73
No opinion	3	3	3

As a result of his State of the Union address, do you have more confidence in George Bush's economic leadership, less confidence, or has your confidence in his economic leadership not changed much?

More confidence	14%
Less confidence	16
Not changed much	63
No opinion	7

Note: The results of a new Gallup Poll offer both good news and bad news for President George Bush and Democratic front-runner Bill Clinton. On the positive side for Bush, he now runs better in a test election against an unnamed Democrat than he did last month, before his State of the Union address. Fifty-two percent of registered voters now say that they would vote to reelect Bush; 43% would opt for the Democratic party's presidential candidate. In an early January poll, Bush and the Democratic candidate were statistically tied, 47% to 45%.

On the negative side, the speech appears to have done little to restore voter confidence in the president's economic leadership. When interviewed several days after the State of the Union address, a majority of voters (63%) say that the speech did not much affect their opinion of Bush's economic leadership. In fact, about as many say that they lost confidence in Bush (16%) as say that they gained confidence in him (14%) as a result of his address.

The national media attention that Clinton has received since Gennifer Flowers charged him with having an extramarital affair is somewhat of a mixed blessing for the Arkansas governor. On the one hand, as his name recognition has soared to over 80%, his support among Democratic voters for his party's presidential nomination has also skyrocketed. Only a month ago, Clinton had just 17% support among registered Democrats, placing him second in the field of the party's presidential hopefuls. Since that time, he has picked up 25 percentage points and captured 42% of Democratic voter support nationally. Jerry Brown, the only other Democratic candidate with high name recognition, is currently a distant second with 16%.

On the other hand, the adverse publicity may compromise Clinton's ability to run a strong campaign in the fall. The percentage of all voters, including Republicans, who have an unfavorable opinion of Clinton has tripled since Flowers told her story in the *Star* tabloid (32% now versus 10% in early January).

FEBRUARY 7
ALCOHOLIC BEVERAGES

Interviewing Date: 1/16–19/92
Survey #GO 222035

Do you have occasion to use alcoholic beverages such as liquor, wine, or beer, or are you a total abstainer?

	Those who drink
National	64%

Selected National Trend

	Those who drink
1990	57%
1989	56
1987	65
1984	64
1982	65
1981	70
1979	69
1978	71
1976	71
1974	68
1969	64
1964	63
1960	62
1958	55
1956	60
1947	63
1945	67
1939	58

Selected User Changes, 1990 versus 1992
(Those Who Drink)

	1990	*1992*	*Point change*
Total	57%	64%	+7
By Sex			
Male	64	72	+8
Female	51	57	+6
By Education			
College Graduate	68	78	+10
College Incomplete	65	64	-1
High-School Graduate	57	64	+7
Less Than High-School Graduate	33	49	+16
By Age			
18–29 Years	61	71	+10
30–49 Years	64	68	+4
50 Years and Over	47	56	+9
By Household Income			
$40,000 and Over	76	80	+4
$30,000–$49,999	61	63	+2
$20,000–$29,999	58	64	+6
Under $20,000	44	56	+12

Asked of those who drink (64% of the sample): When did you last take a drink of any kind of alcoholic beverage?

Within last 24 hours	26%
Over one day to one week ago	25
Over one week ago	48
No opinion	1

Selected National Trend

	Last 24 hours	*One day to one week*	*Over one week*	*No opinion*
1990	29%	23%	47%	1%
1987	38	29	32	1
1984	39	29	31	1

Also asked of those who drink: Approximately how many drinks of any kind of alcoholic beverage did you drink in the past seven days?

None	51%
1 to 7 drinks	36
8 to 19 drinks	10
20 or more	2
No opinion	1

Selected National Trend

	None	*1 to 7*	*8 to 19*	*20 or more**
1990	50%	40%	6%	3%
1989	33	47	13	5
1988	32	49	10	6
1987	29	50	11	6

*"No opinion"—at 4% or less—is omitted.

Also asked of those who drink: Do you most often drink liquor, wine, or beer?

Beer	47%
Wine	27
Liquor	21
All about equally (volunteered)	3
Cordials (volunteered)	1
No opinion	1

Also asked of those who drink: Do you sometimes drink more than you think you should?

	Yes
National	29%

Selected National Trend

	Yes
1990	23%
1989	35
1987	29
1985	32
1978	23

Also asked of those who drink: Do you plan to cut down or quit drinking within the next year?

Yes, cut down	17%
Yes, quit	9
Neither (volunteered)	74
No opinion	*

*Less than 1%

Selected National Trend

	Yes, cut down	Yes, quit	Neither	No opinion
1990	12%	8%	78%	2%
1989	18	7	74	1
1987	12	3	82	3
1984	14	2	83	1

Asked of the entire sample: Has drinking ever been a cause of trouble in your family?

	Yes
National	24%

Selected National Trend

	Yes
1990	23%
1989	19
1987	24
1985	21
1984	17
1981	22
1978	22
1976	17
1974	12
1966	12
1950	14

Have you heard or read about the scientific study that found moderate drinkers to have lower rates of heart disease than those who do not drink alcoholic beverages?

	Yes
National	58%

Asked of the aware group (58%): As a result of what you have heard or read about the study, are you more likely to have one or two drinks on a daily basis, or not?

Yes, more likely	5%
No, less likely	53
Can't say	*
	58%

*Less than 1%

Note: After two years of declines, Americans appear to be returning to alcoholic consumption on a level last seen in the mid-1980s Nearly two thirds (64%) of those interviewed in the latest Gallup Poll now identify themselves as drinkers, up from 57% in 1990.

The 1992 numbers are still well below those of a decade ago. In 1981, when Gallup's survey also was conducted in mid-January (with holiday hangovers and brave New Year's resolutions still in mind), 70% identified themselves as drinkers, some 6 points higher than in 1992.

This escalation may be related to the country's current economic malaise. The increases are particularly striking among those groups most affected by the hard economic times: the young (up from 61% to 71%); those making less than $20,000 (44% to 56%); and those without a high-school diploma, up from 33% to 49% since Gallup's last survey in December 1990.

The percentage of those who admit to sometimes drinking more than they should has also risen from 1990. At that time 23% responded affirmatively; now, the figure is 29%. However, the current figures are not out of line with those from most of the last three decades, suggesting that 1989 and 1990—when people seemed particularly conscious of the campaigns of MADD and other anti-excess groups—were, in fact, the anomalous years.

Fifty-eight percent are aware of recent research linking moderate drinking to lower rates of heart disease. Thus far, the overall impact of this research does not appear to be significant: only 5% of all respondents say that the studies are more likely to make them drink moderately.

Although beer continues to be the beverage of choice—preferred by 47% (and by a whopping 71% of those under age 30)—its adherents have declined slightly (from 51% in 1990), while those favoring wine have increased (from 22% to 27%). The numbers opting for liquor remain virtually the same (23% in 1990, 21% today). Wine is now the drink of choice for four in ten college graduates, up from three in ten in 1990; by contrast, among those without a high-school diploma, beer (53%) continues as the beverage preferred over wine (15%).

Over the last decade, there has been little change among women or among Gallup's various demographic subgroups on the question: "Has drinking ever been a cause of trouble in your family?" The significant exception in 1992 is men. In 1981 only 15% of men replied affirmatively; as recently as 1990 the figure was only 18%. But in the latest poll, as many men as women (24%) so reply.

FEBRUARY 9
NEW HAMPSHIRE PRIMARY

Interviewing Date: 2/4–6/92*
Survey #GO 222039

Asked of those who plan to vote in the New Hampshire Republican primary: Suppose the Republican primary election for president were being held today. If you had to choose between George Bush and Pat Buchanan, which candidate would you vote for? [Those who were undecided were asked: As of today, to which of the Republican candidates do you lean most?]

Bush	62%
Buchanan	30
Undecided; other	8

Also asked of those who plan to vote in the New Hampshire Republican primary: Would you say your choice is more of a vote for George Bush or Pat Buchanan or more of a vote against Bush or Buchanan?

	Bush voters	*Buchanan voters*
For candidate	81%	24%
Against other candidate	15	74
No opinion	4	2

Also asked of those who plan to vote in the New Hampshire Republican primary: Tell me whether you have a favorable or unfavorable opinion of each of the following Republican candidates:

*Gallup survey for CNN/*USA Today*

George Bush?

Favorable	66%
Unfavorable	31
No opinion	3

Pat Buchanan?

Favorable	49%
Unfavorable	38
No opinion	13

Asked of those who plan to vote in the New Hampshire Democratic primary: Suppose the Democratic primary election for president were being held today. If you had to choose among Bill Clinton, Paul Tsongas, Bob Kerrey, Jerry Brown, or Tom Harkin, which candidate would you vote for? [Those who were undecided were asked: As of today, to which of the Democratic candidates do you lean most?]

Clinton	37%
Tsongas	24
Kerrey	12
Brown	8
Harkin	8
Undecided; other	11

Also asked of those who plan to vote in the New Hampshire Democratic primary: Tell me whether you have a favorable or unfavorable opinion of each of the following Democratic candidates:

Bill Clinton?

Favorable	73%
Unfavorable	20
No opinion	7

Paul Tsongas?

Favorable	71%
Unfavorable	18
No opinion	11

Bob Kerrey?

Favorable	66%
Unfavorable	19
No opinion	15

Tom Harkin?

Favorable	52%
Unfavorable	27
No opinion	21

Jerry Brown?

Favorable	41%
Unfavorable	39
No opinion	20

Also asked of those who plan to vote in the New Hampshire Democratic primary: Do the allegations about Bill Clinton's personal conduct and his handling of them make you more likely or less likely to vote for him, or will they not have much effect on your vote?

More likely	4%
Less likely	15
Not much effect	78
No opinion	3

Also asked of those who plan to vote in the New Hampshire Democratic primary: Are you pretty satisfied with the current field of Democratic presidential candidates, or would you like to see some other candidate enter the race? [Those who said "some other candidate" were then asked: Who in particular would you like to see enter the race?]

Satisfied with field	48%
Want some other candidate	48
Mario Cuomo	19
Other	10
Not certain	19
No opinion	4

Note: President George Bush and Arkansas Governor Bill Clinton hold big leads in New Hampshire, less than two weeks before that state's February 18 primary. A Gallup Poll of New Hampshire voters shows Bush with a 2-to-1 edge (62% versus 30%) over conservative political commentator Pat Buchanan. On the Democratic side, Clinton outpolls former Massachusetts Senator Paul Tsongas, in second place, by 37% to 24%.

Among New Hampshire Republicans four years ago, a weak commitment to Robert Dole's candidacy gave Bush the opportunity to swing the vote his way in the final days of the campaign. In the state's 1984 Democratic primary, Gary Hart pulled off a stunning 39%-to-29% victory, overcoming Walter Mondale's commanding lead in polls released only a few days before the election.

Although Buchanan seems unlikely to defeat Bush in the primary, he has a chance to win a respectable share of the vote. His support level is already at the 30% mark; capturing 40% does not seem beyond his reach. Moreover, the recession's effects on New Hampshire's economy appear to have hurt President Bush's popularity among Republicans in the state.

The Buchanan vote is essentially one of protest; three fourths (74%) of his backers say that their vote is more an expression of anti-Bush sentiment than a positive statement for the former cohost of CNN's "Crossfire." Candidate preferences in the Republican primary do not follow ideological lines. Despite his hard-line position on taxes, Buchanan shows no special appeal for self-described conservatives. Furthermore, Buchanan's favorability ratings are lower than Bush's among New Hampshire GOP voters. Overall, 49% have a favorable opinion of Buchanan, while 38% have an unfavorable opinion. The Republican challenger, however, may have an advantage over the incumbent among undecided voters.

In the Democratic race, Clinton's lead seems tenuous. The front-runner does not have a big advantage in overall favorability over the second-place challenger: 73% of Democratic primary voters have a favorable opinion of Clinton, while 71% have a favorable opinion of Tsongas.

Almost one half of Democratic voters (48%) say that they are unhappy with the field of party candidates and would like to see someone else run. A well-organized write-in campaign for New York Governor Mario Cuomo might have some success in the Granite State. Among those who want some other candidate, 19% cite Cuomo as someone they would like to see enter the race.

Although Nebraska Senator Bob Kerrey is now a distant third with 12% of the vote, he shows potential for making gains if either of the two leaders falter. Kerrey is well regarded by most Democratic voters: 66% have positive views of him, while only 19% see him negatively. As for the other contenders, Iowa Senator Tom Harkin and former California Governor Jerry Brown have failed to attract significant support in New Hampshire: each receives only 8% of the vote overall. Harkin, who has campaigned as a standard-bearer for traditional liberalism, gets only 13% among self-described liberals. Brown, running an antiestablishment campaign, may find some of the voter anger he is trying to harness directed back at himself. About as many Democratic primary voters regard him unfavorably (39%) as favorably (41%).

FEBRUARY 12
PRESIDENT BUSH/PRESIDENTIAL TRIAL HEAT

Interviewing Date: 2/6–9/92
Survey #GO 222040

Do you approve or disapprove of the way George Bush is handling his job as president?

Approve....................................44%
Disapprove....................................48
No opinion....................................8

Asked of registered voters: Suppose the 1992 presidential election were being held today. If George Bush were the Republican candidate and Bill Clinton were the Democratic candidate, whom would you vote for?

Bush....................................53%
Clinton....................................38
Undecided; other....................................9

	Bush	*Clinton*	*Undecided; other*
By Sex			
Male	55%	38%	7%
Female	52	38	10
By Ethnic Background			
White	56	36	8
Nonwhite	31	58	11
By Education			
College Graduate	51	37	12
College Incomplete	62	32	6
High-School Graduate	59	33	8
Less Than High-School Graduate	35	57	8
By Region			
East	50	38	12
Midwest	57	36	7
South	56	36	8
West	47	46	7
By Age			
18–29 Years	49	45	6
30–49 Years	59	33	8
50 Years and Over	51	39	10
By Household Income			
$50,000 and Over	64	29	7
$30,000–$49,999	59	33	8
$20,000–$29,999	57	36	7
Under $20,000	35	55	10
By Politics			
Republicans	87	8	5
Democrats	18	70	12
Independents	56	35	9
By Political Ideology			
Liberal	36	54	10
Moderate	50	41	9
Conservative	66	28	6
By Community Size			
Large City	50	37	13
Medium City	51	41	8
Suburbs	59	33	8
Small Town	51	42	7
Rural Area	61	31	8
By Sex/Education			
College Male	58	35	7
College Female	53	35	12
Noncollege Male	52	40	8
Noncollege Female	51	41	8

Note: George Bush's approval rating in the Gallup Poll has dipped to 44%, slightly below his previous low of 46% recorded in mid-January. But as the presidential primary season begins, the Democratic party is still without a candidate who shows the potential for defeating Bush in November.

Arkansas Governor Bill Clinton, who surged to the top of the Democratic preference polls last month, fails the "electability" test in a recent Gallup survey. If an election between Bush and Clinton were held today, 53% would vote for the president, while 38% would back the governor.

Interviewing for the poll took place after Clinton came under fire for allegedly evading the military draft in the Vietnam era. Because respondents were not questioned specifically about the allegations, the poll provides no direct evidence that they have been politically damaging. Clinton's standing among older voters, however, who may be more sensitive to issues of military service, suggests that some damage may have occurred.

Bush would seem especially vulnerable among older voters. Only 29% of adults over age 50 approve of the president's job performance, yet Bush has a 51%-to-39% advantage over Clinton among voters in this age group. Clinton also has political problems among voters of his own generation. Those age 30 to 49 prefer Bush over Clinton by nearly a 2-to-1 margin, 59% to 33%. Only among the youngest group of voters—those under 30—does Clinton's support (45%) roughly equal Bush's (49%).

Bush tops Clinton among political moderates (50% versus 41%) and independents (56% versus 35%), two groups that can swing an election one way or the other. The president has an edge in all regions of the country except the West, where the race is statistically even (47% Bush versus 46% Clinton).

FEBRUARY 12
PRESIDENT BUSH AND CONGRESS

Interviewing Date: 2/6–9/92
Survey #GO 222040

Do you think President Bush is too quick to blame Congress for the country's economic problems, or not?

Yes	50%
No	44
No opinion	6

	Yes	*No*	*No opinion*
By Politics			
Republicans	28%	67%	5%
Democrats	72	21	7
Independents	51	44	5

Do you think Congress will have an economic legislation package ready in time to meet the March 20 deadline set by President Bush in his State of the Union address, or not?

Yes	20%
No	73
No opinion	7

	Yes	*No*	*No opinion*
By Politics			
Republicans	18%	76%	6%
Democrats	22	69	9
Independents	20	75	5

Note: While President George Bush waits for congressional Democrats to pass an economic package this spring, the American public is not holding its breath. Already pessimistic about the future of the economy and their own personal finances, respondents are skeptical that Congress will produce an economic legislation package by the March 20 deadline set by the president in his State of the Union address.

This skepticism cuts across party lines. Only 20% of the public (including 18% of Republicans and 22% of Democrats) believe that Congress will meet the deadline, while three quarters (73%) say that it will not.

Meanwhile, partisan politics surface when the Gallup Poll asks whether the president is too quick to blame Congress for the state of the economy. Democrats are nearly three times as likely as Republicans to reply that Bush is too quick to point to Congress (72% versus 28%). Independents are in the middle, reflecting the opinion of the overall population which is split on the question: 51% say that the president is too quick to blame Congress, while 44% reply that he is not.

FEBRUARY 13
PARTY BETTER FOR PEACE AND PROSPERITY

Interviewing Date: 2/6–9/92
Survey #GO 222040

Looking ahead for the next few years, which political party do you think would be more likely to keep the United States out of war—the Republican or the Democratic party?*

Republican....................................39%
Democratic....................................39
No difference; no opinion.....................22

*The wording of the question changes in 1992 from that used in earlier surveys: ". . . more likely to keep the United States out of World War III."

Selected National Trend

	Repub-lican	*Demo-cratic*	*No difference; no opinion*
October 1991	45%	38%	17%
July 1991	42	33	25
October 1990	34	36	30
August 1990*	36	34	30
September 1988*	43	33	24
July 1988*	39	36	25
May 1988*	31	39	30
January 1988*	36	35	29
August 1984	36	40	24
April 1984	30	42	28
September 1983	26	39	35
October 1982	29	38	33
April 1981	29	34	37
September 1980	25	42	33
August 1976	29	32	39
September 1972	32	28	40
October 1968	37	24	39
October 1964	22	45	33
October 1960	40	25	35
October 1956	46	16	38
January 1952	36	15	49
September 1951	28	21	51

*Asked of registered voters

Which political party—the Republican or the Democratic—will do a better job of keeping the country prosperous?

Republican....................................41%
Democratic....................................43
No difference; no opinion.....................16

Selected National Trend

	Repub-lican	*Demo-cratic*	*No difference; no opinion*
October 1991	44%	41%	15%
July 1991	49	32	19
October 1990	37	35	28
August 1990*	45	30	25
September 1988*	52	34	14
July 1988*	46	39	15
May 1988*	41	39	20
January 1988*	42	35	23
August 1984	48	36	16
April 1984	44	36	20
September 1983	33	40	27
October 1982	34	43	23
April 1981	41	28	31
September 1980	35	36	29
August 1976	23	47	30
September 1972	38	35	27
October 1968	34	37	29
October 1964	21	53	26
October 1960	31	46	23
October 1956	39	39	22
January 1952	31	35	34
September 1951	29	37	34

*Asked of registered voters

Note: While the recession has left President George Bush and the Republican party on the ropes, the Democrats have yet to win back the title of "party of prosperity." Americans today are about as likely to name the Republicans (41%) as the Democrats (43%) when asked which party can better keep the country prosperous.

The Democrats' failure to appropriate the prosperity issue in this election year does not bode well for their chances of defeating Bush in November. Despite the president's low approval ratings on the economy—overwhelmingly regarded by voters as the critical issue in this year's campaign—the findings of Gallup surveys over the past forty years suggest that Bush will be returned to office unless voters become convinced that the Democrats are more likely to bring about prosperity.

Since Gallup began asking the prosperity question in 1951, it has proved to be a reliable barometer of the parties' presidential prospects. Since that time Democratic candidates have won three of ten presidential elections—John Kennedy in 1960, Lyndon Johnson in 1964, and Jimmy Carter in 1976. During all three of these election years the Democrats held a significant advantage over the Republicans as the party of prosperity in the Gallup Poll. (For example, in August 1976, the Democrats had a 47%-to-23% advantage.) In the other seven presidential elections since 1952, all Republican victories, the GOP statistically equaled or surpassed the Democrats on this measure.

It has been almost nine years since the Democrats last enjoyed a significant advantage on the prosperity issue. In September 1983, when the effects of the Reagan recession were still being felt, the Democrats led by 40% to 33%. For most of the period between 1984 and late 1990, when the current recession began, the GOP had a significant edge as the party of prosperity.

The two parties are also even on another key Gallup barometer of their strength: 39% believe that the GOP is more likely to keep the country out of war; an identical 39% see the Democratic party as the party of peace. History shows that this measure is less predictive of the outcome of presidential elections, except when the country is at war or involved in an international crisis.

FEBRUARY 16
NEW HAMPSHIRE PRIMARY

Interviewing Dates: 2/4–6; 8–10; 11–13/92*
Various Surveys

Asked of those who plan to vote in the New Hampshire Republican primary: Suppose the Republican primary election for president were being held today. If you had to choose between George Bush and Pat Buchanan, which candidate would you vote for? [Those who were undecided were asked: As of today, to which of the Republican candidates do you lean most?]

Bush	60%
Buchanan	30
Undecided; other	10

Selected State Trend

	Bush	Buchanan	Undecided; other
1992			
February 8–10	64%	27%	9%
February 4–6	62	30	8

Also asked of those who plan to vote in the New Hampshire Republican primary: Tell me whether you have a favorable or unfavorable opinion of each of the following Republican candidates:

George Bush?

	Favorable
State's Republican voters	67%

Selected State Trend

	Favorable
1992	
February 8–10	70%
February 4–6	66

*Gallup surveys for CNN/*USA Today*

Pat Buchanan?

	Favorable
State's Republican voters	49%

Selected State Trend

	Favorable
1992	
February 8–10	46%
February 4–6	49

Asked of those who plan to vote in the New Hampshire Democratic primary: Suppose the Democratic primary election for president were being held today. If you had to choose among Bill Clinton, Paul Tsongas, Bob Kerrey, Jerry Brown, or Tom Harkin, which candidate would you vote for? [Those who were undecided were asked: As of today, to which of the Democratic candidates do you lean most?]

Tsongas	37%
Clinton	22
Harkin	13
Kerrey	10
Brown	7
Undecided; other	11

Selected State Trend

	Feb. 8–10	*Feb. 4–6*
Tsongas	33%	24%
Clinton	26	37
Harkin	11	8
Kerrey	13	12
Brown	8	8
Undecided; other	9	11

Also asked of those who plan to vote in the New Hampshire Democratic primary: Tell me whether you have a favorable or unfavorable opinion of each of the following Democratic candidates:

Paul Tsongas?

	Favorable
State's Democratic voters	79%

Selected State Trend

	Favorable
1992	
February 8–10	75%
February 4–6	71

Bill Clinton?

	Favorable
State's Democratic voters	61%

Selected State Trend

	Favorable
1992	
February 8–10	60%
February 4–6	73

Bob Kerrey?

	Favorable
State's Democratic voters	64%

Selected State Trend

	Favorable
1992	
February 8–10	64%
February 4–6	66

Tom Harkin?

	Favorable
State's Democratic voters	54%

Selected State Trend

	Favorable
1992	
February 8–10	47%
February 4–6	52

Jerry Brown?

	Favorable
State's Democratic voters	42%

Selected State Trend

	Favorable
1992	
February 8–10	41%
February 4–6	41

Also asked of those who plan to vote in the New Hampshire Democratic primary: Do the allegations about Bill Clinton's draft status during the Vietnam War, and the way he has handled these allegations, make you more likely or less likely to vote for him, or will they not have much effect on your vote?

More likely	5%
Less likely	20
Not much effect	73
No opinion	2

Note: George Bush and Paul Tsongas lead in their respective primary races as the New Hampshire campaign enters its final days. Although it appears unlikely that Pat Buchanan can defeat the president in the GOP primary, the conservative commentator might receive as much as 35% of the Republican vote. The final outcome may well hinge on the effectiveness of the Bush and Buchanan organizations in getting their supporters to the polls this Tuesday (February 18).

In the Democratic race, the Tsongas lead has held up since last weekend, when the former Massachusetts senator surged past former front-runner Bill Clinton. Sunday night's (February 16) televised debate, sponsored by CNN, gives Clinton and the other Democratic candidates a final shot at cutting into the Tsongas lead. Clinton's dramatic loss of support, coupled with some late movement toward Iowa Senator Tom Harkin, has made the race for second and third place more interesting. Voter support for these candidates is so soft that candidate standings could easily shift in the final days.

The Gallup tracking poll of voter preferences shows Bush maintaining a 2-to-1 lead over Buchanan (60% versus 30%). Candidate support levels have changed little in the past two weeks; Bush led by 62% to 30% one week ago. Buchanan's failure to gain additional ground in the past week may result from his relative unpopularity with New Hampshire's Republican voters. While one half (49%) of these voters have favorable views of Buchanan, about four in ten (39%) regard him unfavorably. The president's favorability ratings among these same voters are more positive: 67% favorable versus 29% unfavorable.

In the past week the president's support among New Hampshire Republicans has firmed up. Over one half (53%) of those who prefer the president over his rival say that they support Bush strongly. Buchanan support—much of it a protest vote—remains very soft. Only a little more than one third (35%) of Buchanan voters supports him strongly.

Since the controversy arose over Clinton's draft deferments during the Vietnam War, Tsongas has surged to the top of the Democratic field. Earlier this month, before the story about Clinton and the draft initially appeared in the *Wall Street Journal*, the Arkansas governor led Tsongas by 37% to 24% among those who planned to vote in the New Hampshire Democratic primary. Late last week, Clinton's support began to drop, and by Monday (February 10), Tsongas took the lead. As of Thursday (February 13), Tsongas led by 37% to 22%.

The only other Democrat to gain ground in the past week is Tom Harkin, who has moved from 8% to 13% over the course of Gallup's tracking. Perhaps helped by the publicity from Monday's Iowa caucuses, which he won easily as the other candidates chose not to compete, Harkin's rise might spell trouble for Bob Kerrey who, with 10%, has dropped to fourth place in the poll. Many observers think that the Nebraska senator must finish no lower than third in order to stay in the race.

Given his sharp decline in the polls, Clinton's survival is also in question; even a second-place finish may not be a sure thing. Harkin is now within 9 points of Clinton and has an opportunity to close the gap in the final weekend. With the candidates this close in overall support, and given the softness of their support, organizational efforts to get out the vote on Tuesday will be critical to the New Hampshire primary's outcome.

FEBRUARY 21
AMERICAN-JAPANESE RELATIONS

Interviewing Date: 2/6–9/92
Survey #GO 222040

What is your opinion about the country of Japan? Is your overall opinion of it very favorable, mostly favorable, mostly unfavorable, or very unfavorable?

Very favorable....................................9%
Mostly favorable................................38
Mostly unfavorable.............................28
Very unfavorable.................................22
No opinion...3

Opinion of Japan Compared to Other Nations
(Very, Mostly Favorable Combined)

	Japan	Canada	CIS*	Germany	Israel
1992					
Feb.	47%	91%	57%	74%	48%
1991					
Nov.	48	–	52	–	47
March	65	91	50	77	69
Feb.	62	–	57	75	79
1990					
Feb.	61	89	64	–	48
1989					
Aug.	58	93	51	–	45
March	69	92	62	–	49

*Commonwealth of Independent States, known before 1992 as the Soviet Union

Do you agree or disagree with each of the following statements:

Many American workers are lazy and lack the work ethic they had in the past?

Agree 45%
Disagree...54
No opinion...1

Too much illiteracy among U.S. workers hurts the country's ability to compete internationally?

Agree 71%
Disagree...26
No opinion...3

I am going to read two statements. Please tell me whether you think each statement is very true, somewhat true, or not at all true:

I try to buy the best product for me whether it is American-made or imported?

Very true 46%
Somewhat true 31
Not at all true....................................22
No opinion...1

I will only buy an imported product if there is no comparable American product available?

Very true 37%
Somewhat true 36
Not at all true....................................26
No opinion...1

Thinking about your experience with Japanese products, would you say they are generally good to excellent, average, or below average?

Good to excellent 57%
Average 32
Below average 8
No opinion...3

Thinking about your experience with American products, would you say they are generally good to excellent, average, or below average?

Good to excellent 51%
Average 44
Below average 4
No opinion...1

Note: Despite recent negative publicity generated by the relationship between Japanese economic policies and the U.S. recession, Americans exhibit decidedly mixed reactions toward the Asian superpower. A new Gallup Poll shows that overall attitudes toward Japan remain low, down from the more friendly ones of recent years. At the same time, admiration for Japanese products and goods is up, and many Americans agree with the widely quoted critical statements about U.S. workers made recently by Japanese officials.

Japan's favorability rating—now at 47%—is statistically the same as last November's (48%) but significantly down from those of 1989 and 1990. In the latest poll, in fact, Japan has substantially lower ratings than Germany, Canada, and even the new Commonwealth of Independent States (the former Soviet Union). Japan's favorability rating is now on a par with that of another controversial American ally, Israel.

Reasons for the unfavorable attitudes of Americans toward Japan are primarily business-related. In a poll conducted late in 1991, prior to the fiftieth anniversary of Pearl Harbor, Americans were most likely to base their unfavorable opinions of Japan on perceptions of unbalanced trade and the banning of imports between the two nations and on a dislike of Japanese real estate investments and business buy-outs in this country.

Recent anti-Japanese sentiment may have been fueled by widely quoted comments from Japanese officials about the poor quality of American workmanship. Still, the poll shows that many respondents agree with the Japanese assessments: over four in ten (45%) think that American workers are lazy or lack the work ethic they had in the past, and a much higher number (71%) agrees with the comment that worker illiteracy hurts our competitive situation.

Despite Japan's lukewarm national image, respondents maintain respect for Japanese manufactured goods and products. Fifty-seven percent rate those products as good or excellent, higher than the 51% who rate American products as good or excellent. The perceived quality of Japanese goods, in fact, has gone up over the past six years compared to previous Gallup surveys.

The poll shows only a slight increase in protectionist "Buy American" sentiment, compared to 1983: 46% now say that it is very true that they buy products regardless of origin, down only slightly from the 53% who so agreed in 1983. Similarly, there has been very little change in reaction to the statement "I will only buy an imported product if there is no comparable American product available"; 37% say now that this is very true, but 40% said in 1983 that it was very true.

FEBRUARY 23
PRESIDENT BUSH/PRESIDENTIAL TRIAL HEATS/PRESIDENTIAL CANDIDATES

Interviewing Date: 2/19–20/92*
Survey #GO 222042

Do you approve or disapprove of the way George Bush is handling his job as president?

Approve	39%
Disapprove	47
No opinion	14

Selected National Trend

	Approve	*Dis-approve*	*No opinion*
1992			
February 6–9	44%	48%	8%
January 16–19	46	47	7
January 3–6	46	47	7
1991			
December 5–8	52	42	6
November 7–10	56	36	8
October 3–6	65	27	8
September 5–8	70	21	9
February 28–March 3	89	8	3

Asked of registered voters: Suppose the 1992 presidential election were being held today. If George Bush were the Republican candidate and Bill Clinton were the Democratic candidate, whom would you be more likely to vote for? [Those who were undecided were asked: As of today, do you lean more to Bush, the Republican, or to Clinton, the Democrat?]

	Feb. 19–20, 1992	*Feb. 6–9, 1992*
Bush	53%	53%
Clinton	43	38
Undecided; other	4	9

*Gallup survey for CNN/*USA Today*

Also asked of registered voters: Suppose the 1992 presidential election were being held today. If George Bush were the Republican candidate and Paul Tsongas were the Democratic candidate, whom would you be more likely to vote for? [Those who were undecided were asked: As of today, do you lean more to Bush, the Republican, or to Tsongas, the Democrat?]

Bush	54%
Tsongas	39
Undecided; other	7

Asked of registered Democrats and those who lean Democratic: I will read off the names of five Democratic candidates for president. After I read all five names, please tell me which one you would like to see nominated as the Democratic party's candidate for president. [Those who were undecided were asked: As of today, to which Democratic candidate do you lean most?]

Bill Clinton	41%
Paul Tsongas	31
Jerry Brown	7
Bob Kerrey	6
Tom Harkin	5
Undecided; other	10

Selected National Trend

	Jan. 31–Feb. 2, 1992	*Jan. 3–6, 1992*	*Oct. 31–Nov. 3, 1991*
Clinton	42%	17%	9%
Tsongas	9	6	7
Brown	16	21	21
Kerrey	10	11	10
Harkin	9	9	10
Undecided; other	14	36	43

Also asked of registered Democrats and those who lean Democratic: Regardless of which Democratic presidential candidate you may personally prefer, which one do you think is most likely to defeat George Bush in November?

	Feb. 19–20, 1992	*Jan. 31–Feb. 2, 1992*
Bill Clinton	36%	45%
Paul Tsongas	31	5
Jerry Brown	2	11
Bob Kerrey	2	7
Tom Harkin	1	4
Other	5	5
No opinion	23	23

Asked of registered Republicans and those who lean Republican: I will read off the names of three Republican candidates for president. After I read all three names, please tell me which one you would like to see nominated as the Republican party's candidate for president. [Those who were undecided were asked: As of today, to which Republican candidate do you lean most?]

George Bush	78%
Pat Buchanan	20
David Duke	–
Undecided; other	2

Selected National Trend

	Jan. 31–Feb. 2, 1992	*Jan. 3–6, 1992*	*Dec. 5–8, 1991*
Bush	84%	85%	86%
Buchanan	11	10	5
Duke	4	3	6
Undecided; other	1	2	3

Asked of registered voters: Are you unlikely to vote for Bill Clinton because of questions about his character?

Yes, unlikely	24%
No, not unlikely	64
Would not vote for Clinton for other reasons (volunteered)	5
No opinion	7

Also asked of registered voters: Are you unlikely to vote for Paul Tsongas because you are worried about his health?

Yes, unlikely	10%
No, not unlikely	76

Would not vote for Tsongas for
other reasons (volunteered) 5
No opinion 9

Also asked of registered voters: Are you unlikely to vote for Pat Buchanan because you think his views are too extreme?

Yes, unlikely 33%
No, not unlikely 43
Would not vote for Buchanan for
other reasons (volunteered) 8
No opinion 16

Note: In the aftermath of the New Hampshire primary on February 18, President George Bush's standing among the American public has slipped further. His approval rating has declined to 39%, his all-time low. The percentage of voters who think that Bush deserves to be reelected has fallen to 42%, after hovering around the 50% mark earlier this year.

The New Hampshire results dramatize the extent. to which the recession has hurt the president. Conservative political commentator Pat Buchanan, who was unknown to many of the state's voters prior to his presidential bid, captured 37% of the GOP vote largely by capitalizing on the economic distress that New Hampshire's citizens are suffering. As long as the recession continues, and especially in those parts of the country most severely hurt by it, there will be an anti-Bush vote for either a Democratic or a Republican challenger to exploit.

At present, however, neither Buchanan nor the two leading Democratic presidential hopefuls—Bill Clinton and Paul Tsongas—have enough stature with the voters to fully take advantage of Bush's political vulnerability. Support for Buchanan as the GOP's 1992 presidential nominee has about doubled since the New Hampshire primary, but the challenger still trails the president by an 80%-to-20% margin. In test elections for the fall, Bush defeats both Clinton and Tsongas. His margin against Clinton is 53% to 43%; matched against Tsongas, Bush wins by 54% to 39%.

Nationally, there is no evidence that Buchanan, who sees himself as a conservative in the tradition of Barry Goldwater and Ronald Reagan, has captured the hearts of like-minded GOP voters. Indeed, his staunchly conservative views may limit his appeal among the broader electorate: one third (33%) say that they are unlikely to support Buchanan because his views are too extreme.

As the campaign moves south, Clinton's fortunes are likely to rise, but he may have to deal further with the character issue. While his overall support level has held up, his electability seems more in question to the voters. Fewer now say that Clinton is the Democrat best able to defeat Bush than did so three weeks ago (36% versus 45%), and 24% say that questions about Clinton's character make them unlikely to vote for him. By comparison, only 10% think that concerns about Tsongas's health will lose him votes.

At least until results from future primaries disturb the status quo, New Hampshire winner Tsongas and runner-up Clinton seem to be in a two-man race for the Democratic party's nomination. Clinton remains the front-runner nationally, winning 41% support among registered Democrats and those who lean Democratic. Clinton's support has held despite the allegations of the past month of adultery and draft-dodging. A poll completed earlier this month showed him at 42%.

While Clinton remains on top, Tsongas is close behind with 31%. Like past New Hampshire primary victors, his win has provided a big boost in support among Democratic voters nationally. He has gained 22 percentage points since the last poll. Interestingly, eight years ago another Democrat registering low support nationally—Gary Hart—had an even more spectacular rise in the national polls after victory in New Hampshire. A March 1984 Gallup/*Newsweek* Poll showed Hart's support increasing by 33 percentage points (from 2% to 35%) after he defeated Walter Mondale.

MARCH 1
IMMIGRATION

Interviewing Date: 1/6–9/92*
Survey #GO 22203402

*Gallup survey for CNN/*USA Today*

Asked of registered voters: Would you be more likely or less likely to vote for a presidential candidate who favored tougher laws to limit immigration into the United States, or would it not make much difference?

More likely	64%
Less likely	19
Not much difference	14
No opinion	3

Interviewing Date: 2/6–9/92
Survey #GO 222040

Thinking about immigration into this country from various parts of the world, do you think the number of immigrants now entering the United States from each of the following areas is too many, too few, or about the right amount:

Latin America?

Too many	69%
Too few	5
About right	22
No opinion	4

Asia?

Too many	58%
Too few	4
About right	32
No opinion	6

Africa?

Too many	47%
Too few	10
About right	36
No opinion	7

Europe?

Too many	36%
Too few	7
About right	52
No opinion	5

Please tell me whether you agree or disagree with each of the following statements about immigrants and immigration:

Many immigrants work hard, often taking jobs that Americans don't want?

Agree	84%
Disagree	15
No opinion	1

Many immigrants wind up on welfare and raise taxes for Americans?

Agree	64%
Disagree	32
No opinion	4

Immigrants take the jobs of U.S. workers?

Agree	62%
Disagree	36
No opinion	2

Immigrants help improve our country with their different cultures and talents?

Agree	61%
Disagree	37
No opinion	2

Do you agree or disagree with the recent U.S. decision to refuse to allow Haitian refugees to immigrate to the United States?

Agree	67%
Disagree	27
No opinion	6

	Agree	*Dis-agree*	*No opinion*
By Sex			
Male	70%	26%	4%
Female	64	29	7
By Ethnic Background			
White	70	24	6
Nonwhite	42	52	6
Black	33	61	6

By Education			
College Graduate......62	31	7
College Incomplete...68	24	8
High-School Graduate..............71	24	5
Less Than High-School Graduate....63	33	4
By Region		
East......................63	30	7
Midwest.................68	27	5
South....................70	26	4
West.....................67	27	6
By Age		
18–29 Years............65	30	5
30–49 Years............67	28	5
50 Years and Over.....68	25	7
By Household Income		
$50,000 and Over.....71	24	5
$30,000–$49,999....74	23	3
$20,000–$29,999....69	25	6
Under $20,000.........59	35	6
By Politics		
Republicans............72	23	5
Democrats..............62	31	7
Independents...........67	28	5
By Religion		
Protestants.............68	27	5
Catholics...............75	21	4
By Political Ideology		
Liberal...................56	41	3
Moderate................71	23	6
Conservative...........69	25	6
By Bush Approval		
Approve.................72	23	5
Disapprove.............63	32	5

Note: Immigration has yet to develop into a major issue in this year's presidential campaign. As the campaign battleground moves to the South and West, however, the immigration issue could heat up, especially now that Pat Buchanan's success in New Hampshire has made him a focus of media attention. Recent Gallup surveys find widespread public support for Buchanan's call to restrict the flow into this country of Third World immigrants.

Since the mid-1980s the number of respondents who believe that too many foreigners are allowed into the United States has increased significantly. Concern is greatest about immigration from Latin America, followed by immigration from Asia. Recent government statistics show that a majority of foreigners now entering the country were born in Mexico or some other Latin American country. Close to three in ten new immigrants come from Asian countries.

A January Gallup survey finds almost two thirds (64%) saying that they would be more likely to vote for a presidential candidate who favored tougher laws to limit immigration. Only one in five (19%) would be less likely to support such a candidate.

Especially in southern states like Georgia, which allows registered voters to participate in either party's primary, Buchanan's position on immigration and related issues might attract votes among those who would otherwise stay home or vote in the Democratic primary. (Georgia holds its primary on Tuesday, March 3.) White Protestant voters, small-town voters, and rural voters all are more apt to cast their ballots for a candidate who wants to restrict immigration. These categories are important segments of the white southern electorate that is likely to participate in Republican primaries.

Many Americans share Buchanan's view that the flow of immigration from the Third World should be stemmed. Seven in ten (69%) interviewed in a February poll think that there is too much immigration into the United States from Latin America. Six in ten (58%) believe that there are too many Asians, and about one half (47%) says that there are too many Africans entering this country. Far fewer (36%) have problems with the level of immigration from European countries, which now accounts for less than 10% of the total immigrant pool.

Anti-immigrant sentiment has clearly risen since the mid-1980s. A 1984 Gallup/*Newsweek* Poll showed lower levels of public concern about immigration from all parts of the world. The increase is greatest for Latin America and Africa (a 16-percentage point increase for each), although there has also been a significant increase in concern about Asian (9 percentage points) and European (10 percentage points) immigration.

Today, majorities of Americans fear that immigrants take the jobs of U.S. workers (62%) or often wind up on welfare, thus raising people's taxes (64%). Somewhat surprisingly, the percentage saying that immigrants take jobs away from Americans is not significantly higher today than it was in 1984 (only 1 point). But while people may be no more likely to believe that immigrants take people's jobs, the threat may seem more serious in today's recessionary climate.

Americans' more restrictive views on immigration are bad news for the Haitian boat people who were deported by the U.S. government early last month. Two thirds (67%) of respondents agree with Washington's decision to refuse to allow them to immigrate to this country. The United States refused entry on the grounds that the Haitians were "economic" rather than "political" refugees. They were attempting to flee Haiti after the United States and its allies placed economic sanctions on the country in response to a military overthrow of a popularly elected government in late 1990.

Opinion on the Haitians divides sharply by race. Seventy percent of whites, compared with 42% of blacks, approve of the decision to send them back to their homeland.

MARCH 1
PRESIDENTIAL CANDIDATES

Interviewing Date: 2/20–21/92*
Special Survey

*From what you know about the following presidential candidates, do you think each of the following descriptions applies?***

	George Bush	*Pat Buchanan*	*Bill Clinton*	*Paul Tsongas*
Could be elected	83%	44%	44%	38%
Cares about people	66	61	60	60
Personally honest	65	57	39	56
Strong leader	63	45	45	32
Appeals to me	49	32	33	31
Has good plans	46	47	51	47

*Gallup/*Newsweek* Poll
**Multiple replies were given.

Interviewing Date: 2/19–20/92*
Survey #GO 222042

Asked of registered Republicans and those who lean Republican: I will read off the names of three Republican candidates for president. After I read all three names, please tell me which one you would like to see nominated as the Republican party's candidate for president. [Those who were undecided were asked: As of today, to which Republican candidate do you lean most?]

	Non-South	*South*
George Bush	76%	82%
Pat Buchanan	21	18
David Duke	–	–
Undecided; other	3	**

**Less than 1%

Asked of registered Democrats and those who lean Democratic: After I read all five names, please tell me which one you would like to see nominated as the Democratic party's candidate for president. [Those who were undecided were asked: As of today, to which Democratic candidate do you lean most?]

	Non-South	*South*
Bill Clinton	34%	57%
Paul Tsongas	35	24
Bob Kerrey	7	5
Tom Harkin	5	5
Jerry Brown	7	5
Undecided; other	12	4

*Gallup survey for CNN/*USA Today*

Also asked of registered Democrats and those who lean Democratic: Are you unlikely to vote for Bill Clinton because of questions about his character?

	Non-South	*South*
Yes, unlikely	18%	17%
No, not unlikely	74	73
Would not vote for Clinton for other reasons (volunteered)	*	5
No opinion	8	5

*Less than 1%

Note: As the presidential campaign enters the next phase, both the Republican challenger and the Democratic front-runner face key tests. Pat Buchanan must prove that his success in the New Hampshire primary was not a fluke, by showing strength in states that have been less severely hurt by the recession and by doing so without the benefit of extended campaigning. Bill Clinton must demonstrate his organizational and political skills by sweeping the upcoming southern primaries and show convincingly that he has put the "character" issues of marital infidelity and draft-dodging behind him.

The next two weeks should clear up much of the uncertainty about the Republican and Democratic presidential races. Delegates in twenty states will be up for grabs between now and Super Tuesday on March 10. This day marks the first multicontest event of the campaign, when Georgia, Maryland, and Colorado hold primaries.

The high level of support for uncommitted delegates (31%) in this week's South Dakota Republican primary has led some observers to downplay Buchanan's effectiveness as a presidential candidate. His results in New Hampshire were only 6 percentage points higher than the uncommitted vote in South Dakota. Buchanan's voters, some argue, were expressing no confidence in George Bush, with little regard for Buchanan the man or for his political views. Recent Gallup Polls, however, show that while Buchanan is unquestionably a beneficiary of anti-Bush sentiment, he wins the respect of many Americans for his ideas and abilities.

A Gallup Poll conducted for *Newsweek* magazine after the New Hampshire primary shows Buchanan to be more than a match for leading Democratic candidates Clinton and Paul Tsongas on key qualities that Americans look for in a president. Buchanan is Clinton's equal on perceptions of leadership ability (each 45%), but far fewer see Tsongas in this light (32%). Buchanan is more likely than Clinton to be seen as personally honest (57% versus 39%), while 56% say that Tsongas is personally honest.

Buchanan's more extreme views may not yet be well known to the general public. But for now, the *Newsweek* Poll shows that about as many respondents think that Buchanan has good plans for the country (47%) as Clinton (51%) or Tsongas (47%). On this issue, Buchanan also runs even with the president (47% for Buchanan versus 46% for Bush). Despite his hardline positions on issues such as welfare and immigration, Buchanan is about as likely as the two leading Democrats to be seen as someone who cares about people (61% versus 60% each for Clinton and Tsongas).

The increased visibility that Buchanan received from his New Hampshire showing should help his chances in the South. He is as well regarded in the South as he is outside of the region, but he faces more of an uphill struggle there since Bush remains more popular in the South than he does in any other part of the country. A Gallup Poll taken in the days following the New Hampshire primary found Buchanan gaining as much ground in the South as he did elsewhere. Among all registered Republicans in the region, he trails Bush by 82% to 18%. But in states that have open primaries, such as Georgia, Buchanan might surprise the public, especially if many apathetic Bush supporters stay home and if Buchanan's opposition to the Gulf War—now the subject of the president's television ads—does not prove especially damaging to him in this promilitary region.

After New Hampshire, the Gallup Poll found Clinton losing his lead among Democratic voters outside of the South: Tsongas pulled into a statistical tie among Democratic voters who live in the East, Midwest, or West, capturing 35% support to Clinton's 34%. But in the South, Clinton has held his ground. After the New Hampshire primary, his support edged upward to 57%, from 50% in early February before the Gennifer Flowers and draft-evasion stories broke. Tsongas gained in the South but remains well behind with 24%. No other candidate received more than 5% among southern Democratic voters, although the poll was completed before Bob Kerrey's recent victory in South Dakota.

Kerrey, who has decided to challenge Clinton on the draft issue, may be in the best position to cut into the Arkansas governor's big lead in the South. So far, the character issue does not seem to have done major damage to Clinton, at least among the Democratic electorate. About three in four (73%) southern Democratic voters say that questions about Clinton's character do not make them less likely to vote for him.

MARCH 3
DEMOCRATIC PRESIDENTIAL CANDIDATES

Interviewing Date: 2/28–3/1/92
Survey #GO 222041

Asked of registered Democrats and those who lean Democratic: I will read off the names of some people in politics. As I read each name, tell me if you have a favorable or unfavorable opinion of this person, or if you have never heard of him:

Bill Clinton?

	Total	*Non-South*	*South*
Favorable	44%	40%	51%
Unfavorable	35	37	31
No opinion	13	15	9
Never heard of	8	8	9

Selected National Trend
(Total)

1992	*Favor-able*	*Unfavor-able*	*No opinion*	*Never heard of*
Jan. 31–Feb. 2	51%	24%	14%	11%
Jan. 3–6	28	11	16	45

(Non-South)

1992	*Favor-able*	*Unfavor-able*	*No opinion*	*Never heard of*
Jan. 31–Feb. 2	51%	23%	15%	11%
Jan. 3–6	26	11	17	46

(South)

1992	*Favor-able*	*Unfavor-able*	*No opinion*	*Never heard of*
Jan. 31–Feb. 2	51%	27%	9%	13%
Jan. 3–6	33	9	14	44

Paul Tsongas?

	Total	*Non-South*	*South*
Favorable	39%	40%	37%
Unfavorable	21	19	23
No opinion	18	20	15
Never heard of	22	21	25

Selected National Trend
(Total)

1992	*Favor-able*	*Unfavor-able*	*No opinion*	*Never heard of*
Jan. 31–Feb. 2	25%	16%	18%	41%
Jan. 3–6	22	13	14	51

(Non-South)

1992	*Favor-able*	*Unfavor-able*	*No opinion*	*Never heard of*
Jan. 31–Feb. 2	27%	14%	20%	39%
Jan. 3–6	24	14	13	49

(South)

1992	*Favor-able*	*Unfavor-able*	*No opinion*	*Never heard of*
Jan. 31–Feb. 2	20%	19%	17%	44%
Jan. 3–6	17	10	17	56

Jerry Brown?

Favorable	34%
Unfavorable	37
No opinion	14
Never heard of	15

Selected National Trend

	Favor-able	Unfavor-able	No opinion	Never heard of
1992				
Jan. 31–Feb. 2	39%	30%	17%	14%
Jan. 3–6	35	30	13	22

Bob Kerrey?

Favorable	30%
Unfavorable	17
No opinion	25
Never heard of	28

Selected National Trend

	Favor-able	Unfavor-able	No opinion	Never heard of
1992				
Jan. 31–Feb. 2	31%	11%	20%	38%
Jan. 3–6	29	9	17	45

Tom Harkin?

Favorable	27%
Unfavorable	20
No opinion	25
Never heard of	28

Selected National Trend

	Favor-able	Unfavor-able	No opinion	Never heard of
1992				
Jan. 31–Feb. 2	23%	12%	25%	40%
Jan. 3–6	24	11	15	50

Also asked of registered Democrats and those who lean Democratic: Do you think any of the Democratic candidates for president has much chance of defeating George Bush in November, or not? [Those who answered "yes" were asked: Which of the following three candidates do you think has the best chance of defeating George Bush in November?]

	Total	Non-South	South
Bill Clinton	28%	25%	36%
Paul Tsongas	23	25	18
Bob Kerrey	9	9	8
Other	2	2	1
All the same (volunteered)	*	*	1
None	34	33	34
No opinion	4	6	2

*Less than 1%

Also asked of registered Democrats and those who lean Democratic: Are you satisfied with Bill Clinton's explanation of his draft status during the Vietnam War, or not?

	Total	Non-South	South
Yes	53%	49%	61%
No	31	36	21
No opinion	16	15	18

Note: Democratic presidential candidate Bill Clinton still seems to be on track to win big in the southern primaries, including, in particular, the important Super Tuesday votes of March 10. The Arkansas governor, however, is in serious trouble outside of his own region. After the early primaries, Clinton has maintained his popularity among the southern Democratic electorate, but outside the South his popularity has taken a dive.

The Arkansas governor's vulnerability in other parts of the country increases the pressure on him to win big in the southern primaries held on Super Tuesday. If he falls short, then bouncing back will be much more difficult as the campaign moves to the less friendly industrial Midwest. (Illinois and Michigan hold primaries on March 17.)

Southern Democratic voters seem to be sticking by Clinton despite the draft-evasion charges against him that surfaced last month. Opinion of Clinton among registered Democrats in the South divides 51% favorable to 31% unfavorable. These results are essentially unchanged from those of one month ago (51% favorable, 27% unfavorable).

Six in ten (61%) southern Democratic voters say that they are satisfied with Clinton's explanation of his draft status during the Vietnam War, while two in ten (21%) are dissatisfied. And he is seen as the most electable Democrat. By a 2-to-1 margin (36% versus 18%) southern Democratic voters pick Clinton over Paul Tsongas as the candidate with the best chance of defeating George Bush in November.

Outside the South, Democratic voters see Clinton in a much less positive light. Forty percent of Democratic voters who live in the East, Midwest, or West have favorable views of him and 37% unfavorable. Only one month ago these nonsouthern voters were much more charitable in their appraisals of Clinton: twice as many had a favorable (51%) as had an unfavorable opinion (23%).

Democratic voters in the non-South also seem less willing than southern Democrats to give Clinton the benefit of the doubt on the military draft issue. More than one third of Democratic voters (36%) who live outside of the South, compared with only one fifth of southern Democratic voters (21%), are not satisfied with Clinton's explanation of his past draft status.

Former Massachusetts Senator Tsongas is less well known than Clinton but receives positive favorability ratings in both the South (37% favorable versus 23% unfavorable) and the non-South (40% versus 19%). Nonetheless, while Clinton has been damaged by the rumors of marital infidelity and draft evasion, Tsongas may have his own electability problems. Even though Democratic voters outside the South have much more positive views of Tsongas than of Clinton, they are evenly divided on whether Tsongas (25%) or Clinton (25%) has a better chance to be elected in November.

MARCH 5
CONGRESS

Interviewing Date: 2/28–3/1/92
Survey #GO 222041

In general, whom do you trust more on the issue of taxes—George Bush or the Democratic leaders in Congress?

George Bush....................................38%
Democratic leaders..............................40
Both equally (volunteered)......................1
Neither (volunteered)...........................16
No opinion..5

As I read off some economic and tax proposals now being discussed in Congress, please tell me whether you favor or oppose each one:

Providing tax credits and incentives for first-time home buyers?

Favor...84%
Oppose...14
No opinion..2

Cutting taxes for middle-income families?

Favor...80%
Oppose...18
No opinion..2

Creating jobs through government-financed public works programs?

Favor...77%
Oppose...20
No opinion..3

Increasing taxes on those making high incomes?

Favor...75%
Oppose...22
No opinion..3

Using available extra money to reduce the federal deficit?

Favor...73%
Oppose...21
No opinion..6

Cutting taxes on capital gains?

Favor	52%
Oppose	38
No opinion	10

Giving business and real estate developers tax breaks and incentives?

Favor	47%
Oppose	48
No opinion	5

*Which action do you think is the most important that Congress pass:**

Cutting taxes for middle-income families?	27%
Creating jobs through government-financed public works programs?	27
Increasing taxes on those making high incomes?	15
Using available extra money to reduce the federal deficit?	11
Providing tax credits and incentives for first-time home buyers?	9
Giving business and real estate developers tax breaks and incentives?	5
Cutting taxes on capital gains?	4
No opinion	2

*Multiple replies were given.

Note: President George Bush and congressional Democrats draw similar levels of public support in their dispute over taxes and the economy. In a new Gallup Poll, about four in ten Americans (38%) say that they trust Bush more on taxes, while another four in ten (40%) place greater trust in Democratic leaders in Congress. The Democrats, however, may be winning the battle of ideas; their approaches to stimulating the economy win broader public support than do those of the Republicans.

Tax cuts for the middle class, part of the Democratic legislation that narrowly passed the House last week, are broadly popular. Eight in ten (80%) say that they favor cutting taxes for middle-income families, while only 18% oppose such a cut. Democrats also can find reassurance in the high level of public support (75%) for increasing taxes on the rich, proposed as a means to offset the cost of tax breaks for the middle class.

By contrast, opinion on cutting the capital gains tax, a Bush priority, is more closely divided. Roughly one half (52%) would favor a capital gains cut, but four in ten (38%) would oppose it.

President Bush's proposal to give tax credits to first-time home buyers, announced in his State of the Union message, is favored by 84%. But, compared with a middle-class tax cut and other Democratic proposals, this tax break is seen as less urgent. When asked to choose among seven economic proposals, the public rates a middle-class tax cut (27%) and job creation through public works programs (27%) as most important. Tax credits for first-time home buyers rates fifth (9%), after increasing taxes for upper-income people (15%) and using extra money to reduce the federal budget deficit (11%). Tax incentives for business and real estate developers (5%) and cuts in capital gains rates (4%) rank lowest with the public as legislative priorities.

MARCH 8
PRESIDENT BUSH/PRESIDENTIAL CANDIDATES

Interviewing Date: 2/28–3/1/92
Survey #GO 222041

Do you approve or disapprove of the way George Bush is handling his job as president?

Approve	41%
Disapprove	53
No opinion	6

	Approve	*Dis-approve*	*No opinion*
By Sex			
Male	70%	26%	4%
Female	66	30	4
By Education			
College Graduate	67	28	5
College Incomplete	73	22	5
No College	65	31	4

By Region			
South	74	25	1
Non-South	66	29	5
By Age			
Under 40	74	24	2
40 Years and Over	64	31	5
By Income			
$30,000 and Over	71	24	5
Under $30,000	63	34	3
By Political Ideology			
Conservative	74	23	3
Moderate; Liberal	63	32	5

Selected National Trend

	Approve	Dis-approve	No opinion
1992			
February 19–20	39%	47%	14%
February 6–9	44	48	8

*Asked of registered Republicans and those who lean Republican: Please tell me if you have a favorable or unfavorable opinion of this person, or if you have never heard of him:**

George Bush?

Favorable 85%
Unfavorable 14

	Favor-able	Unfavor-able
By Sex		
Male	86%	13%
Female	84	15
By Education		
College Graduate	86	14
College Incomplete	89	9
No College	83	15
By Region		
South	88	11
Non-South	84	15
By Age		
Under 40	87	13
40 Years and Over	84	14
By Income		
$30,000 and Over	88	11
Under $30,000	81	17
By Political Ideology		
Conservative	91	8
Moderate; Liberal	81	18

Pat Buchanan?

Favorable 38%
Unfavorable 45

	Favor-able	Unfavor-able
By Sex		
Male	45%	41%
Female	33	48
By Education		
College Graduate	43	48
College Incomplete	37	46
No College	35	42
By Region		
South	37	46
Non-South	39	44
By Age		
Under 40	41	45
40 Years and Over	37	45
By Income		
$30,000 and Over	39	49
Under $30,000	38	38
By Political Ideology		
Conservative	44	46
Moderate; Liberal	35	45

*"No opinion" and "never heard of" are omitted.

Asked of registered Democrats and those who lean Democratic: Please tell me if you *have a favorable or unfavorable opinion of this person, or if you have never heard of him:**

Bill Clinton?

Favorable	44%
Unfavorable	35

	Favorable	*Unfavorable*
By Sex		
Male	48%	35%
Female	40	35
By Ethnic Background		
White	44	37
Nonwhite	45	25
By Education		
College Graduate	45	41
College Incomplete	43	41
No College	43	31
By Region		
South	51	31
Non-South	40	37
By Age		
Under 50	40	38
50 Years and Over	49	30
By Income		
$30,000 and Over	40	50
Under $30,000	47	24
By Political Ideology		
Liberal	44	38
Moderate	41	37
Conservative	47	29

Paul Tsongas?

Favorable	39%
Unfavorable	21

	Favorable	*Unfavorable*
By Sex		
Male	35%	24%
Female	43	18
By Ethnic Background		
White	43	21
Nonwhite	25	16
By Education		
College Graduate	60	18
College Incomplete	41	23
No College	32	21
By Region		
South	37	23
Non-South	40	19
By Age		
Under 50	38	18
50 Years and Over	42	25
By Income		
$30,000 and Over	51	24
Under $30,000	31	19
By Political Ideology		
Liberal	50	16
Moderate	41	18
Conservative	28	28

*"No opinion" and "never heard of" are omitted.

Note: By capturing 36% of the Republican primary vote in Georgia, and receiving close to 30% in other GOP primaries held on Tuesday, March 3, Pat Buchanan has proved that his showing in New Hampshire is no fluke. He has evoked conservative themes in his campaign by attacking George Bush for giving in on his "no new taxes" pledge and by taking issue with the president on racial quotas and government funding of controversial art.

A recent Gallup Poll, however, suggests that the major factor behind Buchanan's success is not disillusionment with Bush among conservative Republicans. Instead, it appears to be more a protest vote against the president and his administration, who are tagged with the blame for tough economic times.

Buchanan's personal support does tilt conservative; 44% of conservatives view him favorably compared with only 35% of moderate and liberal Republicans. However, it appears that many of these same conservatives who view him favorably remain pragmatic when it comes to their vote. According to an earlier Gallup Poll (February 19–20), only 19% of the conservative vote goes to Buchanan, while the remainder stays with Bush.

Buchanan's strength and Bush's problems at the polls can be traced to shaky favorability ratings of the president within his own party. Nearly one third (28%) of Republican voters now say that they disapprove of the way Bush is handling his job. Yet these critics tend to describe themselves as moderate-to-liberal Republicans, not conservatives. Just 23% of conservative Republicans say that they disapprove of Bush, compared with 32% of moderate and liberal Republicans.

The major factor which distinguishes Bush's supporters from his detractors within his own party is household income: 24% of Republicans making over $30,000 per year disapprove of his job performance, compared with 34% of Republicans of lower incomes. The anti-Bush group also tends to be older and less well educated, thus suggesting that Bush's problems are based on the disaffection of a social and economic class—more discouraged than the rest of its party with the state of the economy—rather than on Buchanan's conservative appeal.

Class lines also help define the base of support for each of the major Democratic candidates seeking the presidency this year. The survey shows Bill Clinton to be better regarded by the traditional Democratic base of older, lower-income, and minority voters. His favorable rating generally runs 10 percentage points higher with these groups than does Paul Tsongas's.

Tsongas's appeal is sharper and more concentrated. His favorability rating is highest among upscale, younger, mostly white, better educated, and more liberal blocs of voters, who tend to live outside the South. His rating among these groups runs some 20 percentage points higher than Clinton's.

Despite the conservative label being applied to Tsongas on the basis of his economic views, it is actually Clinton who receives higher ratings from Democrats who see themselves as conservative. Tsongas is viewed favorably by just 28% of conservatives in his own party, while Clinton receives a favorable response from 47% of the same group.

The downside for Clinton is his unfavorable ratings among self-described liberal and higher-income voters. One half (50%) of Democrats in the higher-income category views Clinton unfavorably; 38% of liberals regard him poorly as well. Tsongas does not have high unfavorable ratings with any particular social or economic group within his own party.

MARCH 10
PRESIDENT BUSH

Interviewing Date: 2/28–3/1/92
Survey #GO 222041

Do you approve or disapprove of the way George Bush is handling his job as president?

	Approve
National	41%

Selected National Trend

	Approve
1992	
January 31– February 2	46%
January 3–6	46
1991	
December 5–8	52
October 24–27	62
October 3–6	65
September 13–15	68
August 23–25	74
August 8–11	71
July 18–21	70
June 27–30	72
March 7–10	87
February 28–March 3	89
1990	
July 6–8	63
1989	
November 2–5	70
March 10–13	56

Please tell me whether you approve or disapprove of the way George Bush is handling some specific problems facing the country:

Foreign policy?

	Approve
National	55%

Selected National Trend

	Approve
1992	
January 31– February 2	65%
January 3–6	64
1991	
December 5–8	64
October 24–27	68
October 3–6	70
September 13–15	70
August 23–25	74
August 8–11	68
July 18–21	71
June 27–30	64
March 7–10	79
February 28–March 3	84
1990	
July 6–8	62
1989	
November 2–5	65
March 10–13	62

Economy?

	Approve
National	21%

Selected National Trend

	Approve
1992	
January 31– February 2	22%
January 3–6	24
1991	
December 5–8	22
October 24–27	28
October 3–6	29
September 13–15	32
August 23–25	36
August 8–11	33
July 18–21	34
June 27–30	36
March 7–10	37
February 28–March 3	51
1990	
July 6–8	40
1989	
November 2–5	40
March 10–13	52

Note: President George Bush's foreign policy ratings, which had remained high in the aftermath of popular support for the Gulf War, have declined sharply in recent weeks. The percentage of those who approve of the way Bush is handling foreign policy fell from 65% in January to 55% in the most recent Gallup survey.

At the end of the Gulf War, 84% expressed approval of Bush's handling of foreign policy. While this record high rating—as well as Bush's 89% overall approval rating—was not sustained, his approval on foreign policy stabilized by the summer of 1991 at between 60% and 70% and stayed at that high level through January. Bush's foreign policy rating remained strong across most social and political groups, including his otherwise harshest critics: Democrats and self-described liberals.

The recent decline in Bush's foreign policy rating is most evident among Democrats, independents, and political moderates, who are also the most critical of his handling of the economy. Election-year partisanship may provide a partial explanation for their sudden withdrawal of approval for the president's foreign policy.

Bush's overall approval rating of 41% and the percentage who approve of his handling of the economy (21%) are statistically unchanged from January.

MARCH 12
SATISFACTION INDEX

Interviewing Date: 2/28–3/1/92
Survey #GO 222041

In general, are you satisfied or dissatisfied with the way things are going in the United States at this time?

Satisfied	21%
Dissatisfied	78
No opinion	1

Selected National Trend

	Satisfied	Dis-satisfied	No opinion
1992			
January 31–February 2	24%	75%	1%
1991			
December	37	60	3
October	39	57	4
August	49	45	6
March	52	43	5
January 17–20	62	33	5
January 3–6	32	61	7
1990			
October	29	67	4
July	45	51	4
February	55	39	6
1989			
February	45	50	5
1988			
September	56	40	4
May	41	54	5
1987			
August	45	49	6
1986			
December	47	49	4
March	66	30	4
1985			
November	51	46	3
1984			
September	48	45	7
February	50	46	4
1983			
August	35	59	6
1982			
November	24	72	4
April	25	71	4
1981			
June	33	61	6
January	17	78	5
1979			
July	12	84	4
February	26	69	5

In general, are you satisfied or dissatisfied with the way things are going in your own personal life?

Satisfied	79%
Dissatisfied	20
No opinion	1

Selected National Trend

	Satisfied	Dis-satisfied	No opinion
1992			
January	77%	22%	1%
1991			
October	81	18	1
August	82	16	2
March	87	12	1
January 17–20	86	12	2
January 3–6	84	14	2
1990			
October	82	16	2
July	81	17	2
February	83	16	1
1988			
September	87	12	1
May	80	16	4
1987			
August	83	15	2
1986			
March	84	15	1
1985			
November	82	17	1
1984			
February	79	19	2
1983			
August	77	20	3
1982			
November	75	23	2
April	76	22	2
1981			
June	81	16	3
January	81	17	2
1979			
July	73	23	4
February	77	21	2

Note: At the beginning of this election year, Americans take a very dim view of the state of affairs in this country. In a recent Gallup Poll, only one in five adults (21%) says that he is satisfied with the way things are going in the United States. Indeed, public satisfaction with the state of the nation is at a ten-year low. The last time so few respondents felt good about conditions in this country was in November 1982, during the last recession. A Gallup Poll taken at that time found a satisfaction level of 24%, statistically similar to the current results.

In presidential elections, voters usually take out their frustrations on the incumbent—bad news for George Bush. Eight years ago, when

Ronald Reagan easily won reelection, the public mood was upbeat. A February 1984 Gallup survey found 50% feeling positive about the state of the nation.

The current level of public contentment is not yet as low as it was at the end of Jimmy Carter's presidency. Satisfaction with the country dropped to 12% in mid-1979, before Carter delivered his "malaise" speech.

Respondents' satisfaction with their personal lives contrasts sharply with their views on the nation as a whole. No matter how bad things seem to be going in the country, they tend to say that they are happy with their own lives. Eight in ten (79%) now reply that they are satisfied with their personal life, somewhat below the 87% level reported one year ago during the post-Gulf War victory euphoria. Since Gallup began asking these questions in 1979, personal satisfaction has never dropped below the mid-70s.

MARCH 13
SILICONE-GEL BREAST IMPLANTS

Interviewing Date: 2/28–3/1/92
Survey #GO 222041

Have you heard or read about the recent controversy over the safety of silicone breast implants?

	Yes
National	92%

	Yes
By Sex	
Male	91%
Female	93

Asked of those who replied in the affirmative: Do you think silicone breast implants should be legally available to all women who want them, legally available only in special circumstances (such as when a woman has had a mastectomy), or should silicone breast implants be banned entirely because of safety concerns?

	Total	*Women*	*Men*
Legally available to all women who want them	37%	31%	44%
Legally available only in special circumstances	29	31	27
Should be banned entirely	31	36	24
No opinion	3	2	5

*Also asked of those who replied in the affirmative: Which of the following do you blame for the current problems over silicone breast implants?**

	Total	*Women*	*Men*
Companies that make the implants	40%	40%	41%
Women who were too eager to change their physical appearance	31	30	31
Government agencies which regulate public health and safety	26	30	21
The medical profession and doctors	19	18	20
No opinion	3	3	3
None of the above	2	1	2

*Multiple replies were given.

Note: Americans are divided over whether access to silicone-gel breast implants should be restricted because of concerns about safety. According to a recent Gallup Poll, public opinion splits three ways on implants: more than one third (37%) of adults aware of the controversy believe that implant surgery should be available to all women who request it, three in ten (29%) think that the procedure should be available only on a limited basis, and another three in ten (31%) say that it should be banned entirely because of safety concerns.

Last month a federal advisory panel took a middle position on access to implants. The Food and Drug Administration panel recommended allowing women who have had cancer surgery to get them but restricting access for otherwise healthy women who seek to increase their breast size.

While Dow, Corning, and other manufacturers have been most widely criticized in the media coverage of this controversy, the public tends to spread the blame for problems that may have resulted from implants. Manufacturers are most often singled out, but less than one half (40%) of aware respondents finds at fault the companies making the product. Women themselves blame other women too eager to change their physical appearance (30%), and another 30% hold government regulators of public health and safety responsible. Doctors and the medical profession are least likely to be seen by women as culpable (18%).

MARCH 15
PRESIDENTIAL CANDIDATES/ PRESIDENTIAL TRIAL HEATS

Interviewing Date: 3/11–12/92*
Survey #GO 222044

Asked of registered Democrats and those who lean Democratic: Which one of the following would you like to see nominated as the Democratic party's candidate for president? [Those who were undecided were asked: As of today, to which Democratic candidate do you lean most?]

Bill Clinton	54%
Paul Tsongas	23
Jerry Brown	18
Undecided; other	5

	Clinton	*Tsongas*	*Brown***
By Sex			
Male	49%	26%	20%
Female	58	20	17
By Ethnic Background			
White	53	25	18
Nonwhite	55	16	21
By Education			
College Graduate	48	31	18
College Incomplete	52	33	13
No College	56	18	20
By Region			
East	53	21	22
Midwest	59	23	16
South	58	21	13
West	41	28	27
By Age			
18–29 Years	60	14	22
30–49 Years	47	29	23
50–64 Years	52	23	15
65 Years and Over	63	19	14
By Household Income			
$50,000 and Over	41	30	24
$30,000–$49,999	53	29	14
$20,000–$29,999	59	17	21
Under $20,000	62	19	14
By Political Ideology			
Liberal	62	17	15
Moderate	57	24	15
Conservative	41	27	24
By 1988 Vote			
George Bush	65	16	13
Michael Dukakis	47	27	21
By State Primary			
Held primary or caucus	55	24	13
Still to come	52	22	26

*Gallup survey for CNN/*USA Today*

**"Undecided" and "other" are omitted.

Selected National Trend

	Clinton	*Tsongas*	*Brown*	*Undecided; other*
1992				
Feb. 19–20	41%	31%	7%	21%
Jan. 31–Feb. 2	42	9	16	33
Jan. 3–9	27	6	21	46
1991				
Oct. 31–Nov. 3	9	7	21	63

Asked of registered Republicans and those who lean Republican: Which one of the following would you like to see nominated as the Republican party's candidate for president? [Those who were undecided were asked: As of today, to which Republican candidate do you lean most?]

George Bush....................................86%
Pat Buchanan....................................11
David Duke 1
Undecided; other................................. 2

	Bush	*Buchanan*	*Duke**
By Sex			
Male 84%		12%	3%
Female..................87		10	–
By Ethnic Background			
White....................85		11	2
Nonwhite 99		–	–
By Education			
College Graduate 93		5	1
College Incomplete...88		10	–
No College 80		16	1
By Region			
East 79		15	4
Midwest................87		11	–
South 86		10	1
West 90		8	1
By Age			
18–29 Years...........90		6	2
30–49 Years...........88		11	–
50–64 Years...........83		15	1
65 Years and Over.....79		11	4
By Household Income			
$50,000 and Over.....90		8	1
$30,000–$49,999....86		10	1
$20,000–$29,999....87		13	–
Under $20,000........78		14	4
By Political Ideology			
Liberal..................88		12	–
Moderate................88		11	–
Conservative..........86		11	1
By 1988 Vote			
George Bush...........85		11	2
Michael Dukakis 91		9	–
By State Primary			
Held primary or caucus................86		13	1
Still to come 85		10	2

*"Undecided" and "other" are omitted.

Selected National Trend

	Bush	Buchanan	Duke	Undecided; other
1992				
Feb. 19–20	78%	20%	–	2%
Jan. 31–Feb. 2	84	11	4	1
Jan. 3–9	85	10	3	2
1991				
Oct. 31–Nov. 3	86	5	6	3

Also asked of registered Republicans and those who lean Republican: In your opinion, should Pat Buchanan stay in the race for the Republican nomination for president, or should he drop out?

Stay in..37%
Drop out..57
No opinion.. 6

Asked of registered voters: Suppose the 1992 presidential election were being held today. If George Bush were the Republican candidate and Bill Clinton were the Democratic candidate, whom would you vote for? [Those who were undecided were asked: As of today, do you lean more to Bush, the Republican, or to Clinton, the Democrat?]

Bush 50%
Clinton...44
Undecided; other................................ 6

Selected National Trend

1992	Bush	Clinton	Undecided; other
February 19–20	53%	43%	4%
February 6–9	53	38	9

Also asked of registered voters: Suppose the 1992 presidential election were being held today. If George Bush were the Republican candidate and Paul Tsongas were the Democratic candidate, whom would you vote for? [Those who were undecided were asked: As of today, do you lean more to Bush, the Republican, or to Tsongas, the Democrat?]

Bush	55%
Tsongas	38
No opinion	7

Also asked of registered voters: Suppose the 1992 presidential election were being held today. If George Bush were the Republican candidate and Jerry Brown were the Democratic candidate, whom would you vote for? [Those who were undecided were asked: As of today, do you lean more to Bush, the Republican, or to Brown, the Democrat?]

Bush	59%
Brown	34
No opinion	7

Also asked of registered voters: Regardless of how you might vote, who do you think is more likely to win in November—George Bush or the Democratic party's candidate for president?

Bush	71%
Democratic candidate	22
No opinion	7

Note: After sweeping the southern primaries on Super Tuesday, Bill Clinton has taken the momentum away from his chief rival, Paul Tsongas, in the race for the Democratic nomination. A national Gallup Poll finds Democratic voters favoring Clinton over Tsongas by a 2-to-1 margin (54% versus 23%). Combined with his advantage in campaign finances and organization, Clinton's post-Super Tuesday surge increases his chances of success in the upcoming Illinois and Michigan primaries on March 17.

Clinton continues to run closest to George Bush in test elections. But even after Super Tuesday, Clinton manages only a statistical tie, receiving 44% to Bush's 50%. Tsongas loses to Bush by 55% to 38%; Jerry Brown loses by 59% to 34%.

Super Tuesday's other big winner—President Bush—now seems virtually assured of his party's nomination. In fact, after his solid victories in this week's primaries and caucuses, a majority (57%) of GOP voters says that it is time for conservative challenger Pat Buchanan to end his campaign.

Buchanan is far less welcome in the Republican race for president today than he was just three weeks ago, after the New Hampshire primary. At that time, one out of five Republican voters (20%) supported the conservative commentator for the GOP nomination and more than six in ten (62%) thought that he should continue his challenge against Bush. Now, 37% of Republicans want Buchanan to stay in, while 57% prefer that he bow out.

The Bush campaign's efforts to portray Buchanan as an extremist may have played a role in his loss of support. Since New Hampshire, the proportion of GOP voters who say they are unlikely to vote for Buchanan because his views are too extreme has increased from one third (33%) to one half (50%).

MARCH 19
CRIME

Interviewing Date: 2/28–3/1/92
Survey #GO 222041

Is there more crime in the United States than there was a year ago, or less?

More	89%
Less	3
Same (volunteered)	4
No opinion	4

Selected National Trend

	More	Less	Same	No opinion
September 1990	84%	3%	7%	6%
June 1989	84	5	5	6

Is there more crime in your area than there was a year ago, or less?

More	54%
Less	19
Same (volunteered)	23
No opinion	4

	More	Less	Same	No opinion
By Community Size				
Large City	64%	15%	16%	5%
Medium City	57	21	17	5
Suburbs	46	21	28	5
Small Town	47	23	27	3
Rural	58	14	24	4

Selected National Trend

	More	Less	Same	No opinion
1990				
September	51%	18%	24%	8%
1989				
June	53	18	22	7
January	47	21	27	5
1983	37	17	36	10
1981	54	8	29	9
1977	43	17	32	8
1975	50	12	29	9
1972	51	10	27	12

Is there any area near where you live—that is, within a mile—where you would be afraid to walk alone at night?

	Yes
National	44%

	Yes
By Community Size	
Large City	60%
Medium City	56
Suburbs	42
Small Town	36
Rural	31

Selected National Trend

	Yes
1990	40%
1989	43
1983	45
1981	45
1977	45
1975	45
1972	42
1967	31
1965	34

How about at home at night—do you feel safe and secure, or not?

	Yes
National	89%

	Yes
By Community Size	
Large City	85%
Medium City	88
Suburbs	91
Small Town	92
Rural	87

Selected National Trend

	Yes
1990	90%
1989	90
1983	84
1981	84
1977	85
1975	80
1972	83

Note: A new Gallup Poll shows that perceptions of a crime problem at the national level continue to exceed worries about it at the local level. Nine in ten adults (89%) believe that crime in America is on the increase. Perceptions of a growing problem at the national level are even more widespread today than they were a few years ago. In both 1989 and 1990 Gallup Polls, 84% thought that crime was on the rise in the country as a whole.

People's beliefs about crime in America, however, are probably more a reflection of news coverage than of personal experience. Respondents are much less apt to think that crime has gone up at the local level. Just over one half (54%) now say that there is more crime in their area, not a significant increase over 1989 and 1990 poll results.

The percentage of those who feel personally threatened by crime has not increased significantly in more than a decade. Slightly less than one half (44%) of adults know of an area within a mile of their home where they would not feel safe walking alone at night. That percentage has been relatively stable since the early 1970s.

While 89% claim to feel safe and secure at night, 11% do not. In the mid-1970s a larger percentage (20%) did not feel secure at home after dark. Concern about crime is highest among big-city dwellers (60%) who do not feel entirely safe walking alone at night in their neighborhoods.

MARCH 22
PRESIDENT BUSH—AN ANALYSIS

Interviewing Date: 3/11–12/92
Survey #GO 222044

Do you approve or disapprove of the way George Bush is handling his job as president?

Approve	41%
Disapprove	47
No opinion	12

Presidential Approval Ratings
(In March of Election Year)

	Year	*Approval rating*	*Election outcome*
Bush	1992	41%	?
Reagan	1984	54	Won
Carter	1980	43	Lost
Ford	1976	46	Lost
Nixon	1972	46	Won
Johnson	1964	77	Won
Eisenhower	1956	72	Won
Truman	1948*	36	Won

*Approval figures for April (not available for March)

Incumbent's Advantage in Early Test Elections, 1948–1992

Incumbent	*Challenger*	*Point difference*	*Margin of victory/ defeat*
Bush(50%)	Clinton(44%)	+6	?
Reagan(50%)	Mondale(45%)	+5	+18
Carter(50%)	Reagan(42%)	+8	-10
Ford(46%)	Carter(47%)	-1	-2
Nixon(46%)	McGovern(31%)*	+15	+23
Johnson(77%)	Goldwater(18%)	+59	+23
Eisenhower(61%)	Stevenson(37%)	+24	+15
Truman(39%)	Dewey(47%)**	-8	+5

*The 1972 test election included a third candidate, George Wallace.
**The 1948 test election included a third candidate, Henry Wallace.

Note: As Bill Clinton's nomination seems more certain, doubts about his electability persist. It remains to be seen how the allegations of draft dodging, marital infidelity, and conflicts of interest will play out. At this early stage of the campaign, however, it does not appear that the Clinton character issues are seriously affecting his voter appeal. The Arkansas governor runs no better or worse against George Bush than other recent challengers did against incumbent presidents in early Gallup test elections.

In the most recent Gallup Poll, President Bush leads Clinton by 6 percentage points, 50% to 44%. During the last two presidential races with an incumbent running—1984 and 1980—the challenger trailed the incumbent by an almost identical margin in an early Gallup trial heat. Eight years ago at this time, Ronald Reagan led Walter Mondale by 5 percentage points, 50% to 45%. Twelve years ago, Jimmy Carter led then-challenger Reagan by 8 percentage points, 50% to 42%.

These early polls are not too predictive of the November election's outcome. Although they led by similar margins at first, incumbent Reagan ended by winning in a landslide while incumbent Carter lost by 10 percentage points. However, these polls do show the value of incumbency. During the postwar era no challenger has received more than 47% of the vote against an incumbent in any of the surveys taken at this time in the campaign.

Between 1948 and 1988 incumbents have been on the ballot in seven presidential elections. Only twice in that period have incumbents lost—Carter in 1980 and Gerald Ford in 1976. Both men had approval ratings below 50% early in the campaign, as Bush does today. But approval ratings can reverse themselves. Richard Nixon recovered from a 46% approval rating in March 1972 to receive 61% of the vote that year. In early 1948, Harry Truman's approval rating fell below 40%, but he rebounded to defeat Thomas Dewey by 50% to 45% in November.

The incumbency factor in presidential elections strongly suggests that the state of the economy, rather than Clinton's character, will be the deciding issue this year. If the voters see real improvement in the economy between now and the fall, Bush could win as Reagan did in 1984. If voters see the economy as stalled, however, this election might turn out like 1976, the last time a Democrat won the White House.

MARCH 25
PRESIDENT BUSH/CONGRESS/PRESIDENTIAL TRIAL HEAT

Interviewing Date: 3/20–22/92*
Survey #GO 222046

Do you approve or disapprove of the way George Bush is handling his job as president?

Approve	41%
Disapprove	49
No opinion	10

*Gallup survey for CNN/*USA Today*

Selected National Trend
(Post-Gulf War)

	Approve	*Disapprove*	*No opinion*
1992			
March 11–12	41%	47%	12%
February 28–March 1	41	53	6
February 6–9	44	48	8
January 3–6	46	47	7
1991			
December 5–8	52	42	6
November 7–10	56	36	8
October 3–6	65	27	8
September 5–8	70	21	9
August 8–11	71	22	7
July 11–14	72	21	7
May 30–June 2	74	17	9
May 2–5	74	19	7
April 4–6	83	12	5
February 28–March 3	89	8	3

Asked of registered voters: Please tell me whether or not you think each of the following political officeholders deserves to be reelected:

The U.S. representative in your congressional district?

Yes	56%
No	30
No opinion	14

Selected National Trend

	Yes	*No*	*No opinion*
1992			
January 31–February 2	64%	24%	12%
January 3–9	61	25	14
1991			
November	58	25	17

Most members of the U.S. House of Representatives?

Yes	31%
No	58
No opinion	11

Selected National Trend

	Yes	No	No opinion
1992			
January 31–			
February 2	43%	43%	14%
January 3–9	43	42	15
1991			
November	38	48	14

Also asked of registered voters: Suppose the 1992 presidential election were being held today. If George Bush were the Republican candidate and Bill Clinton were the Democratic candidate, whom would you vote for? [Those who were undecided were asked: As of today, do you lean more to Bush, the Republican, or to Clinton, the Democrat?]

Bush	52%
Clinton	43
Undecided; other	5

	Bush	Clinton	Undecided; other
By Sex			
Male	56%	39%	5%
Female	48	46	6
By Ethnic Background			
White	56	39	5
Nonwhite	25	69	6
By Education			
College Graduate	58	38	4
College Incomplete	54	40	6
No College	48	47	5
By Region			
East	54	39	7
Midwest	52	44	4
South	49	46	5
West	53	41	6
By Age			
18–29 Years	52	45	3
30–49 Years	56	41	3
50 Years and Over	47	46	7
By Household Income			
$50,000 and Over	65	31	4
$30,000–$49,999	53	43	4
$20,000–$29,999	46	48	6
Under $20,000	42	52	6
By Politics			
Republicans	85	12	3
Democrats	17	79	4
Independents	50	42	8
By Political Ideology			
Liberal	28	66	6
Moderate	43	52	5
Conservative	69	27	4
By 1988 Vote			
George Bush	74	23	3
Michael Dukakis	10	83	7

Note: President George Bush's approval rating has stabilized after months of steady decline. Three consecutive surveys conducted in February and March by the Gallup Poll found that 41% of adults nationwide approve of the way that he is handling his job.

His ability to stave off further erosion of his appeal as president seems to have come just in time to help him edge out Bill Clinton in Gallup's first presidential test election since Paul Tsongas withdrew from the race. Bush beats Clinton, his likely opponent in November, by 52% to 43% among registered voters nationwide.

For now, voters are remaining loyal to their own party's candidate: Bush receives 85% of the Republican vote, just slightly better than Clinton's 79% of the Democratic vote. The important bloc who identify with neither party, calling themselves independents, now favors Bush over Clinton, 50% to 42%.

Consistent with the demographic makeup of Republicans, Bush runs strongest among men (56%) and with voters under 50 years of age. He does especially well on the East and West coasts with 15 and 12 percentage point advantages over Clinton. The Bush lead is smallest among women (48% versus 46%), with voters age 50 and over (47% versus 46%), and in the South, where he leads Clinton by just 3 percentage points (49% versus 46%).

While the check-bouncing scandal in the U.S. House of Representatives has taken its toll on Congress as an institution, individual members seem to be Teflon-coated. The number of people who believe that most House members do not deserve reelection is up dramatically, from 43% to 58% since January—a 15-percentage point rise. But most people believe that their own incumbent has done the job. Only 30% say that they would turn out their own congressmen, up just 6 percentage points from the January measure.

MARCH 29
DEMOCRATIC PRESIDENTIAL CANDIDATES

Interviewing Date: 3/20–22/92*
Survey #GO 222046

Asked of registered Democrats and those who lean Democratic: Which one of the following would you like to see nominated as the Democratic party's candidate for president? [Those who were undecided were asked: As of today, to which Democratic candidate do you lean most?]

Bill Clinton..71%
Jerry Brown..25
Undecided; other.................................. 4

	Clinton	*Brown*	*Undecided; other*
By Region			
Non-South	65%	32%	3%
South	86	8	6

Also asked of registered Democrats and those who lean Democratic: Next, I'd like your opinion of some people in politics. As I read each name, please tell me if you have a favorable or unfavorable opinion of this person, or if you have never heard of him:

Jerry Brown?

Favorable..49%
Unfavorable..36
No opinion; never heard of.......................15

	Favorable	*Unfavorable*	*No opinion, never heard of*
By Region			
Non-South	56%	31%	13%
South	32	47	21

Bill Clinton?

Favorable..73%
Unfavorable..19
No opinion; never heard of....................... 8

	Favorable	*Unfavorable*	*No opinion, never heard of*
By Region			
Non-South	70%	23%	7%
South	79	10	11

Also asked of registered Democrats and those who lean Democratic: I'm going to read off some personal characteristics and qualities. As I read each one, tell me whether you think it strongly applies, somewhat applies, or does not apply to Bill Clinton:

Clinton's Character
(Those Who Say "Strongly Applies")

	Total	*Non-South*	*South*
Is intelligent?	67%	64%	74%
Has likable personality?	56	52	67
Has charisma?	54	54	56
Has strong leadership qualities?	50	47	57
Cares about needs of people like you?	46	43	54
Is willing to do anything to get elected?	44	47	38
Is tough?	38	37	42

*Gallup survey for CNN/*USA Today*

Can get things done?	38	35	44
Would display good judgment in crisis?	36	31	46
Can bring about changes this country needs?	35	32	44
Upholds family values?	33	28	43
Is honest and trustworthy?	25	21	34
Does not seem to stand for anything	14	16	9

Note: Jerry Brown's upset victory over Bill Clinton in Connecticut on March 24 reflected the front-runner's political vulnerability outside of his native South. A Gallup Poll completed before Connecticut voters gave Brown renewed life found major differences in attitudes toward Clinton between Democratic voters in southern states and those who live outside of the South.

This national poll found Clinton leading Brown by 71% to 25% among registered Democrats. In the South, Brown is barely a factor, registering only 8% support among Democratic voters to Clinton's 86%. But outside of the South, where most of the remaining primaries will be held, Brown is more competitive. The former California governor received one third of the vote (32%) in the non-South before his victory in Connecticut; Clinton received 65%.

Clinton's native-son advantage and Brown's unpopularity in the South give the front-runner a virtual lock on his home region. Close to one half (47%) of southern Democratic voters has an unfavorable opinion of Brown. But once again the candidate does better elsewhere: Brown's ratings are 56% favorable, 31% unfavorable in the non-South; Clinton's are 70% favorable, 23% unfavorable.

Much of Clinton's support outside the South may be the result of pure momentum. His victories on Super Tuesday and subsequent wins in Illinois and Michigan made him the presumptive nominee, for the moment suppressing any doubts that many voters may have had about him.

Voters in other parts of the country have not warmed up to Clinton as have those in his native South. Moreover, he has more difficulty passing the character test with nonsouthern voters. There is a 15 point difference in the percentage of southerners (67%) and nonsoutherners (52%) who think "likable personality" strongly applies to Clinton. Similarly, there are gaps of 13 and 15 points, respectively, in the percentage of southerners and nonsoutherners who think that "honest and trustworthy" (34% versus 21%) and "upholds family values" (43% versus 28%) strongly apply to Clinton.

MARCH 31
CONGRESSIONAL CHECK-CASHING SCANDAL

Interviewing Date: 3/26–29/92
Survey #GO 222047

As you may know, Congress has voted to publicly identify all members who wrote checks beyond the amounts in their private House bank accounts. How likely are you to vote to reelect the current House member from your district if his or her name is on the list—very likely, somewhat likely, not too likely, or not at all likely:

On list of worst offenders?

	March 26–29	*March 13*
Very likely	4%	5%
Somewhat likely	16	13
Not too likely	22	19
Not at all likely	54	60
Don't vote (volunteered)	2	1
No opinion	2	2

On list of average offenders?

	March 26–29	*March 13*
Very likely	8%	8%
Somewhat likely	27	30

Not too likely	24	23
Not at all likely	34	36
Don't vote (volunteered)	2	1
No opinion	5	2

On list of minor offenders?

	March 26–29	*March 13*
Very likely	20%	22%
Somewhat likely	36	40
Not too likely	14	12
Not at all likely	25	23
Don't vote (volunteered)	2	1
No opinion	3	2

Which of the following concerns you most about members of Congress writing bad checks on their House bank accounts:

Members who mismanage personal finances making decisions about spending federal tax dollars?....41%
Members granting themselves privileges?....22
Members displaying low ethical standards?....16
All of the above equally....17
No opinion....4

To the best of your knowledge, did members of Congress earn interest on the checks they deposited in their House bank accounts, or not?

Yes....23%
No (correct)....33
No opinion....44

Were any public funds used to cover the overdraft checks written by members of Congress, or not?

Yes....31%
No (correct)....31
No opinion....38

I am going to read some explanations that have been offered by members of Congress who wrote overdraft checks to defend themselves against charges of wrongdoing. As I read each one, please tell me whether you believe this is a satisfactory explanation, or not:

Their spouse or a staff member handled their account?

Yes, satisfactory....13%
No....85
No opinion....2

The House bank did not operate like a commercial bank and paid no interest on deposits?

Yes, satisfactory....18%
No....78
No opinion....4

They were not informed by the House bank that their account was overdrawn?

Yes, satisfactory....21%
No....77
No opinion....2

No public funds were used to cover overdrafts?

Yes, satisfactory....22%
No....74
No opinion....4

Note: Members of Congress who engaged in check-kiting cannot be having an easy time explaining their actions to their constituents. According to a Gallup Poll, none of the major reasons being offered to justify the practice has much credibility with the public.

Fewer than one in four (22%) say that they are satisfied with the explanation that no public funds were used to cover the overdraft checks. Moreover, only small percentages are inclined to excuse members of Congress who argue that the House bank failed to inform them that their accounts were overdrawn (21%) or who point out that their accounts earned no interest (18%). Those who try to evade responsibility by blaming someone else are even less likely to win sympathy: only 13% of the public would excuse an offending House member who claimed that a spouse or staff member handled the account.

To the public, the "Rubbergate" scandal is as much about congressional competence as it is about ethics or the abuse of privilege. When asked what bothers them most about House members writing bad checks, 16% of adults express concern about low ethical standards; another 22% say that Congress goes too far in granting itself special privileges which other Americans do not have. But the largest number (41%) is most concerned about House members who mismanage personal finances and then make decisions about how to spend everyone's tax dollars.

Members of Congress included on the list of worst offenders face serious problems if they choose to run for reelection this fall. Only 20% of poll respondents say that they are very or somewhat likely to vote to reelect a congressional representative who is one of the worst offenders; over one half (54%) are not at all likely to do so.

Average offenders face difficulties as well; while 35% would be at least somewhat likely to reelect someone in this category, an equal proportion (34%) says that this is not at all likely. Minor offenders may escape serious damage. A majority (56%) would be very or somewhat likely to reelect their representative provided that he or she were only a minor offender. Perceptions of how this scandal might affect the vote for Congress have not changed significantly since a *Newsweek*/Gallup Poll conducted two weeks ago.

The most damaging aspect of the scandal for Congress may be its reinforcement of existing stereotypes of institutional ineptitude. While few are reluctant to offer opinions on the check-kiting controversy, the public seems inattentive to the details of what actually happened. For example, only one third (33%) of poll respondents is aware that members did not earn interest on their accounts with the House bank. And less than one third (31%) knows that no public funds were used to cover the overdraft checks. An equal number (31%), in fact, has the mistaken impression that public funds were involved.

Lack of information may contribute to harshness of public perceptions toward Congress. But for those representatives who took the most liberties in writing overdraft checks, educating the public may not be enough to clear their names. As previously mentioned, when offered the factual information that some House members have offered as a defense, the overwhelming majority of Americans says that it is not enough to excuse their behavior.

MARCH 31
BUSH'S TAX VETO

Interviewing Date: 3/26–29/92
Survey #GO 222047

President Bush recently vetoed a Democratic-sponsored bill that would have cut taxes for some Americans and raised taxes for others. From what you know about the bill, do you approve of Bush's veto, or do you think he should have signed the bill?

Approve veto	31%
Bush should have signed	44
No opinion	25

	Approve veto	*Bush should have signed*	*No opinion*
By Politics			
Republicans	50%	28%	22%
Democrats	16	60	24
Independents	27	44	29

Note: President George Bush's swift veto of the recent tax bill sponsored by congressional Democrats stirs predictably partisan responses among the public. The bill would have given tax cuts to middle-income wage earners and raised taxes on those with higher incomes.

Overall, just three in ten (31%) approve of Bush's veto, while more than four in ten (44%) think that he should have signed the bill. One quarter of the public expresses no opinion (25%).

Republicans approve of Bush's veto by a nearly 2-to-1 margin (50% to 28%), but Democrats oppose it by an even larger margin:

16% to 60%. The largest bloc of respondents—those calling themselves independents—is closer to Democrats than to Republicans on this question; only 27% approve of Bush's veto, while 44% reply that he should have signed the bill.

APRIL 3
MOST IMPORTANT PROBLEM/REPUBLICAN AND DEMOCRATIC PARTIES

Interviewing Date: 3/26–29/92
Survey #GO 222047

*What do you think is the most important problem facing this country today?**

	March 1992	November 1991
Economic problems		
Economy in general	42%	32%
Unemployment	25	23
Federal budget deficit	8	4
Taxes	6	3
Trade deficit	4	4
Recession	3	5
Noneconomic problems		
Poverty; homelessness	15%	16%
Health care	12	6
Drugs; drug abuse	8	10
Dissatisfaction with government	8	5
Education	8	4
Crime	5	6
Ethics, moral decline	5	4
AIDS	3	5
Environment	3	3
International situation	3	3
No opinion	2	3

*Total adds to more than 100% due to multiple replies. None of the other replies draws more than 2%.

Which political party do you think can do a better job of handling the problem you have just mentioned—the Republican party or the Democratic party?

Republican	34%
Democratic	40
No difference (volunteered); no opinion	26

Selected National Trend

	Republican	Democratic	No difference; no opinion
November 1991	32%	33%	35%
May 1988	27	40	33
February 1984	30	32	38
April 1980	28	32	40
April 1976	18	39	43
August 1972	28	34	38
May 1968	30	28	42
April 1964	16	40	44
February 1960	24	32	44
September 1956	55	45	*

*Less than 1%

Note: As the 1992 election year enters its fourth month, the economy continues to dominate all other issues as the most important problem facing the country. Some 42% mention the economy in general, while one fourth (25%) cites unemployment as the worst evil.

Following these two major concerns, most often mentioned are the federal budget deficit (8%), taxes (6%), the trade deficit (4%), and the recession (3%). Other problems cited are poverty and homelessness (15%), health care (12%, up from 6% in November), and dissatisfaction with government, the quality of education, and drugs (mentioned by 8% each).

Asked which party they think would do a better job of handling the nation's top problem, respondents give the Democrats a 6-percentage point edge over the Republicans, 40% to 34%. To one quarter (26%), it makes no difference.

This measure of the party better able to handle the nation's number-one problem is not necessarily predictive of the fall presidential election. Democrats have traditionally led Republicans on this political indicator but have lost all but one presidential election since 1968.

APRIL 5
AIDS

Interviewing Date: 1/3–6/92
Survey #GO 222034

Asked of registered voters: We'd like to know which issues you think are important for the presidential candidates to discuss and debate in the 1992 campaign. As I read a list of issues, please rate each as very important, somewhat important, not too important, or not at all important:

	Very important
Economy	93%
Education	87
Unemployment	84
Health care	80
Federal budget deficit	79
Crime	77
Drugs; drug abuse	77
Poverty; homelessness	76
Taxes	70
AIDS	67
Environment	60
Foreign trade	53
Race relations	48
National defense	43
Abortion	38
Foreign affairs	37

Interviewing Date: 3/26–29/92
Survey #GO 222047

What would you say is the most urgent health problem facing this country at the present time?

AIDS	41%
Cancer	5
Heart disease	2
Health-care costs	30
Other	18
No opinion	4

If you had a say in making up the federal budget, would you increase spending for the following types of medical research, decrease spending, or keep spending at about the same level:

AIDS research?

Increase	70%
Keep same	23
Decrease	5
No opinion	2

Cancer research?

Increase	63%
Keep same	34
Decrease	2
No opinion	1

Research on heart disease?

Increase	46%
Keep same	49
Decrease	3
No opinion	2

Now, I will read a list of things some people say the government should do to prevent the spread of AIDS. Please tell me whether you approve or disapprove of each:

Begin teaching children about AIDS and other sexually transmitted diseases in the early grades?

Approve	87%
Disapprove	12
No opinion	1

	Approve	*Dis-approve*	*No opinion*
By Sex			
Male	86%	13%	1%
Female	87	11	2
By Ethnic Background			
White	86	13	1
Nonwhite	94	5	1
Black	95	5	*
By Education			
College Graduate	90	10	*
College Incomplete	87	12	1

High-School Graduate	86	13	1
Less Than High-School Graduate	86	12	2
By Region			
East	86	14	*
Midwest	90	7	3
South	86	13	1
West	86	13	1
By Age			
18–29 Years	89	11	*
30–49 Years	88	12	*
50 Years and Over	85	12	3
By Household Income			
$50,000 and Over	90	10	*
$30,000–$49,999	84	14	2
$20,000–$29,999	86	12	2
Under $20,000	89	10	1
By Politics			
Republicans	85	14	1
Democrats	93	7	*
Independents	84	14	2
By Religion			
Protestants	87	11	2
Catholics	89	11	*
By Political Ideology			
Liberal	90	9	1
Moderate	92	7	1
Conservative	81	17	2

*Less than 1%

Make condoms available to high-school students as part of an AIDS-prevention program?

Approve	63%
Disapprove	35
No opinion	2

	Approve	Dis-approve	No opinion
By Sex			
Male	62%	36%	2%
Female	65	33	2
By Ethnic Background			
White	61	37	2
Nonwhite	84	15	1
Black	84	16	*
By Education			
College Graduate	64	35	1
College Incomplete	65	34	1
High-School Graduate	64	34	2
Less Than High-School Graduate	62	36	2
By Region			
East	58	40	2
Midwest	63	36	1
South	65	33	2
West	69	29	2
By Age			
18–29 Years	81	18	1
30–49 Years	65	33	2
50 Years and Over	50	48	2
By Household Income			
$50,000 and Over	59	40	1
$30,000–$49,999	62	37	1
$20,000–$29,999	64	34	2
Under $20,000	70	28	2
By Politics			
Republicans	53	46	1
Democrats	71	28	1
Independents	66	31	3
By Religion			
Protestants	63	36	1
Catholics	61	37	2
By Political Ideology			
Liberal	79	20	1
Moderate	70	28	2
Conservative	51	48	1

*Less than 1%

Dispense free needles and syringes to IV drug users to cut down on shared needles?

Approve	41%
Disapprove	55
No opinion	4

	Approve	Dis-approve	No opinion
By Sex			
Male	36%	61%	3%
Female	46	50	4
By Ethnic Background			
White	40	57	3
Nonwhite	52	44	4
Black	56	42	2
By Education			
College Graduate	45	53	2
College Incomplete	41	56	3
High-School Graduate	39	58	3
Less Than High-School Graduate	41	53	6
By Region			
East	39	57	4
Midwest	39	58	3
South	40	56	4
West	48	50	2
By Age			
18–29 Years	46	53	1
30–49 Years	42	55	3
50 Years and Over	37	58	5
By Household Income			
$50,000 and Over	42	57	1
$30,000–$49,999	37	62	1
$20,000–$29,999	42	53	5
Under $20,000	45	51	4
By Politics			
Republicans	36	62	2
Democrats	49	49	2
Independents	39	56	5
By Religion			
Protestants	38	58	4
Catholics	40	56	4
By Political Ideology			
Liberal	55	41	4
Moderate	40	57	3
Conservative	36	62	2

Asked of registered voters: Which presidential candidate do you think would do a better job of handling the problem of AIDS—George Bush or Bill Clinton?

Clinton	40%
Bush	34
Both equally (volunteered)	3
Neither (volunteered)	7
No opinion	16

Asked of registered Democrats and those who lean Democratic: Which Democratic presidential candidate do you think would do a better job of handling the problem of AIDS—Bill Clinton or Jerry Brown?

Clinton	49%
Brown	36
Both equally (volunteered)	2
Neither (volunteered)	2
No opinion	11

Note: Once of great concern only in the gay community, AIDS has emerged in recent years as a key national political issue. A new Gallup Poll finds AIDS perceived to be the nation's number-one health problem. Seven in ten (70%) respondents now support new federal spending on AIDS research, and once-controversial measures to combat AIDS, such as giving out condoms in high schools and educating children in the early grades about the disease, now win majority support. In this presidential election year Gallup surveys have also shown AIDS to be of greater concern to voters than more publicized issues such as the environment, abortion, foreign trade, and race relations.

Over the past five years Gallup has consistently ranked AIDS as the nation's most urgent health problem. In the latest poll, 41% place AIDS at the top, down from the 55% recorded last November when Earvin "Magic" Johnson's dramatic announcement that he is HIV-positive elevated public concern about the disease.

When respondents are asked to name the country's most pressing health problems, AIDS has little competition, even from cancer and heart disease, the two leading killers; only

5% and 2%, respectively, name these two life-threatening illnesses as their top concern. Paying for health care is the only health concern that rivals AIDS (30%), up from 12% last fall.

As a political issue, voters rate AIDS below the economy, education, and health-care policy, but high proportions do think that AIDS deserves serious attention from the presidential candidates. In a January poll, two thirds (67%) of all voters said that it is very important for AIDS to be discussed in this year's campaign. Fewer gave priority to such issues as the environment (60%), foreign trade (53%), race relations (48%), and abortion (38%).

With the New York primary on April 7 shaping up as pivotal to the Democratic presidential race, the candidates' positions on AIDS have received more attention. For months, Jerry Brown has worn a red ribbon to demonstrate his concern. The new poll suggests, however, that the former California governor has had mixed success so far in making the issue his own. Front-runner Bill Clinton has an edge over Brown among all Democratic voters by a margin of 49% to 36%, and he is seen as better able to deal with AIDS by the two groups most concerned about the disease: those under age 30 (55% versus 31%) and nonwhites (47% to 34%). Indeed, in the fall campaign, AIDS may be an issue that the Democrats can use to their advantage. Currently, voters prefer Clinton over George Bush by a margin of 40% to 34% on this problem.

In addition to endorsing bigger budgets for AIDS research, the public gives overwhelming support to early education as an AIDS-prevention measure. Nine in ten (87%) approve of teaching children about sexually transmitted diseases in the early grades. A smaller majority (63%) approves of making condoms available to high-school students as a preventative measure. Less than a majority (41%) approves of going so far as to dispense free needles to intravenous, or IV, drug users to cut down on shared needles.

Not surprisingly, the public divides along generational lines in its willingness to support condom distribution and needle dispensation for AIDS prevention. Respondents over the age of 50 are evenly divided on making condoms available in high schools (50% approve versus 48% disapprove). In contrast, those under 30 solidly approve (81% versus 18%). Approval for giving out needles ranges from 46% among those under 30 to 37% among those over 50.

APRIL 5
PRESIDENTIAL TRIAL HEATS/H. ROSS PEROT

Interviewing Date: 3/31–4/1/92*
Survey #GO 222048

Asked of registered voters: Suppose the 1992 presidential election were being held today. If George Bush were the Republican candidate and Bill Clinton were the Democratic candidate, whom would you vote for? [Those who were undecided were asked: As of today, do you lean more to Bush, the Republican, or to Clinton, the Democrat?]

Bush	54%
Clinton	34
Undecided; other	12

Selected National Trend

	Bush	*Clinton*	*Undecided; other*
1992			
March 20–22	52%	43%	5%
March 11–12	50	44	6
February 19–20	53	43	4
February 6–9	53	38	9

Thinking about the presidential primaries and caucuses that have taken place so far this year, in general do you think they have been a good way of determining who the best qualified nominees are, or not?

Yes	35%
No	54
No opinion	11

*Gallup survey for CNN/*USA Today*

Selected National Trend

	Yes	No	No opinion
June 1988	48%	37%	15%
June 1980	40	48	12

Do you have a favorable or an unfavorable opinion of H. Ross Perot, or have you never heard of him?

	March 31– April 1	March 20–22
Favorable	32%	20%
Unfavorable	10	12
No opinion (volunteered)	24	13
Never heard of	34	55

Asked of registered voters who had heard or read about Perot (66% of the sample): I am going to read you some statements about H. Ross Perot. As I read each one, please tell me if this makes you more likely to vote for Perot for president, less likely, or if it would not have much effect on your vote:

He takes a "pro-choice" position on abortion?

More likely	40%
Less likely	26
Not much effect	29
No opinion	5

	More likely	Less likely	Not much effect	No opinion
By Sex				
Male	41%	22%	33%	4%
Female	38	29	27	6
By Education				
College Graduate	51	19	28	2
College Incomplete	53	16	30	1
No College	29	33	30	8
By Region				
East	43	26	26	5
Midwest	34	29	31	6
South	34	27	33	6
West	53	20	25	2
By Age				
18–29 Years	48	21	31	*
30–49 Years	44	26	27	3
50–64 Years	37	25	32	6
65 Years and Over	26	32	29	13
By Household Income				
$50,000 and Over	51	18	30	1
$30,000–$49,999	47	21	28	4
$20,000–$29,999	36	30	28	6
Under $20,000	26	36	30	8
By Politics				
Republicans	32	33	31	4
Democrats	42	24	25	9
Independents	46	20	32	2
By Political Ideology				
Liberal	50	23	22	5
Moderate	49	19	28	4
Conservative	26	38	31	5

*Less than 1%

He opposed the Persian Gulf War?

More likely	21%
Less likely	39
Not much effect	36
No opinion	4

	More likely	Less likely	Not much effect	No opinion
By Sex				
Male	18%	45%	34%	3%
Female	23	35	37	5
By Education				
College Graduate	22	42	35	1
College Incomplete	27	35	37	1
No College	18	40	36	6

By Region				
East	23	37	32	8
Midwest	14	41	43	2
South	17	39	39	5
West	32	42	26	*
By Age				
18–29 Years	31	32	36	1
30–49 Years	20	46	32	2
50–64 Years	17	37	40	6
65 Years and Over	16	37	38	9
By Household Income				
$50,000 and Over	22	41	36	1
$30,000–$49,999	20	43	35	2
$20,000–$29,999	22	38	36	4
Under $20,000	22	32	38	8
By Politics				
Republicans	9	53	36	2
Democrats	29	29	35	7
Independents	26	34	37	3
By Political Ideology				
Liberal	42	32	26	*
Moderate	18	39	40	3
Conservative	15	47	35	3

*Less than 1%

He has never held or run for political office?

More likely....................................16%
Less likely....................................34
Not much effect................................46
No opinion.....................................4

	More likely	Less likely	Not much effect	No opinion
By Sex				
Male	16%	34%	46%	4%
Female	18	30	48	4
By Education				
College Graduate	17	30	52	1
College Incomplete	15	36	48	1
No College	16	35	43	6
By Region				
East	20	31	46	3
Midwest	14	37	43	6
South	14	37	44	5
West	17	29	54	*
By Age				
18–29 Years	14	37	48	1
30–49 Years	17	30	51	2
50–64 Years	17	35	40	8
65 Years and Over	16	38	39	7
By Household Income				
$50,000 and Over	17	34	49	*
$30,000–$49,999	17	33	48	2
$20,000–$29,999	19	32	46	3
Under $20,000	14	34	44	8
By Politics				
Republicans	13	35	50	2
Democrats	13	35	45	7
Independents	23	31	43	3
By Political Ideology				
Liberal	18	33	41	8
Moderate	14	34	51	1
Conservative	19	35	43	3

*Less than 1%

He is a billionaire?

More likely....................................10%
Less likely....................................22
Not much effect................................66
No opinion.....................................2

	More likely	*Less likely*	*Not much effect*	*No opinion*
By Sex				
Male	13%	18%	68%	1%
Female	8	25	64	3
By Education				
College Graduate	11	16	72	1
College Incomplete	9	15	76	*
No College	11	27	59	3
By Region				
East	12	17	69	2
Midwest	9	26	63	2
South	9	26	61	4
West	11	15	74	*
By Age				
18–29 Years	4	19	77	*
30–49 Years	10	23	66	1
50–64 Years	13	19	63	5
65 Years and Over	14	24	59	3
By Household Income				
$50,000 and Over	14	10	76	*
$30,000–$49,999	8	22	69	1
$20,000–$29,999	11	24	62	3
Under $20,000	8	30	57	5
By Politics				
Republicans	10	17	72	1
Democrats	11	26	59	4
Independents	11	22	66	1
By Political Ideology				
Liberal	9	28	61	2
Moderate	9	20	70	1
Conservative	13	20	66	1

*Less than 1%

Asked of registered voters: Suppose the 1992 presidential election were being held today. If George Bush were the Republican candidate and Bill Clinton were the Democratic candidate and H. Ross Perot were an independent candidate, whom would you vote for? [Those who were undecided were asked: As of today, do you lean more to Bush, the Republican; to Clinton, the Democrat; or to Perot, the independent?]

	Total	*Bush voters*	*Clinton voters*	*Undecided; other voters*
Bush	44%	81%	1%	6%
Clinton	25	*	70	7
Perot	24	18	25	47
Undecided; other	7	1	4	40

*Less than 1%

Note: H. Ross Perot says that it is up to the voters to decide whether he should mount an independent campaign for president. The results of this week's Gallup Poll should encourage the Texas entrepreneur to throw his hat into the ring. Matched up against President George Bush and Arkansas Governor Bill Clinton in a trial heat, Perot wins about one quarter of the vote (24%). That puts him in a virtual tie for second place with Clinton (25%), even though one voter in three (34%) still does not recognize Perot's name. Bush captures 44% in this hypothetical three-way race.

In politics, timing is everything. Perot is contemplating running for president at a time when voters are looking for alternatives to the likely nominees of the two major parties. A late March poll shows Bush approval at 41%, well below the 50% level usually considered safe for an incumbent seeking reelection, but Democratic front-runner Clinton is not in a position to capitalize on the president's electoral vulnerability. Since Jerry Brown won a stunning upset in the Connecticut primary two weeks ago, Clinton has lost ground to the president in test elections. Support for Clinton in a two-way race against Bush has fallen from 43% in a poll completed before the Connecticut primary to 34% in this week's poll.

Voters today appear even less satisfied with the two major parties' processes for selecting nominees than they were in 1980. In that year,

Ohio Republican John Anderson ran as an independent against Democrat Jimmy Carter, an unpopular incumbent, and Republican Ronald Reagan, whose age and hawkishness on military matters made many uncomfortable about sending him to the White House. In June 1980, when support for Anderson reached its peak of 24% in the Gallup Poll, nearly one half (48%) of the voters said that the primary process had not done a good job of determining the best-qualified candidates. Today, a majority (54%) sees the process as failing to produce good candidates.

Does Perot have much chance to win? One could argue that the decline of the parties and the level of voter dissatisfaction evident in 1992 make past electoral history irrelevant, but history suggests that Perot would have a difficult time realizing the voter potential reflected in early polls. Anderson's support held at around 20% between April and July 1980, but after the nominating conventions in August his support level dropped to 14%. He ended up with only 7% of the votes cast for president that November.

At this point, most voters have only good things to say about Perot. Poll respondents with a favorable opinion of him outnumber those with an unfavorable opinion by a 3-to-1 margin (32% versus 10%). However, that may well change if Perot enters the race and subjects himself to media scrutiny. His opposition to the Gulf War, for example, might not play well with the voters. Four in ten (39%) say that Perot's opposition to the war makes them less likely to vote for him, while only about one half as many (21%) say that it increases their chances of voting for him.

Perot's status as a nonpolitician—never having held or run for political office—may not be an advantage. Lack of experience in politics is more of a negative with the broader electorate: 16% say that this makes them more likely to vote for Perot, but 34% say less likely.

APRIL 8
FEDERAL TAXES

Interviewing Date: 3/26–29/92
Survey #GO 22204

Do you consider the amount of federal income tax you have to pay as too high, about right, or too low?

Too high...56%
About right......................................39
Too low...2
No opinion.......................................3

	Too high	*About right*	*Too low*	*No opinion*
By Income				
$50,000 and Over	60%	37%	3%	*
$30,000–$49,999	61	36	1	2
$20,000–$29,999	53	42	2	3
Under $20,000	50	42	2	6

Selected National Trend

	Too high	*About right*	*Too low*	*No opinion*
1991	55%	37%	2%	6%
1990	63	31	2	4
1973	65	28	1	6
1969	69	25	*	6
1967	58	38	1	3
1961	46	45	1	8
1957	61	31	*	8
1953	59	37	*	4
1951	52	43	1	4
1948	57	38	1	4

*Less than 1%

Do you think you will pay more or less in federal income taxes than last year?

More...63%
Less..26
No opinion......................................11

As I read off some different groups, please tell me whether you think they are paying their fair share in federal taxes, paying too much, or paying too little:

	Fair share	Too much	Too little	No opinion
Large corporations	15%	4%	75%	6%
Upper-income people	16	4	77	3
Lower-income people	32	57	8	3
Middle-income people	36	57	5	2
Small businesses	40	46	6	8

Note: Americans rushing to file their IRS returns this year are inclined to believe that they are paying more than their fair share in taxes and that large corporations and the affluent are paying less than they should. In a new Gallup Poll, 56% say that the amount of federal income tax they pay is too high, while 39% think that it is about right. Only 2% admit to paying less in federal taxes than seems appropriate.

Respondents are more convinced this year than last that their own tax burden is going up. More than six in ten (63%) expect to pay more in federal income taxes than they did last year, compared with 56% who said so in 1991.

Asked to evaluate the equity of the federal tax at varying income levels, majorities see middle-income (57%) and lower-income people (57%) paying too much. However, only 4% say that upper-income families pay too much; indeed, 77% think that upper-income families pay too little.

Americans also believe that large corporations are getting off more easily than small businesses. Three quarters (75%) say that corporations pay too little, while most think that small businesses pay too much (46%) or about the right amount (40%) in federal taxes.

APRIL 9
TALK-SHOW HOSTS

Interviewing Date: 3/26–29/92
Survey #GO 222047

*I'm going to mention the names of some television talk-show hosts. For each, please tell me if you recognize the name and, if so, whether you have a generally favorable or unfavorable impression of that person:**

	Favorable**	Unfavorable	Total recognition
Oprah Winfrey	78%	14%	98%
Johnny Carson	71	19	98
Phil Donahue	68	26	99
Sally Jessy Raphael	60	15	89
Arsenio Hall	52	22	89
David Letterman	52	26	93
Jay Leno	46	17	75
Kathie Lee Gifford	41	10	65
Regis Philbin	41	14	69
Geraldo Rivera	39	50	95
Dennis Miller	16	9	37

*Excluded from the table are those who recognize the person but have no impression, those who are unsure if they recognize the person, and refusals.
**"Strongly favorable" is omitted.

Note: Oprah Winfrey reigns supreme as the most popular talk-show host in America, according to a new Gallup Poll. When respondents are asked to give their opinion of eleven television talk-show hosts, Winfrey comes out on top, followed by Johnny Carson, daytime hosts Phil Donahue and Sally Jessy Raphael, and late-night television's Arsenio Hall and David Letterman.

Winfrey's number-one status is primarily due to her very strong appeal to women, the core audience of her afternoon show. An extraordinary 83% of all women say that they have a favorable opinion of Oprah, with 41% of them strongly favorable. The others rounding out the top five among women are Raphael, Donahue, Carson, and Hall.

For men, it is a different story: Carson is first, followed by Donahue, Winfrey, Letterman, and Jay Leno. Oprah is number one in all age categories, but the rank of other hosts varies by age. Hall is in the top five only for 18-to-29-year-old viewers, while Regis Philbin and Kathie Lee Gifford make the top five among viewers over 50 years of age.

Only one talk-show host generates significant negative reaction—Geraldo Rivera, viewed unfavorably by 50%. The next most negatively evaluated hosts are Letterman (26% unfavorable), Donahue (26%), and Hall (22%).

Most of the hosts tested have near universal recognition among respondents, with four exceptions. Despite the fact that he is soon to replace Carson as full-time host of the "Tonight Show," Leno is known by only 75% of the population. Others who have relatively low recognition levels are Dennis Miller (by only 37% of the population), Regis Philbin (69%), and Kathie Lee Gifford (65%).

APRIL 12
PRESIDENTIAL CANDIDATES

Interviewing Date: 3/26–29/92
Survey #GO 222047

I'd like you to rate [NAME] on a scale. If you have a favorable opinion of him, name a number between +1 and +5—the higher the number, the more favorable your opinion. If you have an unfavorable opinion of him, name a number between -1 and -5—the lower the number, the more unfavorable your opinion. How would you rate [NAME] on this scale?

	Highly, mildly favor-able (+5 to +1)	*Mildly highly unfavor-able (-1 to -5)*	*No opinion*
George Bush	64%	35%	1%
Bill Clinton	58	33	9

Selected National Trend
(Presidential Incumbents and Their Challengers)

	Highly, mildly favor-able (+5 to +1)	*Mildly highly unfavor-able (-1 to -5)*	*No opinion*
April 1984			
Reagan	73%	25%	2%
Mondale	69	27	4
April 1980			
Carter	66	31	3
Reagan	66	26	8
March 1976			
Ford	68	28	4
Carter	64	10	26
August 1972			
Nixon	81	17	2
McGovern	68	27	5
August 1964			
Johnson	89	6	5
Goldwater	51	38	11
March 1956			
Eisenhower	88	11	1
Stevenson	63	23	14

Note: Bill Clinton's primary victories this past week (April 7) in New York, Wisconsin, and Kansas put him another step closer to winning his party's presidential nomination. In terms of the delegate count, Clinton is about as close to the nomination today as Michael Dukakis was four years ago at this time, but the primary campaign has taken a heavy toll on Clinton's image with the voters. Gallup surveys of the last month have shown roughly four in ten registered voters expressing unfavorable opinions of Clinton; at this time four years ago, only one half as many had a negative opinion of Dukakis. Analysis of Gallup Polls taken over three decades, however, suggests that it would be premature to rule out a Clinton victory in November because of his high negative rating at this point in the campaign.

The year 1992 does seem to be the time of the angry voter. While the primary process has been bruising for Clinton, the recession has had a similar effect on George Bush's image. Both men are regarded more unfavorably by the public than were their counterparts in previous presidential elections. At this stage of the campaign, Clinton is rated more negatively than any presidential challenger since Barry Goldwater, but Bush receives higher negative ratings than any incumbent president of the postwar era, including Jimmy Carter and Gerald Ford, the last two incumbents to suffer defeat.

Since the 1950s, Gallup has used a "scalometer" to measure favorability toward public figures. This kind of question tends to produce a lower percentage of "unfavorable" replies than questions that ask simply: "Do you have a favorable or unfavorable opinion of Bill Clinton?"

When Gallup asked a national sample of adults to rate Clinton on this scale in a recent poll, roughly six in ten (58%) give him a positive, or favorable, rating and one third (33%) a negative, or unfavorable, rating. Bush's ratings on the same scale are similar: 64% favorable versus 35% unfavorable.

Gallup began asking the scalometer question about presidential candidates in 1956. This is the first time that both the incumbent president and his major party challenger have scored negative ratings above 30% at this early stage of the campaign. Carter is the only incumbent to be rated so negatively (31% rated him unfavorably in April 1980). Goldwater, who lost to Lyndon Johnson by a landslide in 1964, received the most negative rating on record: 38% unfavorable in August 1964. (That increased to 46% in October.)

The Gallup Poll shows that presidential candidates' ratings can move both up and down over the course of a campaign. Four years ago, Bush's unfavorable ratings climbed during the primary season but went down in August after the GOP convention. They never reverted to preconvention levels in the fall campaign.

APRIL 15
PRESIDENT BUSH/PRESIDENTIAL TRIAL HEAT/PRESIDENTIAL CANDIDATES

Interviewing Date: 4/9–12/92
Survey #GO 222049

Do you approve or disapprove of the way George Bush is handling his job as president?

Approve	39%
Disapprove	54
No opinion	7

	Approve	*Disapprove*	*No opinion*
By Sex			
Male	41%	52%	7%
Female	38	55	7
By Ethnic Background			
White	41	52	7
Nonwhite	25	68	7
Black	17	74	9
By Education			
College Graduate	36	59	5
College Incomplete	42	51	7
High-School Graduate	41	52	7
Less Than High-School Graduate	35	55	10
By Region			
East	37	57	6
Midwest	37	56	7
South	44	48	8
West	38	56	6
By Age			
18–29 Years	47	45	8
30–49 Years	42	54	4
50 Years and Over	32	59	9
By Household Income			
$50,000 and Over	45	52	3
$30,000–$49,999	44	52	4
$20,000–$29,999	39	49	12
Under $20,000	33	58	9
By Politics			
Republicans	74	23	3
Democrats	17	74	9
Independents	34	58	8
By Religion			
Protestants	41	52	7
Catholics	41	53	6
By Political Ideology			
Liberal	25	66	9
Moderate	39	57	4
Conservative	48	44	8

Selected National Trend

	Approve	Dis-approve	No opinion
1992			
March 26–29	42%	51%	7%
March 20–22	41	49	10
March 11–12	41	47	12
February 28– March 1	41	53	6
February 19–20	39	47	14
February 6–9	44	48	8
January 31– February 2	47	48	5
January 16–19	46	48	6
January 3–6	46	47	7

Asked of registered voters: Suppose the 1992 presidential election were being held today. If George Bush were the Republican candidate and Bill Clinton were the Democratic candidate, whom would you vote for? [Those who were undecided were asked: As of today, do you lean more to Bush, the Republican, or to Clinton, the Democrat?]

Bush	48%
Clinton	41
Undecided; other	11

Selected National Trend

	Bush	Clinton	Undecided; other
1992			
March 26–29	54%	38%	8%
March 11–12	50	44	6
February 19–20	53	43	4
February 6–9	53	38	9

Do you have a favorable or unfavorable opinion of:

George Bush?

	April 9–12	March 26–29
Favorable	48%	49%
Unfavorable	44	44
No opinion	8	7

Bill Clinton?

	April 9–12	March 26–29
Favorable	34%	37%
Unfavorable	47	40
No opinion	19	23

Asked of registered Democrats and those who lean Democratic: Some people think that the Democrats may have an open convention this summer, meaning that no Democratic candidate will be able to get the nomination on the first ballot. If that happens, how do you think they should choose a candidate? Should they limit their choice to one of the candidates who ran in the primaries, or should they consider others who did not choose to run?

Limit to candidates who ran in primaries	31%
Consider others	61
No opinion	8

Asked of registered voters: If the Democratic party nominates a candidate who did not run in the presidential primaries, would that make you more likely or less likely to vote Democratic in the November presidential election, or would it not have much effect on your vote?

	Total	Now prefer Bush	Now prefer Clinton	Now un-decided
More likely	23%	18%	25%	36%
Less likely	9	11	7	6
Not much effect	60	62	62	47
No opinion	8	9	6	11

Also asked of registered voters: I'm going to read you a statement about Bill Clinton. Please tell me whether you strongly agree, agree, disagree, or strongly disagree with the following statement: Bill Clinton has the honesty and integrity to serve as president.

	Total	Registered Democrats
Strongly agree	6%	9%
Agree	39	53
Disagree	34	25
Strongly disagree	13	6
No opinion	8	7

Note: Despite high unfavorable ratings from voters, Arkansas Governor Bill Clinton runs close to President George Bush in a Gallup test election. If the November election were held today, 48% of registered voters say that they would support Bush, while 41% would back Clinton; 11% are undecided or plan to vote for another candidate. A Gallup Poll taken in late March, before the New York primary, showed Bush with a more comfortable lead, 54% to 38%.

Clinton is competitive in a test election against Bush even though nearly one half (47%) of all voters say that they have an unfavorable opinion of him. Only one in three (34%) has a favorable opinion of Clinton; about one in five (19%) has no opinion at all. In the March poll, voters divided about equally in their opinion of the Arkansas governor: 37% favorable, 40% unfavorable, and 23% no opinion.

High percentages of voters in the national Gallup Poll express doubts about Clinton's character, consistent with findings of exit polls in primary states. Voters are about evenly divided on the question of whether Clinton has the honesty and integrity to serve as president: 45% agree, while 47% disagree. Although some of these doubts can be explained by partisanship, even among registered Democrats and those who lean Democratic three in ten (31%) disagree that Clinton is honest, and these doubts are clearly limiting his ability to capitalize on Bush's political vulnerability at this time.

Voter unhappiness with Bush's performance keeps the race close, and history suggests that there is plenty of time for Clinton to overtake Bush. The president's approval rating is now 39%—identical to the rating that President Jimmy Carter received in the Gallup Poll at this time in 1980. Bush's current margin over Clinton resembles Carter's margin over Ronald Reagan in a Gallup survey taken at a similar point in 1980. Although Reagan ended by easily winning the presidential election that year, he trailed Carter by 49% to 43% in an April 1980 poll.

Given their criticism of the primary process, it is no surprise that voters are willing to support a presidential candidate who did not run in the primaries. Fully 61% of all registered Democrats say that, in the event of an open convention, the party should consider nominating someone who did not enter any primaries. Close to one quarter (23%) of all voters say that they would be more likely to vote Democratic in the fall presidential election if the party nominates someone who has not been an active candidate, while only 9% say that this would make them less inclined to vote Democratic.

APRIL 19
BILL CLINTON

Interviewing Date: 4/9–12/92
Survey #GO 222049

Asked of registered voters: I'm going to read you a statement about Bill Clinton. Please tell me whether you strongly agree, agree, disagree, or strongly disagree with the following statement: Bill Clinton has the honesty and integrity to serve as president.

Agree	45%
Disagree	47
No opinion	8

	Agree	Dis-agree	No opinion
By Sex			
Male	47%	46%	7%
Female	44	48	8
By Ethnic Background			
White	43	49	8
Nonwhite	62	33	5
By Education			
College Graduate	45	50	5
College Incomplete	33	57	10
No College	51	41	8

By Region			
East.......................43	48	9
Midwest.................44	49	7
South....................52	42	6
West.....................40	51	9
By Age			
18–29 Years...........47	47	6
30–49 Years...........43	51	6
50 Years and Over.....47	43	10
By Household Income			
$50,000 and Over.....37	60	3
$30,000–$49,999....41	51	8
$20,000–$29,999....54	40	6
Under $20,000.........53	37	10
By Politics			
Republicans............28	66	6
Democrats..............63	30	7
Independents...........42	49	9
By Political Ideology			
Liberal..................56	41	3
Moderate................48	45	7
Conservative...........38	55	7
By Community Size			
Large City..............48	44	8
Medium City...........43	51	6
Suburbs..................36	57	7
Small Town............49	42	9
Rural Area..............47	43	10
By Presidential Preference			
Bush.....................23	69	8
Clinton.................78	17	5
Undecided; other.......21	61	18

Note: The character issue has been particularly damaging to Bill Clinton among more affluent and suburban voters. These groups, who mostly backed Paul Tsongas over Clinton in the Democratic primaries, could well determine the outcome of the November presidential election. To build a winning coalition, Clinton will have to expand his appeal beyond the big-city, minority, and blue-collar coalition that has been the key to his success in the primaries.

In a Gallup Poll taken after Clinton won the New York primary on April 7, six in ten voters (60%) with household incomes over $50,000 disagree with the statement that the Arkansas governor has the honesty and integrity to serve as president. A similar proportion (57%) of suburban voters says that Clinton lacks the honesty necessary to be president.

Among all registered voters, opinion on Clinton's character is about evenly divided; 45% think that he is honest enough to be president, while 47% do not. Two thirds (66%) of Republicans doubt Clinton's honesty, but this might be explained by simple partisanship. More worrisome for him is the finding that three in ten (30%) Democrats express doubts about the character of their party's likely nominee. And about one half (49%) of political independents, another group that tended to back Tsongas in the Democratic primaries, says that Clinton fails the honesty test.

APRIL 23
AID TO THE FORMER SOVIET UNION

Interviewing Date: 4/9–12/92
Survey #GO 222049

*Do you think the United States is doing too much, not enough, or about the right amount to help the former Soviet republics in their current economic crisis?**

Too much..	36%
Not enough......................................	21
Right amount...................................	39
No opinion.......................................	4

Selected National Trend

	Too much	*Not enough*	*Right amount*	*No opinion*
1991				
December......35%		16%	44%	5%
August..........19		15	62	4
July.............20		9	64	7

*The wording of the question changes in 1992 from that used in earlier surveys: ". . . to help the Soviet Union in its current economic crisis."

President Bush recently announced that the United States will join six other nations in providing financial aid and loans as well as food and humanitarian and technical assistance to the former Soviet Union. Generally speaking, do you favor or oppose this plan?

Favor	53%
Oppose	43
No opinion	4

	Favor	Oppose	No opinion
By Politics			
Republicans	64%	33%	3%
Democrats	46	50	4
Independents	50	45	5

How concerned are you that if the former Soviet Union does not receive enough help from the United States and its allies that each of the following may happen:

An unfriendly government will take power there?

Very concerned	27%
Somewhat concerned	40
Not too concerned	21
Not at all concerned	10
No opinion	2

There will be serious shortages of food and medical supplies to people in the former Soviet republics?

Very concerned	35%
Somewhat concerned	44
Not too concerned	13
Not at all concerned	6
No opinion	2

Soviet nuclear weapons and technology will spread to other countries?

Very concerned	56%
Somewhat concerned	23
Not too concerned	13
Not at all concerned	5
No opinion	3

Note: Public opinion is closely divided on the new U.S. commitment to help Russia and the other former Soviet republics weather their current economic crisis. Earlier this month, President George Bush announced that the United States would participate in an international consortium to provide financial aid, loans, and other forms of assistance to the new governments of the former Soviet Union. According to a recent Gallup Poll, a majority (53%) supports the aid plan outlined by Bush; however, a large minority (43%) opposes it.

New foreign aid is a hard sell to a public that feels battered by the recent recession, and the number of Americans who think that the United States is doing too much to help the Russians (36%) continues to exceed the number who thinks that we are not doing enough (21%). Thirty-nine percent say that the level of effort is about right.

Public attitudes toward aid to the former Soviet Union have changed little since last December, despite extensive reporting of former President Richard Nixon's outspoken views on this issue. Nixon argues that by failing to help the Russians through these difficult times, the United States risks dangerous consequences for the world's future, including a takeover of their country by an unfriendly government.

This is a classic case of international priorities competing with domestic priorities. Those groups of Americans who themselves feel most economically pressured seem least willing to extend a hand to help the less fortunate in another part of the world. Opinion on aid to the former Soviet republics divides along the lines of race, education, income, gender, and party identification: whites, college graduates, the most prosperous, men, and Republicans are more generous on this issue than nonwhites, those without a high-school diploma, those earning less than $20,000, women, and Democrats.

The public's biggest worry about the consequences of not doing enough to help the former Soviet republics is that nuclear materials might fall into the wrong hands. A majority (56%) is very concerned that Soviet nuclear weapons and technology might spread to other countries. By comparison, roughly one third (35%) is very concerned that inadequate U.S. assistance might lead to serious shortages of food and medical supplies in the republics. Finally, one quarter (27%) is very concerned that an unfriendly government might seize power in the former Soviet Union.

APRIL 26
PRESIDENTIAL TRIAL HEATS/PRESIDENTIAL CANDIDATES/PRESIDENT BUSH

Interviewing Date: 4/20–22/92*
Survey #GO 222050

Asked of registered voters: Suppose the 1992 presidential election were being held today. If George Bush were the Republican candidate and Bill Clinton were the Democratic candidate, whom would you vote for? [Those who were undecided were asked: As of today, do you lean more to Bush, the Republican, or to Clinton, the Democrat?]

Bush	50%
Clinton	34
Undecided; other	16

Selected National Trend

	Bush	Clinton	Undecided; other
1992			
April 9–12	48%	41%	11%
March 31–April 1	54	34	12
March 26–29	54	38	8
March 20–22	52	43	5
March 11–12	50	44	6
February 19–20	53	43	4
February 6–9	53	38	9

Also asked of registered voters: Suppose the 1992 presidential election were being held today. If George Bush were the Republican candidate and Bill Clinton were the Democratic candidate and H. Ross Perot were an independent candidate, whom would you vote for? [Those who were undecided were asked: As of today, do you lean more to Bush, the Republican; to Clinton, the Democrat; or to Perot, the independent?]

Bush	41%
Clinton	26
Perot	25
Undecided; other	8

	Bush	Clinton	Perot	Undecided; other
By Sex				
Male	38%	26%	31%	5%
Female	44	26	19	11
By Ethnic Background				
White	44	23	25	8
Nonwhite	21	50	18	11
Black	14	58	18	10
By Education				
College Graduate	38	25	31	6
College Incomplete	41	22	30	7
No College	43	28	19	10
By Region				
East	48	24	22	6
Midwest	37	22	27	14
South	41	31	23	5
West	37	27	27	9
By Age				
18–29 Years	47	30	17	6
30–49 Years	42	26	26	6
50–64 Years	40	23	30	7
65 Years and Over	35	26	23	16
By Household Income				
$50,000 and Over	39	21	37	3
$30,000–$49,999	45	25	25	5
$20,000–$29,999	41	24	24	11
Under $20,000	40	33	16	11

*Gallup survey for CNN/*USA Today*

By Politics				
Republicans	73	6	16	5
Democrats	15	55	20	10
Independents	30	19	40	11

By Political Ideology				
Liberal	25	39	26	10
Moderate	37	28	28	7
Conservative	53	18	22	7

By Bush Approval				
Approve	74	8	13	5
Disapprove	15	42	35	8

By 1988 Vote				
George Bush	57	12	25	6
Michael Dukakis	11	52	27	10

Selected National Trend

	Bush	*Clinton*	*Perot*	*Undecided; other*
1992				
April 15–16	42%	27%	20%	11%
March 31–April 1	44	25	24	7

Next, I'd like your opinion of some people in politics. As I read each name, please tell me whether you have a favorable or unfavorable opinion of this person:

George Bush?

Favorable	55%
Unfavorable	41
No opinion	4

Selected National Trend

	Favor-able	*Unfavor-able*	*No opinion*
1992			
April 9–12	48%	44%	8%
March 26–29	49	44	7

Bill Clinton?

Favorable	42%
Unfavorable	49
No opinion	9

Selected National Trend

	Favor-able	*Unfavor-able*	*No opinion*
1992			
April 9–12	34%	47%	19%
March 26–29	37	40	23

H. Ross Perot?

Favorable	41%
Unfavorable	23
No opinion	25
Never heard of	11

	Favor-able	*Unfavor-able*	*No opinion; never heard of*
By Sex			
Male	48%	25%	27%
Female	35	21	44
By Ethnic Background			
White	43	23	34
Nonwhite	30	25	45
Black	33	24	43
By Education			
College Graduate	59	18	23
College Incomplete	44	21	35
No College	31	26	43
By Region			
East	35	25	40
Midwest	45	21	34
South	41	24	35
West	44	22	34
By Age			
18–29 Years	37	23	40
30–49 Years	47	23	30
50–64 Years	45	24	31
65 Years and Over	30	23	47
By Household Income			
$50,000 and Over	63	18	19
$30,000–$49,999	40	27	33
$20,000–$29,999	39	22	39
Under $20,000	27	24	49
By Politics			
Republicans	39	26	35

Democrats	35	24	41
Independents	51	17	32
By Political Ideology			
Liberal	47	19	34
Moderate	44	20	36
Conservative	39	29	32
By Bush Approval			
Approve	37	27	36
Disapprove	46	21	33
By 1988 Vote			
George Bush	43	23	34
Michael Dukakis	43	25	32

Do you approve or disapprove of the way George Bush is handling his job as president?

Approve....................42%
Disapprove....................48
No opinion....................10

Selected National Trend

	Approve	Dis-approve	No opinion
1992			
April 9–12	39%	54%	7%
March 26–29	42	51	7
March 20–22	41	49	10
March 11–12	41	47	12
February 28–March 1	41	53	6

Asked of registered voters: Please tell me whether you approve or disapprove of the way George Bush is handling some specific problems facing the country:

Foreign affairs?

Approve....................60%
Disapprove....................35
No opinion....................5

Education?

Approve....................36%
Disapprove....................57
No opinion....................7

Taxes?

Approve....................27%
Disapprove....................67
No opinion....................6

Health care?

Approve....................24%
Disapprove....................69
No opinion....................7

Economy?

Approve....................22%
Disapprove....................73
No opinion....................5

Also asked of registered voters: How would you rate economic conditions in this country today—excellent, good, only fair, or poor?

	April 20–22	Jan. 3–6
Excellent	1%	*
Good	11	12
Fair	40	46
Poor	48	41
No opinion	*	1

*Less than 1%

Also asked of registered voters: Right now, do you think that economic conditions in the country as a whole are getting better or getting worse?

Better....................40%
Worse....................45
Same (volunteered)....................13
No opinion....................2

Selected National Trend

	Better	Worse	Same	No opinion
1992				
March 20–22	37%	51%	11%	1%
January 31–February 1	22	70	7	1
January 3–6	22	71	6	1

1991			
December......19	69	9	3
October.........25	64	8	3
September.....27	60	10	3
July............34	51	9	6

Also asked of registered voters: Do you think George Bush or Bill Clinton would do a better job of handling the economy?

	April 20–22	*March 20–22*
Bush	43%	37%
Clinton	36	49
Both equally (volunteered)	1	2
Neither (volunteered); no opinion	20	12

Note: Although Democratic front-runner Bill Clinton is expected to win easily in the Pennsylvania primary on April 28, a new Gallup Poll indicates that the Arkansas governor's prospects for winning the November election have never been gloomier. About one half (49%) of voters nationally now has an unfavorable opinion of him, up from 40% in a poll taken in late March, before the New York primary.

Clinton's support in a two-way race against President George Bush has fallen to 34%, matching his previous low in the Gallup Poll. Bush captures 50% of the vote, despite his overall approval rating of only 42%, and still lower ratings for his handling of specific domestic issues ranging from the economy (22%) to education (36%), taxes (27%), and health care (24%).

Although still unhappy with President Bush's economic performance, respondents no longer seem willing to take their chances with Clinton on the critical issue of the economy. By a margin of 43% to 36%, voters now trust Bush more than Clinton to deal with the economy. In March, Clinton enjoyed a 49%-to-37% advantage over Bush on this measure. The Arkansas governor has slipped most among political independents, moderates, and middle-income voters—groups whose ballots will be critical in November.

Until voters are convinced that the economy is turning around, even a damaged Clinton cannot be counted out, however. The level of economic discontent remains relatively high. Close to one half (48%) gives a "poor" rating to economic conditions in this country; another 40% say that conditions are only fair. Although the number of voters who think that the economy is improving has increased markedly since January, pessimists continue to outnumber optimists: 45% say that the national economy is getting worse, while only 40% think that it is getting better.

Clinton's recent fall in the polls, along with Bush's continuing vulnerability, has created an opening for H. Ross Perot's possible presidential bid. Close to nine in ten voters now say that they have heard of the Texas entrepreneur and, at this point, opinion of him is mostly positive. Four in ten (41%) have a favorable opinion of Perot, 23% have an unfavorable opinion, and 25% recognize his name but have no opinion of him.

In a hypothetical three-way race against Bush and Clinton, Perot draws 25% of the vote, about equal to support for the Arkansas governor (26%); Bush finishes on top with 41%. History shows that independent or third-party candidates are rarely a factor in presidential elections. Nevertheless, if the economy fails to improve significantly and Clinton fails to overcome his negative ratings, Perot can be a serious contender.

Perot voters tend to be male, middle-aged, college educated, affluent, and politically independent. The Texas billionaire's ability to draw adherents from certain income groups reflects the weaknesses of his opponents. He receives about as much support as Bush (37% versus 39%) from voters with incomes over $50,000, a group that generally remains solidly Republican in presidential elections. Although the votes of middle-income families are key to the Democrats' chances of regaining the White House, Perot runs even with Clinton among voters earning $30,000 to $49,999 (25% each) and $20,000 to $29,999 (24% each).

MAY 3
1992: THE YEAR OF THE ANGRY VOTER

Interviewing Date: 4/20–22/92
Survey #GO 222050

Asked of registered voters: Are the presidential candidates talking about issues you really care about, or not?

Yes	53%
No	44
No opinion	3

Also asked of registered voters: Is there any candidate running this year that you think would make a good president, or not?

Yes	49%
No	43
No opinion	8

Also asked of registered voters: Do you feel that any of the presidential candidates have come up with good ideas for solving the country's problems, or not?

Yes	36%
No	60
No opinion	4

Also asked of registered voters: Does the way this year's presidential campaign is being conducted make you feel proud to be an American, or not?

Yes	39%
No	53
No opinion	8

	*Angry voters**	*All other voters*
By Sex		
Male	41%	59%
Female	38	62
By Ethnic Background		
White	41	59
Nonwhite	29	71
By Education		
College Graduate	45	55
Some College	42	58
No College	36	64
By Region		
East	39	61
Midwest	45	55
South	34	66
West	42	58
By Age		
18–29 Years	35	65
30–49 Years	37	63
50–64 Years	47	53
65 Years and Over	39	61
By Household Income		
$50,000 and Over	46	54
$30,000–$49,999	45	55
$20,000–$29,999	39	61
Under $20,000	31	69
By Politics		
Republicans	35	65
Democrats	35	65
Independents	49	51
By Political Ideology		
Liberal	40	60
Moderate	40	60
Conservative	40	60

*"Angry voters" are defined as those who answered "no" to at least three of the four preceding questions.

Asked of registered voters: Do you approve or disapprove of the way George Bush is handling his job as president?

	Angry voters	*All other voters*
Approve	37%	46%
Disapprove	57	42
No opinion	6	12

Asked of registered voters: Next, I'd like your opinion of some people in politics. As I read each name, please tell me whether you have a favorable or unfavorable opinion of this person:

George Bush?

	Angry voters	*All other voters*
Favorable	48%	59%
Unfavorable	49	37
No opinion	3	4

Bill Clinton?

	Angry voters	All other voters
Favorable	29%	50%
Unfavorable	62	41
No opinion	9	9

H. Ross Perot?

	Angry voters	All other voters
Favorable	45%	39%
Unfavorable	21	24
No opinion	34	37

Asked of registered voters: Suppose the presidential election were being held today. If George Bush were the Republican candidate and Bill Clinton were the Democratic candidate, whom would you vote for? [Those who were undecided were asked: As of today, do you lean more to Bush, the Republican, or to Clinton, the Democrat?]

	Angry voters	All other voters
Bush	51%	48%
Clinton	30	37
Undecided; other	19	15

Asked of registered voters: Suppose the 1992 presidential election were being held today. If George Bush were the Republican candidate and Bill Clinton were the Democratic candidate and H. Ross Perot were an independent candidate, whom would you vote for? [Those who were undecided were asked: As of today, do you lean more to Bush, the Republican; to Clinton, the Democrat; or to Perot, the independent?]

	Angry voters	All other voters
Bush	38%	43%
Clinton	22	29
Perot	30	21
Undecided; other	10	7

Asked of registered voters: Please tell me whether or not you think the following political officeholder deserves to be reelected—the U.S. representative in your congressional district?

	Angry voters	All other voters
Yes	45%	54%
No	40	26
No opinion	15	20

Asked of registered voters: In general, how would you rate the job the news media has done in covering the presidential campaign—excellent, good, only fair, or poor?

	Angry voters	All other voters
Excellent	3%	7%
Good	24	36
Fair	41	36
Poor	30	19
No opinion	2	2

Asked of registered voters: We'd like to know how the way things have been going in politics and government this year might affect your vote in November. First, as a result of the way things have been going, are you more likely or less likely to bother to vote at all?

	Angry voters	All other voters
More likely	55%	71%
Less likely	29	13
No difference; no opinion	16	16

Next, if you do vote, does the way things have been going in politics and government make you more likely or less likely to do each of the following:

Vote to reelect incumbent political officeholders?

	Angry voters	All other voters
More likely	20%	32%
Less likely	68	53
No difference; no opinion	12	15

Vote for Republican candidates?

	Angry voters	All other voters
More likely	36%	39%
Less likely	52	45
No difference; no opinion	12	16

Vote for Democratic candidates?

	Angry voters	All other voters
More likely	40%	46%
Less likely	48	42
No difference; no opinion	12	12

Vote for independent or third-party candidates?

	Angry voters	All other voters
More likely	51%	38%
Less likely	38	51
No difference; no opinion	11	11

Note: Like the anchorman in the movie *Network*, they're mad as hell and they're not going to take it anymore. Some seem eager to vote incumbents out of office; others plan to register their displeasure with the status quo by voting for third-party candidates. Still others say that they might sit out the presidential election this time. Who are these people? They are America's angry voters, a group generally critical of President George Bush's performance in office but unfavorably disposed toward his likely Democratic opponent, Bill Clinton.

The results of a recent Gallup Poll show 1992 to be the year of the angry voter. The survey finds widespread dissatisfaction in middle America with the presidential candidates, their campaigns, and the way the news media have covered the race for the White House. The high level of voter irritation is a cause of concern for both the Bush and Clinton campaigns. Backers of a third-party presidential bid by H. Ross Perot, however, may be encouraged by it.

Collectively, the presidential candidates and their messages have failed to impress many voters. More than four in ten (43%) do not think that any of the candidates running this year would make a good president. Six in ten (60%) do not think that any of them has come up with good ideas for solving the country's problems.

The primary campaigns themselves have contributed much to the mood of voter disaffection. In early January, well before the first primary in New Hampshire, only one third (29%) of respondents said that the way the presidential campaigns were being conducted made them proud to be Americans. Now over one half (53%) say that the presidential campaign does not make them feel proud. In addition, 44% of voters now disagree that the candidates talk about issues they really care about, up significantly from 28% in January.

Those most dissatisfied with this year's presidential race do not fit the classic profile of the low-income, less well-educated, alienated voter. Gallup classified close to four in ten poll respondents (39%) as "angry voters." But that proportion is higher among college graduates (45%) and those with household incomes of at least $30,000 (46%). Higher proportions are also found among political independents (49%), voters aged 50 to 64 years (47%), and midwesterners (45%).

These angry voters give President Bush a low overall approval rating (37%), but they think even less of his likely Democratic challenger. Six in ten (62%) have an unfavorable opinion of Clinton, compared with about one half (49%) who look unfavorably on Bush. Angry voters also tend to give the news media low marks for coverage of the campaign itself. Seven in ten rate news coverage of the presidential campaign as only fair (41%) or poor (30%).

In past years the electoral consequences of voter anger were predictable: an unhappy electorate would vote against the incumbent president and his party. The 1992 election, however, is anything but predictable. Incumbents are still the biggest target: two thirds (68%) of angry voters say that they are less likely to vote for incumbent officeholders. And Congress, dominated for years by the Democratic party, is even more unpopular in the aftermath of its check-kiting scandal. While roughly one half (51%) of angry voters say that they would vote for Bush over Clinton, fewer than one half (45%) believe that their own member of Congress deserves reelection.

Angry voters direct their wrath about equally at both major parties. Roughly one half (52%) say that they are less likely to vote for

Republican candidates; almost as many (48%) are less likely to support Democrats. While the appeal of the major parties has waned, angry voters respond positively to the idea of an independent presidential candidate such as Perot: 51% are more likely to vote for independent or third-party candidates, a higher proportion than say that they are more likely to support Republicans (36%) or Democrats (40%).

Even before formally declaring his candidacy, Perot shows an uncanny ability to tap the well of public discontent. While angry voters express mixed views of Bush and harshly negative views of Clinton, Jerry Brown, and Pat Buchanan, they give Perot solidly positive ratings: 45% favorable versus 21% unfavorable. Bush receives more support from angry voters (38%) than does Perot (30%) as an independent in a three-way trial heat, but the Texas entrepreneur outdraws Clinton (22%).

Perot's chances to ride voter discontent into the White House remain a long shot. Third-party presidential candidates often show great promise in the spring, only to fade in the fall. Much will depend on how well Perot weathers the media scrutiny of his public and personal life. And he must also fight apathy: 29% of angry voters say that, because of the way things have been going in politics and government, they are less likely to bother to vote at all in November. But as long as Bush continues to be vulnerable on the economy and Clinton cannot shed his negative baggage, the potential exists for a strong showing by Perot as a third-party candidate.

Bush's Job Rating in Key Regions*

	Approve	*Dis-approve*	*No opinion*
Best States for Democrats in 1988			
Democratic East	38%	54%	8%
Democratic Pacific	38	56	6
Democratic Midwest	38	55	7
Democratic Near West	45	50	5
GOP Stronghold States			
GOP Central	43	51	6
GOP East	45	51	4
GOP Near West	38	55	7
GOP South	45	47	8
GOP Mountain West	38	52	10

**Democratic East:* Connecticut, District of Columbia, Maryland, Massachusetts, New York, Pennsylvania, Rhode Island, Vermont, West Virginia; *Democratic Pacific:* California, Hawaii, Oregon, Washington; *Democratic Midwest:* Illinois, Iowa, Michigan, Minnesota, Missouri, Wisconsin; *Democratic Near West:* Colorado, Montana, New Mexico, South Dakota; *GOP Central:* Indiana, Kentucky, Ohio; *GOP East:* Delaware, Maine, New Hampshire, New Jersey; *GOP Near West:* Kansas, Nebraska, North Dakota; *GOP South:* Alabama, Arkansas, Florida, Georgia, Louisiana, Mississippi, North Carolina, Oklahoma, South Carolina, Tennessee, Texas, Virginia; *GOP Mountain West:* Alaska, Arizona, Idaho, Nevada, Utah, Wyoming

MAY 3
PRESIDENT BUSH/PRESIDENTIAL TRIAL HEATS

Interviewing Date: 3/20–4/22/92
Several Surveys

Asked of registered voters: Do you approve or disapprove of the way George Bush is handling his job as president?

Approve	41%
Disapprove	52
No opinion	7

Also asked of registered voters: Suppose the 1992 presidential election were being held today. If George Bush were the Republican candidate and Bill Clinton were the Democratic candidate, whom would you vote for? [Those who were undecided were asked: As of today, do you lean more to Bush, the Republican, or to Clinton, the Democrat?]

Bush	51%
Clinton	39
Undecided; other	10

Bush versus Clinton in Key Regions

	Bush	Clinton	Undecided; other
Best States for Democrats in 1988			
Democratic East	52%	37%	11%
Democratic Pacific	47	42	11
Democratic Midwest	49	40	11
Democratic Near West	52	41	7
GOP Stronghold States			
GOP Central	55	33	12
GOP East	55	35	10
GOP Near West	49	41	10
GOP South	49	42	9
GOP Mountain West	64	25	11

Also asked of registered voters: Suppose the 1992 presidential election were being held today. If George Bush were the Republican candidate and Bill Clinton were the Democratic candidate and H. Ross Perot were an independent candidate, whom would you vote for? [Those who were undecided were asked: As of today, do you lean more to Bush, the Republican; to Clinton, the Democrat; or to Perot, the independent?]

Bush	42%
Clinton	26
Perot	23
Undecided; other	9

Bush, Clinton, and Perot in Key Regions

	Bush	Clinton	Perot	Undecided; other
Best States for Democrats in 1988				
Democratic East	46%	25%	22%	7%
Democratic Pacific	35	27	30	8
Democratic Midwest	38	21	27	14
Democratic Near West	46	22	25	7
GOP Stronghold States				
GOP Central	42	29	20	9
GOP East	55	19	20	6
GOP Near West	46	31	17	6
GOP South	41	30	20	9
GOP Mountain West	47	20	27	6

Note: With his victory in the Pennsylvania primary, Bill Clinton has virtually clinched the Democratic presidential nomination—but that nomination could be a lot less valuable if H. Ross Perot enters the race as a third-party candidate. A special regional analysis of Gallup test election results suggests that, if the election were held today, Perot would hurt Clinton more than George Bush in the battle for electoral votes.

In the Pacific region, where a California victory is critical for the Democrats, Clinton might even finish third if Perot is on the ballot. Similarly, Perot saps Clinton's strength in the Midwest, where he needs to win big industrial states such as Illinois. And even in the East, where Michael Dukakis showed the most strength in 1988, Perot demonstrates the potential to split the anti-Bush vote with Clinton. On the other hand, Perot's candidacy does not seem likely to upset Bush's stranglehold on the blocs of states that most consistently vote Republican in presidential elections.

In winning five of six presidential elections since 1968, Republican candidates have averaged 52% of the popular vote, compared with 43% for Democrats. Republican dominance of the Electoral College vote—the one that counts—is far more impressive. Over the same period the GOP has won, on average, 78% of the electoral vote. In 1988, Bush won 426 electoral votes to Dukakis's 112. To break the GOP's presidential winning streak, the Clinton campaign must devise a strategy to capture 270 or more electoral votes.

Analysis of Gallup Poll data collected over the past month suggests that Bush is vulnerable in three key Democratic regions. Fewer than four in ten voters (38%) in the Democratic East, Pacific, and Midwest approve of the president's job performance. In a two-way trial heat, Clinton now runs close to Bush in the Democratic Pacific (47% Bush versus 42% Clinton) and Democratic Midwest (49% versus 40%). The Bush lead is larger in the Democratic East (52% versus 37%), but much of this region was Paul Tsongas territory in the early primaries. Clinton might be expected to improve his position in the region by the fall, especially if he selects an easterner such as Senator Bill Bradley for his running mate.

The last time the Democrats won a presidential election, they had a southerner at the top of the ticket, Jimmy Carter, who put together an electoral majority by sweeping much of the South. In 1980, however, Ronald Reagan won back the South for the Republicans, with the exception of Georgia, Carter's home state. In 1988, Bush swept the twelve-state region that includes Oklahoma and the eleven states of the old Confederacy.

Bush remains more popular in the South than he is elsewhere. Indeed, his approval in the region now stands at 45%. If there is better economic news in the months ahead, his rating might well move above 50%, into the political comfort zone. For Clinton, however, except for Arkansas and perhaps a few border states, the South will probably not be fertile ground.

If Perot's support in the early polls holds up in November, Clinton's chances of putting together an electoral majority will be seriously compromised. With Perot in the race, Clinton moves from being a close second to an also-ran in the three most critical Democratic regions. His hopes of winning California might be dashed; with 27% of the vote, Clinton is now behind both Bush (35%) and Perot (30%) in the Democratic Pacific. Similarly, while Clinton needs to win states such as Illinois, Wisconsin, and Minnesota to have a chance at the White House, with Perot in the race he falls to third in the Democratic Midwest (38% for Bush, 27% for Perot, and 21% for Clinton). And Perot might make it even tougher for Clinton to rebound in the Democratic East. The Arkansas governor trails Bush by 46% to 25% in the region with Perot in the race at 22%.

In blocs of states that represent the safest GOP territory, the Perot vote does not threaten Bush's lead. In the GOP South, for example, Bush leads with 41%, followed by Clinton with 30% and Perot with 20%.

MAY 10
RACE RELATIONS/PRESIDENTIAL TRIAL HEATS

Interviewing Date: 1/3–6/92
Survey #GO 222034

We'd like to know which issues you think are important for the presidential candidates to discuss and debate in the 1992 campaign. As I read a list of issues, please rate each as very important, somewhat important, not too important, or not at all important:

	Those Replying "Very Important"		
	Total	*Whites*	*Blacks*
Economy	93%	93%	94%
Education	87	86	97
Unemployment	84	82	97
Health care	80	79	90
Federal budget deficit	79	79	79
Crime	77	76	92
Drugs; drug abuse	77	76	91
Poverty; homelessness	76	75	93
Taxes	70	71	71
AIDS	67	63	92
Environment	60	60	64
Foreign trade	53	55	42
Race relations	48	43	82
National defense	43	42	51
Abortion	38	35	51
Foreign affairs	37	38	36

Interviewing Date: 3/20–22/92
Survey #GO 222046

Asked of registered voters: Please tell me whether you think George Bush or Bill Clinton would do a better job of handling race relations:

	Total	*Whites*	*Non-whites*
Bush	42%	45%	21%
Clinton	40	37	63

Both equally (volunteered)	3	3	3
No opinion	15	15	13

Interviewing Date: 4/30–5/1/92*
Special Survey

Asked of registered voters: Suppose the 1992 presidential election were being held today. If George Bush were the Republican candidate and Bill Clinton were the Democratic candidate and H. Ross Perot were an independent candidate, whom would you vote for? [Those who were undecided were asked: As of today, do you lean more to Bush, the Republican; to Clinton, the Democrat; or to Perot, the independent?]

	Total	*Whites*	*Blacks*
Bush	38%	40%	21%
Clinton	27	24	51
Perot	22	24	9
Undecided; other	13	12	19

Also asked of registered voters: Do you think the Bush administration is doing as much as it can to reduce crime at the local level? And do you think the Bush administration is doing as much as it can to guarantee equal justice for black Americans?

Those Replying "Yes"

	Total	*Whites*	*Blacks*
Reduce crime	23%	24%	18%
Guarantee equal justice	34	37	17

Also asked of registered voters: Would a Democratic administration do more to help blacks get ahead, or would it not be much different than the current Republican administration?

	Total	*Whites*	*Blacks*
Would do more	28%	25%	42%
Not much different	55	58	37
No opinion	17	17	21

*Gallup survey for *Newsweek*

Note: The recent events in Los Angeles have moved race relations to the forefront as a presidential campaign issue. Prior to the Rodney King verdict, Gallup surveys found interest in this problem among the voters to be relatively low. When asked to rate the importance of sixteen issues last January, respondents ranked race relations at thirteenth overall.

Both blacks and whites put the economy near or at the top of their list of issues, where it is likely to remain throughout the campaign. But race relations and other domestic problems such as crime, drugs, poverty, homelessness, and AIDS—all associated with urban America—are much more important political issues to blacks than to whites. The greatest divergence between the races is seen on the question of race relations. The January poll found fewer than one half (43%) of white voters rating race relations as very important, compared with eight in ten (82%) black voters.

A Gallup Poll conducted for *Newsweek*, after the King verdict, found both blacks and whites critical of the Bush administration's efforts to guarantee equal justice for black Americans, as well as its efforts to reduce crime. Only 17% of blacks and 37% of whites think that the current administration is doing enough to guarantee equal justice. Roughly two out of ten blacks (18%) and whites (24%) are satisfied with its efforts to reduce crime.

The same poll, however, found general skepticism that a Democratic administration would act differently. Despite their strong Democratic orientation, fewer than one half of blacks (42%) have confidence that a Democratic administration would do more to help them get ahead; 37% think that it would not be much different. Only one quarter (25%) of whites says that electing a Democratic president would improve conditions for blacks.

While the issues of civil rights and race relations are traditionally Democratic ones—and Bill Clinton has assumed the mantle of racial healer during his presidential campaign—the race issue has not worked thus far to Clinton's advantage. A March survey found George Bush rated almost even with Clinton on his ability to handle race relations (42% versus 40%). Bush had a slight advantage among white voters (45% versus 37%) and

Clinton a larger one among nonwhite voters (63% versus 21%).

Clinton's failure so far to capitalize on disaffection for Bush among blacks is seen in Gallup's most recent three-way test election. The poll for *Newsweek* shows Clinton drawing barely one half of the black vote (51%) against Bush (21%) and H. Ross Perot (9%), with 19% undecided. (By contrast, Walter Mondale received 86% in Gallup's May 1984 test election against Ronald Reagan.)

To win in November, Clinton probably needs close to 90% of the black vote. But his support level among blacks today is on a par with that of Michael Dukakis four years ago, when he was still campaigning against Jesse Jackson for the Democratic nomination. A May 1988 poll found Dukakis leading Bush by 54% to 27% among black voters.

MAY 12
PRESIDENT BUSH/LOS ANGELES RIOTS

Interviewing Date: 5/7–10/92
Survey #GO 222052

Do you approve or disapprove of the way George Bush is handling his job as president?

Approve..40%
Disapprove....................................53
No opinion.....................................7

Selected National Trend

	Approve	Dis-approve	No opinion
1992			
April 20–22	42%	48%	10%
April 9–12	39	54	7
March 26–29	42	51	7
March 11–12	41	47	12
February 19–20	39	47	14
February 6–9	44	48	8
January 3–6	46	47	7

Please tell me whether you approve or disapprove of the way George Bush is handling each of the following issues and problems:

Foreign affairs?

Approve..52%
Disapprove....................................43
No opinion.....................................5

Abortion?

Approve..33%
Disapprove....................................46
No opinion.....................................21

Race relations?

Approve..35%
Disapprove....................................56
No opinion.....................................9

Crime?

Approve..33%
Disapprove....................................62
No opinion.....................................5

Economy?

Approve..20%
Disapprove....................................76
No opinion.....................................4

Asked of registered voters: Next, I'd like your opinion of some people in politics. As I read each name, please tell me whether you have a favorable or unfavorable opinion of this person:

George Bush?

Favorable......................................50%
Unfavorable...................................47
Heard of; no opinion.........................3
Never heard of.................................*

*Less than 1%

Selected National Trend

	Favor-able	Un-favor-able	Heard of; no opinion*
1992			
April 20–22	55%	41%	4%

April 9–12	48	44	8
March 26–29	49	44	7

*"Never heard of"—at less than 1%—is omitted.

Bill Clinton?

Favorable....................51%
Unfavorable....................36
Heard of; no opinion....................11
Never heard of....................2

Selected National Trend

	Favorable	Unfavorable	Heard of; no opinion*
1992			
April 20–22	42%	49%	9%
April 9–12	34	47	19
March 26–29	37	40	23

*"Never heard of"—at less than 1%—is omitted.

H. Ross Perot?

Favorable....................48%
Unfavorable....................16
Heard of; no opinion....................22
Never heard of....................14

Selected National Trend

	Favorable	Unfavorable	Heard of; no opinion*
1992			
April 20–22	41%	23%	25%

*"Never heard of" for Perot is 11%.

Asked of registered voters: Now, turning to the recent events in Los Angeles, do you approve or disapprove of the way George Bush handled recent events following the King verdict and the outbreak of violence in Los Angeles?

Approve....................41%
Disapprove....................51
No opinion....................8

	Approve	Disapprove	No opinion
By Ethnic Background			
White	43%	48%	9%
Black	21	71	8

Also asked of registered voters: Do you think either Bill Clinton or Ross Perot could have done a better job of handling the situation, or not?

Yes, Clinton....................14%
Yes, Perot....................13
Yes, both (volunteered)....................5
No, neither (volunteered)....................49
No opinion....................19

Also asked of registered voters: I'd like to know how the recent events in Los Angeles might affect your vote for president in November. First, how about George Bush—are you more likely or less likely to vote for Bush as a result of the riots, or will the events not have much effect on your vote? Next, how about Bill Clinton? Ross Perot?

	More likely	Less likely	Not much effect	No opinion
Bush	4%	14%	80%	2%
Clinton	10	8	77	5
Perot	9	6	73	12

Also asked of registered voters: Who would do a better job of improving conditions for minorities in urban areas—Bill Clinton, George Bush, or Ross Perot?

Clinton....................36%
Bush....................21
Perot....................20
All the same (volunteered)....................1
None (volunteered)....................7
No opinion....................15

Note: The president's overall approval rating has not changed significantly since the Rodney King verdict and the outbreak of violence that followed in Los Angeles: 40% approve of the way that he is handling his job, while 53% disapprove. George Bush receives similar ratings—41% approve versus 51%

disapprove—for his handling of the situation created by the verdict and subsequent riots.

Bush now has been damaged on two fronts: He is vulnerable to charges that he has not done enough to improve race relations and that he has mishandled the crime problem. Only about one third of the public now approves of the way that he is handling race relations (35%) and crime (33%). His increased vulnerability in these areas only compounds the political problems created by his low ratings on the economy (20% approval) and the abortion issue (33% approve). The riots seem to have brought him down a notch in terms of presidential stature; even on foreign affairs, traditionally his greatest area of strength, Bush's ratings have fallen (52% today versus 60% in late April).

While Bush has been weakened politically, neither Bill Clinton nor H. Ross Perot has been able to take full advantage of the situation. Relatively few voters think that Clinton (14%) or Perot (13%) could have done a better job than Bush in dealing with the recent events in Los Angeles. Among the small proportions of voters who say that the riots affected their chances of voting for Clinton, about as many are less inclined to support him as are more inclined (8% versus 10%). The same holds true for Perot: 9% are more likely to vote for him because of the riots, but 6% are less likely.

Clinton is seen by a plurality (36%) as the candidate best able to improve conditions for minorities in urban areas. By comparison, 21% name Bush and 20% name Perot as best able to deal with the problems of the inner cities. Considering that the Democratic party is traditionally associated with minorities and the cities, however, Clinton's rating does not seem particularly impressive. Looked at from another perspective, more Americans name another candidate (41%) than name Clinton as the candidate who can best deal with urban problems.

Clinton and, to a lesser degree, Perot seem to have benefited from the shift in media coverage from the presidential campaign to the problems of urban America. With less attention being given to the Arkansas governor's character, his favorability ratings have improved substantially. In a late April poll nearly one half of voters (49%) said that they had an unfavorable opinion of Clinton. Now, fewer than four in ten (36%) express negative views. Opinion of Clinton has improved most among men, southerners, and political independents.

As for Perot, even though press scrutiny of his background has increased, his ratings in the Gallup Poll are more positive (48% favorable versus 16% unfavorable) than they were in late April (41% versus 23%). With 30% of the vote, Perot is now capturing a level of support higher than any third-party or independent presidential candidate in Gallup's history. (John Anderson's 24% in June 1980 was the previous high-water mark for an independent.)

MAY 17
PRESIDENTIAL TRIAL HEATS/H. ROSS PEROT

Interviewing Date: 5/7–10/92
Survey #GO 222052

Asked of registered voters: Suppose the 1992 presidential election were being held today. If George Bush were the Republican candidate and Bill Clinton were the Democratic candidate and H. Ross Perot were an independent candidate, whom would you vote for? [Those who were undecided were asked: As of today, do you lean more to Bush, the Republican; to Clinton, the Democrat; or to Perot, the independent?]

Bush	35%
Clinton	29
Perot	30
Undecided; other	6

Selected National Trend

	Bush	*Clinton*	*Perot*	*Undecided; other*
1992				
April 20–22	41%	26%	25%	8%
March 31–April 1	44	25	24	7

Change in Vote for Perot

	April 20–22	*May 7–10*	*Point difference*
Total	25%	30%	+5

By Sex			
Male	31	34	+3
Female	19	26	+7
By Ethnic Background			
White	25	32	+7
Black	–	18	–
By Education			
College	31	31	*
No College	19	28	+9
By Region			
East	22	29	+7
Midwest	27	23	-4
South	23	32	+9
West	27	37	+10
By Age			
18–29 Years	17	25	+8
30–49 Years	26	32	+6
50 Years and Over	30	30	*
By Household Income			
$50,000 and Over	37	32	-5
$30,000–$49,999	25	27	+2
$20,000–$29,999	24	33	+9
Under $20,000	16	30	+14
By Politics			
Republicans	16	20	+4
Democrats	20	25	+5
Independents	40	42	+2
By Political Ideology			
Conservative	22	31	+9
Moderate	28	29	+1
Liberal	26	31	+5

*Less than 1%

Note: Support for Texas entrepreneur H. Ross Perot's nascent presidential candidacy is expanding beyond his male, older, and affluent core constituency. According to the most recent Gallup Poll, three in ten respondents (30%) would vote for Perot if the presidential election were held today. That puts the potential wild-card candidate in a statistical tie with apparent Democratic presidential nominee Bill Clinton (29%) and within 5 percentage points of George Bush (35%). Support for Perot is up from 25% in a late April poll conducted before the Los Angeles riots.

In more than fifty years of polling, no third-party presidential candidate, at any time during a campaign, has ever reached the 30% mark in a Gallup survey. John Anderson, who attempted to capitalize on voter dissatisfaction with major-party candidates Jimmy Carter and Ronald Reagan, held the previous record with 24% support for his independent candidacy in June 1980. George Wallace, who ran as the American Independence party's candidate in 1968, peaked at 21% in September of that year. (Anderson ultimately ended up with only 7% of the vote in November 1980, while Wallace received 14% in 1968.)

Earlier polling showed Perot's support concentrated among specific voter subgroups, but in the latest survey he draws support more evenly across all categories of voters. In fact, his recent gains come almost exclusively from groups that have been least likely to support him in the past: women, young people, and those with lower incomes. Perot now receives roughly one quarter of the women's vote (26%), up from 19% in April. Support among his own age group—50 and older—has held steady at 30%, but he has gained 6 percentage points among voters aged 30 to 49 (from 26% to 32%). The Texas billionaire has picked up 9 percentage points among lower middle-income voters (from 24% to 33% in the $20,000-to-$29,999 category) and 14 points among voters with the lowest incomes (from 16% to 30%).

The latest poll also indicates significant gains for Perot among voters in the Sunbelt. In the South, his support has increased by 9 percentage points, from 23% to 32%. In the West, Perot support is up 10 points, moving from 27% to 37%. These results are consistent with the findings of recent state polls in California and Texas that show Perot with a lead.

MAY 24
PRESIDENTIAL TRIAL HEATS/H. ROSS PEROT

Interviewing Date: 5/18–20/92
Survey #GO 222053

Asked of registered voters: Suppose the 1992 presidential election were being held today. If George Bush were the Republican candidate and Bill Clinton were the Democratic candidate and H. Ross Perot were an independent candidate, whom would you vote for? [Those who were undecided were asked: As of today, do you lean more to Bush, the Republican; to Clinton, the Democrat; or to Perot, the independent?]

Bush	35%
Clinton	25
Perot	35
Undecided; other	5

Also asked of registered voters: Next, I'd like your opinion of some people in politics. As I read each name, please tell me whether you have a favorable or unfavorable opinion of this person:

George Bush?

Favorable	48%
Unfavorable	47
Heard of; no opinion	5
Never heard of	*

*Less than 1%

Selected National Trend

	Favorable	*Unfavorable*	*Heard of; no opinion**
1992			
May 7–10	50%	47%	3%
April 20–22	55	41	4
April 9–12	48	44	8
March 26–29	49	44	7

*"Never heard of"—at less than 1%—is omitted.

Bill Clinton?

Favorable	42%
Unfavorable	48
Heard of; no opinion	9
Never heard of	1

Selected National Trend

	Favorable	*Unfavorable*	*Heard of; no opinion**
1992			
May 7–10	51%	36%	11%
April 20–22	42	49	9
April 9–12	34	47	19
March 26–29	37	40	23

*"Never heard of"—at 2% or less—is omitted.

H. Ross Perot?

Favorable	50%
Unfavorable	25
Heard of; no opinion	18
Never heard of	7

	Favorable	*Unfavorable*	*Heard of, no opinion**
By Sex			
Male	54%	24%	17%
Female	46	25	9
By Ethnic Background			
White	52	24	17
Nonwhite	32	32	27
Black	29	36	29
By Education			
College Graduate	53	28	17
College Incomplete	53	26	15
No College	47	23	20
By Region			
East	50	24	15
Midwest	46	31	17
South	50	26	20
West	53	16	23
By Age			
18–29 Years	48	24	10
30–49 Years	52	25	19
50–64 Years	49	22	22
65 Years and Over	49	28	15
By Household Income			
$50,000 and Over	57	21	18
$30,000–$49,999	52	25	17

$20,000–$29,999	50	32	13
Under $20,000	42	25	21
By Politics			
Republicans	47	26	10
Democrats	48	26	6
Independents	54	23	4
By Political Ideology			
Liberal	51	24	22
Moderate	53	22	18
Conservative	46	29	17
By Bush Approval			
Approve	41	30	20
Disapprove	56	21	17

Selected National Trend

	Favor-able	*Un-favor-able*	*Heard of; no opinion**
1992			
May 7–10	48%	16%	22%
April 20–22	41	23	25

*"Never heard of" is omitted.

Asked of registered voters: Some people feel that only a Democrat or Republican president can govern effectively because he can depend on the support of his party. Others feel that any strong candidate with good leadership abilities could be a good president. How important do you think it is for the president to be from one of the two major parties—very important, somewhat important, not too important, or not at all important?

	Total	*Perot supporters*
Very important	31%	17%
Somewhat important	27	28
Not too important	23	28
Not at all important	17	25
No opinion	2	2

Asked of registered voters: How much do you know about Ross Perot—a lot, some, a little, or nothing at all?

	Total	*Perot supporters*
A lot	5%	11%
Some	39	56
A little	36	31
Nothing at all	20	2
No opinion	*	*

*Less than 1%

Also asked of registered voters: Are you satisfied that Ross Perot has said enough about where he stands on the issues, or does he need to be more specific about where he stands?

	Total	*Perot supporters*
Satisfied	11%	19%
He needs to be more specific	78	79
No opinion	11	2

Also asked of registered voters: I'm going to read off some personal characteristics and qualities. As I read each one, tell me whether you think it strongly applies to Ross Perot, somewhat applies, or does not apply:

Has strong leadership qualities?

	Strongly applies
Current supporters	77%
Potential supporters	45
No chance of supporting Perot	18

Is level-headed?

	Strongly applies
Current supporters	70%
Potential supporters	39
No chance of supporting Perot	15

Can get things done?

	Strongly applies
Current supporters	73%
Potential supporters	32
No chance of supporting Perot	14

Has a likeable personality?

	Strongly applies
Current supporters	56%
Potential supporters	30
No chance of supporting Perot	14

Lets people know where he stands on the issues?

	Strongly applies
Current supporters	51%
Potential supporters	29
No chance of supporting Perot	16

Would display good judgment in a crisis?

	Strongly applies
Current supporters	62%
Potential supporters	28
No chance of supporting Perot	8

Is honest and trustworthy?

	Strongly applies
Current supporters	57%
Potential supporters	27
No chance of supporting Perot	11

Cares about the needs of people like you?

	Strongly applies
Current supporters	53%
Potential supporters	21
No chance of supporting Perot	11

Has a clear understanding of the issues?

	Strongly applies
Current supporters	44%
Potential supporters	20
No chance of supporting Perot	10

Can bring about the changes this country needs?

	Strongly applies
Current supporters	51%
Potential supporters	16
No chance of supporting Perot	5

Is sympathetic to the problems of the poor?

	Strongly applies
Current supporters	37%
Potential supporters	11
No chance of supporting Perot	8

Has the experience it takes to be president?

	Strongly applies
Current supporters	30%
Potential supporters	9
No chance of supporting Perot	5

Note: Texas entrepreneur H. Ross Perot, still an unannounced candidate for president, is now tied with President George Bush in the battle for voter support. In a national Gallup Poll of presidential preferences, Perot and Bush are each favored by 35% of registered voters; likely Democratic nominee Bill Clinton trails with 25%. Support for Perot is up by 10 percentage points in the past month, since the rioting over the Rodney King verdict in Los Angeles. Over the same time period, support for Bush is down by 6 percentage points.

The 35% support recorded for Perot in the latest poll is extraordinary for a third-party or independent presidential candidate. John Anderson, an independent candidate in 1980, held the previous record in the Gallup Poll with a high point of 24%.

It is unlikely that Perot, a man who has never held political office, would show so much strength as a presidential candidate were it not for the weakness of his opposition. President Bush has lost favor with the voters since the outbreak of violence in Los Angeles. About as many voters now have an unfavorable opinion of Bush as have a favorable one (47% versus 48%). Clinton's ratings remain negative: 48% view him unfavorably, 42% favorably. By contrast, twice as many voters have a favorable opinion of Perot (50%) as an unfavorable opinion of him (25%). But impressions of Perot are not well defined: one fourth (25%)

have no opinion of him or claim that they still have not heard of him.

For now, many voters unhappy with Bush and Clinton seem willing to support Perot despite their very limited knowledge about the man. Nearly one half of all voters (56%) and one third (33%) of those who now back Perot say that they know little or nothing about him. Only 5% overall—and 11% of Perot voters—claim to know a lot about him.

These results strongly suggest that Perot's support in early test elections may not hold up over the course of the campaign. Most voters still have doubts about whether a third-party or independent candidate can serve effectively as president. Six in ten (58%) overall say that it is very or somewhat important for a president to come from one of the two major parties; 45% of Perot's current supporters agree. During the fall the Bush and Clinton campaigns may well attempt to exploit those doubts.

Perot also may lose votes as he is forced to be more specific about where he stands on the issues. So far, he has been attracting equal levels of support from liberals, moderates, and conservatives. And despite Perot's assertion that his supporters are not interested in detailed issue positions, 79% of Perot voters polled say that they want to hear more about his views on specific issues.

Perot's supporters, who tend to be male and affluent, see their candidate as a man of action, a leader, and someone with common sense. More than seven in ten Perot supporters say that the following characteristics strongly apply to the Texas entrepreneur: he has strong leadership qualities (77%), he can get things done (73%), and he is level-headed (70%).

Smaller majorities of his supporters say that the phrases "would display good judgment in a crisis" (62%), "is honest and trustworthy" (57%), "has a likeable personality" (56%), "cares about the needs of people like you" (53%), and "can bring about the changes this country needs" (51%) apply to Perot. Even among his own supporters, there are doubts about whether Perot has the experience necessary for the job: only 30% say that the statement "has the experience it takes to be president" strongly applies to Perot. Fewer than one half also feel strongly that he "has a clear understanding of the issues" (44%) and "is sympathetic to the problems of the poor" (37%).

JUNE 7
RACE RELATIONS

Interviewing Date: 5/7–10/92
Survey #GO 222052

Looking back over the last ten years, do you think the quality of life of blacks has gotten better, stayed about the same, or gotten worse?

Better	34%
Stayed the same	29
Worse	33
No opinion	4

	Better	*Same*	*Worse*	*No opinion*
By Ethnic Background				
White	37%	30%	29%	4%
Black	15	23	59	3

Selected National Trend

	Better	*Same*	*Worse*	*No opinion*
June 1991	53%	27%	15%	5%
Oct. 1990	61	21	13	5
July 1990	61	24	8	7
Dec. 1981	77	13	6	4

On the whole, do you think most white people want to see blacks get a better break, or do they want to keep blacks down, or don't you think they care either way?

Better break	52%
Keep down	11
Don't care	28
No opinion	9

	Better break	*Keep down*	*Don't care*	*No opinion*
By Ethnic Background				
White	55%	9%	27%	9%
Black	29	23	36	12

Some people say that our nation is moving toward two societies, one black and one white—separate and unequal. Do you agree with this, or not?

Yes	28%
No	66
No opinion	6

	Yes	No	No opinion
By Ethnic Background			
White	25%	69%	6%
Black	51	44	5

In general, how do you think people in the United States feel about people of other races? Do you think only a few white people dislike blacks, many dislike blacks, or almost all white people dislike blacks?

Few	58%
Many	35
Almost all	3
No opinion	4

	Few	Many	Almost all	No opinion
By Ethnic Background				
White	59%	36%	2%	3%
Black	53	32	8	7

Do you think only a few black people dislike whites, many dislike whites, or almost all black people dislike whites?

Few	39%
Many	46
Almost all	10
No opinion	5

	Few	Many	Almost all	No opinion
By Ethnic Background				
White	37%	48%	10%	5%
Black	53	35	6	6

Do you think there is likely to be any serious racial trouble in your community in the next two or three years?

Yes	22%
No	73
Already exists (volunteered)	2
No opinion	3

	Yes	No	Already exists	No opinion
By Ethnic Background				
White	22%	74%	2%	2%
Black	27	66	2	5

Selected National Trend

	Yes	No	Already exists	No opinion
1990	18%	75%	2%	5%
1963	22	69	1	8

Next, I'd like your opinion of some people in politics. As I read each name, please tell me whether you have a favorable or unfavorable opinion of this person:

New Jersey Senator Bill Bradley?

	Total	Whites	Blacks
Favorable	28%	27%	37%
Unfavorable	7	7	9
Heard of; no opinion	32	32	28
Never heard of	33	34	26

Los Angeles Mayor Tom Bradley?

	Total	Whites	Blacks
Favorable	39%	38%	50%
Unfavorable	28	28	26
Heard of; no opinion	25	27	15
Never heard of	8	7	9

Los Angeles Police Chief Darryl Gates?

	Total	Whites	Blacks
Favorable	17%	19%	7%
Unfavorable	59	58	72
Heard of; no opinion	18	17	8
Never heard of	6	6	13

New York City Mayor David Dinkins?

	Total	Whites	Blacks
Favorable	29%	27%	47%
Unfavorable	14	14	11
Heard of; no opinion	29	30	21
Never heard of	28	29	21

Jesse Jackson?

	Total	Whites	Blacks
Favorable	46%	41%	80%
Unfavorable	42	46	11
Heard of; no opinion	11	12	8
Never heard of	1	1	1

HUD Secretary Jack Kemp?

	Total	Whites	Blacks
Favorable	34%	35%	31%
Unfavorable	17	17	18
Heard of; no opinion	25	25	20
Never heard of	24	23	31

Rev. Al Sharpton?

	Total	Whites	Blacks
Favorable	6%	4%	23%
Unfavorable	28	28	29
Heard of; no opinion	13	12	15
Never heard of	53	56	33

Supreme Court Justice Clarence Thomas?

	Total	Whites	Blacks
Favorable	44%	42%	54%
Unfavorable	30	31	26
Heard of; no opinion	20	21	15
Never heard of	6	6	5

Who do you think is more to blame for the present conditions in which blacks find themselves—white people or blacks themselves?

White people	17%
Blacks themselves	51
Neither (volunteered)	5
Both (volunteered)	20
No opinion	7

	White people	Blacks themselves	Neither; both	No opinion
By Ethnic Background				
White	18%	54%	22%	6%
Black	18	32	36	14

Selected National Trend

	White people	Blacks themselves	Neither; both	No opinion
Dec. 1989	18%	55%	22%	5%
May 1968	24	54	–	22
March 1968	22	58	–	20

Which made you angrier—the Rodney King verdict or the violence that followed, or did neither make you angry?

	Total	Whites	Blacks
King verdict	23%	21%	41%
Violence	40	43	15
Neither (volunteered)	7	6	11
Both (volunteered)	29	29	30
No opinion	1	1	3

As a result of recent events, do you favor more federal spending to help minorities in urban areas, less federal spending, or keeping the level of spending about the same?

	Total	Whites	Blacks
More spending	38%	35%	61%
Less spending	13	14	5
Keeping the same	42	44	27
No opinion	7	7	7

Which would you say is more to blame for today's urban problems—the Great Society programs of the 1960s or the Reagan economic policies of the 1980s?

	Total	Whites	Blacks
Great Society	23%	25%	15%
Reaganomics	53	51	69
Both (volunteered)	4	4	4

	Total	Whites	Blacks
Neither; other (volunteered)	6	6	3
No opinion	14	14	9

On the whole, are you optimistic or pessimistic that this country can ever solve its racial problems?

	Total	Whites	Blacks
Optimistic	73%	73%	70%
Pessimistic	25	25	25
No opinion	2	2	5

Here are several ways people have suggested would help conditions for minorities in urban areas. Do you favor or oppose each of these:

Fund more Head Start programs to provide preschool education?

Favor	82%
Oppose	16
No opinion	2

	Favor	Oppose	No opinion
By Ethnic Background			
White	81%	17%	2%
Black	91	7	2

Fund public-works projects to improve housing and streets in minority neighborhoods?

Favor	81%
Oppose	16
No opinion	3

	Favor	Oppose	No opinion
By Ethnic Background			
White	80%	17%	3%
Black	92	5	3

Give tenants in federal housing more control and responsibility in managing their homes and apartments?

Favor	78%
Oppose	15
No opinion	7

	Favor	Oppose	No opinion
By Ethnic Background			
White	78%	16%	6%
Black	77	14	9

Increase federal spending to improve inner-city school systems?

Favor	77%
Oppose	20
No opinion	3

	Favor	Oppose	No opinion
By Ethnic Background			
White	76%	22%	2%
Black	89	7	4

Automatically increase the minimum wage each year to keep pace with inflation?

Favor	76%
Oppose	21
No opinion	3

	Favor	Oppose	No opinion
By Ethnic Background			
White	75%	22%	3%
Black	83	12	5

Give federal tax incentives to encourage businesses to invest in minority neighborhoods?

Favor	72%
Oppose	24
No opinion	4

	Favor	Oppose	No opinion
By Ethnic Background			
White	71%	25%	4%
Black	83	11	6

Offer parents vouchers to help pay the cost of private or parochial-school education?

Favor	43%
Oppose	52
No opinion	5

	Favor	Oppose	No opinion
By Ethnic Background			
White	41%	54%	5%
Black	54	39	7

Note: In the aftermath of the Los Angeles riots, whites and blacks agree that the federal government should take action to help urban minorities. A recent Gallup Poll shows high levels of public support among both whites and blacks for new government programs targeted at the inner cities, but support for new federal funding falls sharply among whites and, to a lesser degree, among blacks if the spending increase is tied directly to the rioting.

The argument that government programs were in themselves a root cause of today's urban problems does not hold up with many Americans of either race. Only 15% of blacks and 25% of whites agree with the Bush administration's contention that the Great Society programs of the 1960s are chiefly to blame for the cities' ills; in contrast, majorities of whites (51%) and blacks (69%) place greater blame on the Reagan administration's economic policies during the 1980s.

Last month, a Gallup Poll for *Newsweek* found large majorities of whites and blacks opposing the "not guilty" verdict in the Rodney King trial. Neither race condoned the subsequent violence in Los Angeles and other large cities; majorities of both races agreed that, while the jury may have erred, the rioting that followed was not justified. And, in the latest Gallup survey, Los Angeles Police Chief Darryl Gates, who defended the actions of his officers charged with using excessive force against King, is viewed unfavorably by majorities of both blacks (72%) and whites (58%).

However, there were also profound differences in the responses of blacks and whites to the events in Los Angeles. By a margin of 41% to 15%, blacks say that it was the King verdict, not the ensuing violence, that made them most angry. Among whites the figures are reversed: 43% say that the violence angered them more, while 21% cite the verdict.

Black and white Americans have very different perspectives on race relations—and these fundamental attitudes do not appear to have been much affected by recent events. Blacks tend to see whites as indifferent, at best, to the problems of black Americans: 59% say that whites either don't care (36%) or want to keep blacks down (23%). Whites are much less willing to accept blame: only 9% say that whites want to keep blacks down, while 27% say that whites don't care.

Blacks are far more inclined than whites to view our society as racist. By a margin of 51% to 44%, blacks agree that our nation is moving toward two societies, "one black and one white—separate and unequal." Only 25% of whites accept the two-societies view, while 69% reject it.

Neither blacks nor whites, however, hold whites totally responsible for black problems (only 18% of each race agree with a whites-to-blame scenario). The difference comes in terms of shared responsibility: 54% of whites say that blacks themselves are to blame, while 22% say that neither or both share the blame. Thirty-six percent of blacks opt for shared blame, while only 32% target blacks themselves.

The Los Angeles riots—viewed by some as a black rebellion against the dominant white culture—have reinforced an underlying difference in how blacks and whites perceive one another today. Whites are more apt to think that they are the object of dislike by many or almost all blacks (58%) than blacks think they are by many or almost all whites (40%). In this regard, whites seem greatly to overestimate black dislike by some 17 points (41% of blacks say that many or all blacks dislike whites).

Whites' more disparaging views of blacks are reflected in evaluations of several national figures in the latest Gallup Poll. When asked for opinions of prominent black Americans, ranging from Al Sharpton to Clarence Thomas, whites consistently give less favorable ratings than blacks. The same is not necessarily true in blacks' evaluations of white leaders. For example, black mayor Tom Bradley of Los Angeles is viewed favorably by 50% of blacks nationwide, but by only 38% of whites. His New York counterpart, David Dinkins, evokes an even larger racial split; he is viewed favorably by 47% of blacks and only 27% of whites.

The more controversial Jesse Jackson is seen positively by 80% of blacks; among whites, more are unfavorable (46%) than favorable (41%). Less than one half of whites has heard of the extremely controversial Reverend Al Sharpton, and only 4% view him favorably; six times as many blacks (23%) so regard him, although a larger group (29%) has an unfavorable view. Supreme Court Justice Clarence Thomas is rated favorably by 54% of blacks but by only 42% of whites.

That blacks may be less likely to stereotype racially seems evident in their opinions of two white leaders, both of whom have made specific proposals for dealing with inner-city problems. Housing and Urban Development Secretary Jack Kemp is viewed favorably by nearly as many blacks (31%) as whites (35%); and New Jersey's Senator Bill Bradley, an advocate of racial unity, has more black (37%) than white (27%) support.

Blacks and whites clearly diverge on the issue of increased federal spending to attack urban problems as a result of the riots. Sixty-one percent of blacks favor more funds; only 35% of whites agree. And three times as many whites (14%) as blacks (5%) advocate less spending.

With funding only indirectly implied, many programs for dealing with the problems of the urban poor attract great support from both groups: Head Start (81% of whites, 91% of blacks); public-works projects (80% and 92%); greater tenant involvement in managing public housing (78% and 77%); increased spending on urban schools (76% and 89%); automatic minimum-wage increases tied to inflation (75% and 83%); and tax incentives for minority businesses (71% and 83%). Only vouchers for private or parochial schools draws less than majority support from whites (41%), and it attracts only a bare majority (54%) of blacks.

JUNE 7
PRESIDENTIAL TRIAL HEATS/THE PEROT FACTOR

Interviewing Date: 5/7–10; 5/18–20/92
Survey #GO 222052; 222053

Asked of registered voters: Suppose the 1992 presidential election were being held today. If George Bush were the Republican candidate and Bill Clinton were the Democratic candidate and H. Ross Perot were an independent candidate, whom would you vote for? [Those who were undecided were asked: As of today, do you lean more to Bush, the Republican; to Clinton, the Democrat; or to Perot, the independent?]

Bush	35%
Clinton	28
Perot	31
Undecided; other	6

Presidential Trial Heat by Region*

	Bush	*Clinton*	*Perot*	*Undecided; other*
East	37%	27%	30%	6%
New England	36	28	35	1
Middle Atlantic	38	26	30	6
Midwest	37	31	25	7
East Central	39	30	23	8
West Central	36	31	27	6
South	33	27	33	7
Southeast	36	29	29	6
Southwest	28	25	42	5
West	33	25	38	4
Rocky Mountain	36	17	46	1
Pacific	31	30	33	6

**New England:* Connecticut, Maine, Massachusetts, New Hampshire, Rhode Island, Vermont; *Middle Atlantic:* Delaware, District of Columbia, Maryland, New Jersey, New York, Pennsylvania, West Virginia; *East Central:*

Illinois, Indiana, Michigan, Ohio; *West Central:* Iowa, Kansas, Minnesota, Missouri, Nebraska, North Dakota, South Dakota, Wisconsin; *Southeast:* Alabama, Florida, Georgia, Kentucky, Mississippi, North Carolina, South Carolina, Tennessee, Virginia; *Southwest:* Arkansas, Louisiana, Oklahoma, Texas; *Rocky Mountain:* Arizona, Colorado, Idaho, Montana, New Mexico, Nevada, Utah, Wyoming; *Pacific:* Alaska, California, Hawaii, Oregon, Washington

Note: Even if voter enthusiasm for his maverick candidacy eventually wanes, wealthy businessman H. Ross Perot has radically altered this year's presidential race. Over the past month, Gallup Polls have found Perot gaining voter support, mostly at George Bush's expense. The "Perot factor" now seems to be affecting the two major-party candidates about equally. Surveys taken earlier in the campaign had shown Perot doing more damage to Bill Clinton's cause.

A three-way race changes the dynamic of the campaign by putting more emphasis on the geographical strengths and weaknesses of the candidates. Perot shows potential for winning some states outright, such as his native Texas. In addition, by taking away more votes from one opponent than another, his vote might shift other states from the Bush column to the Clinton column and vice versa. Based on interviews with voters over the past month, the Perot factor is shaping up as follows across the various regions of the country.

The Southwest and the Rockies are potentially Perot's best sources for electoral votes. Support for the Texas entrepreneur runs highest in Gallup's Southwest (42%) and Rocky Mountain regions (46%). These findings confirm the results of polls in individual states such as Texas, Oklahoma, New Mexico, and Arizona that reflected Perot's strength before the national polls did. With a few exceptions, Bush would be a heavy favorite to win states in this region if Perot were not a factor. *Bottom line*: Seriously hurts Bush.

The Southeast was George Wallace country in 1968 but is only average in its support for Perot in 1992. Gallup finds 29% of voters in this region supporting Perot, compared with 31% of all voters across the country. Political trends in the South, however, have so favored the Republicans in recent presidential elections that the element of uncertainty brought by Perot to the race can only hurt Bush. Fending off Perot in the South might divert Bush campaign resources from other critical electoral battlegrounds. *Bottom line*: Moderately hurts Bush.

The Pacific region includes California, the biggest prize in terms of electoral votes. Exit polls of voters in the recent California primary suggested that Perot might have won both the Democratic and Republican contests had his name been on the ballot. Gallup now shows the vote in the Pacific region as a whole dividing three ways: Perot 33%, Bush 31%, and Clinton 30%. The severity of the recession in California has led to low approval ratings for Bush in the state and offers a golden opportunity for the Democrats to pull off a victory, but Perot's candidacy gives Californians another means of voicing their discontent. *Bottom line*: Seriously hurts Clinton.

The Midwest ranks as Perot's weakest region: he places third with 25% behind Bush (37%) and Clinton (31%). Gallup's May poll results, however, suggest that here Perot is taking more votes from Clinton than from Bush. A recent poll of "Reagan Democrats" in Illinois, Michigan, and Ohio suggested that this key swing-voter group has become disillusioned with Bush and Ronald Reagan and is ready to return to its Democratic roots. However, Clinton may have to divide that vote with Perot. *Bottom line*: Moderately hurts Clinton.

The East ranks about average in support for Perot. Recent Gallup polling shows him at 30% in the region, placing him behind Bush (37%) and slightly ahead of Clinton (27%). Despite its Democratic history, the East has been slow to embrace Clinton. Jerry Brown's Connecticut primary victory dealt Clinton his last significant loss in the Democratic race. Former Massachusetts Senator Paul Tsongas carried the other primaries in New England, an area severely hit by the recession. The Perot factor seems to cut both ways in the East. The third man in the race gives the Bush campaign hopes of carrying traditionally Democratic states such as New York and Massachusetts, but Perot may deny Bush reliably GOP states such as New Jersey and Connecticut if his support holds up. *Bottom line*: Hurts Bush and Clinton about equally.

As the campaign progresses through the selection of vice presidential candidates and the national party conventions, the effects of the Perot factor by geographic region may change. For the present, however, Perot's candidacy makes Bush's South and Rocky Mountain bases less secure but hurts Clinton's ability to capitalize on voter disaffection in other parts of the country.

JUNE 10
PRESIDENTIAL TRIAL HEATS

Interviewing Date: 6/4–8/92
Survey #GO 222054

Asked of registered voters: Suppose the 1992 presidential election were being held today. If George Bush were the Republican candidate and Bill Clinton were the Democratic candidate, whom would you vote for? [Those who were undecided were asked: As of today, do you lean more to Bush, the Republican, or to Clinton, the Democrat?]

Bush	46%
Clinton	40
Undecided; other	14

Selected National Trend

	Bush	Clinton	Undecided; other
1992			
May 18–29	50%	39%	11%
May 7–10	45	40	15
April 20–22	50	34	16
April 9-12	48	41	11
March 31–April 1	54	34	12
March 26–29	54	38	8
March 20–22	52	43	5
March 11–12	50	44	6
February 19–20	53	43	4
February 6–9	53	38	9

Also asked of registered voters: Suppose the 1992 presidential election were being held today. If George Bush were the Republican candidate and Bill Clinton were the Democratic candidate and H. Ross Perot were an independent candidate, whom would you vote for? [Those who were undecided were asked: As of today, do you lean more to Bush, the Republican; to Clinton, the Democrat; or to Perot, the independent?]

Bush	31%
Clinton	25
Perot	39
Undecided; other	5

Selected National Trend

	Bush	Clinton	Perot	Undecided; other
1992				
May 18–20	35%	25%	35%	5%
May 7–10	35	29	30	6
April 20–22	41	26	25	8
March 31–April 1	44	25	24	7

Asked of registered voters: Thinking about the presidential primaries and caucuses that have taken place this year—in general do you think they have been a good way of determining who the best qualified nominees are, or not?

Yes	38%
No	51
No opinion	11

Selected National Trend

	Yes	No	No opinion
June 1988	48%	37%	15%
June 1980	40	48	12

Asked of Democrats and those who lean Democratic: Are you satisfied that Bill Clinton ended up the winner in the Democratic race, or would you have preferred to see one of the other Democratic presidential candidates win?

	June 1992 (Clinton)	June 1988 (Dukakis)
Satisfied	58%	62%
Preferred other candidate	37	32
Did not like any of them (volunteered)	3	2
No opinion	2	4

Note: For the first time, unannounced presidential candidate H. Ross Perot holds a significant lead in a test election against President George Bush and likely Democratic nominee Bill Clinton. A national survey of registered voters shows 39% supporting Perot; Bush is in second place with 31%, while Clinton trails with 25%. Bush and Perot were tied, with 35% of the vote each, in a Gallup Poll conducted in late May.

The Texas entrepreneur continues to break records in terms of support for an independent or third-party candidate. When Perot captured 30% of the vote in a Gallup test election one month ago, in early May, he exceeded John Anderson's high-water mark (in June 1980) of 24% for an independent. No previous independent or third-party candidate, including Anderson, had ever run second in a Gallup Poll, let alone first.

Perot and Bush have been moving in opposite directions since late April, when the president held a 16-percentage point lead, 41% to 25%, over the self-made billionaire. Clinton has been unable to take advantage of Bush's fall from grace with the voters. The Arkansas governor trails Bush in a two-way race, 40% to 46%. He has never held a lead over Bush in a Gallup test election.

Most voters express dissatisfaction with the primary process and many Democrats see Clinton as a flawed candidate produced by that process. When asked whether the primaries and caucuses have been a good way of determining who the best qualified nominees are, more voters disagree than agree (51% versus 38%). Voters were more likely to be pleased with the process four years ago, when Bush and Michael Dukakis were the major-party presidential candidates (48% responded positively about the primary process in June 1988). The current level of dissatisfaction with the primaries is comparable to that seen in 1980 (40%), when unhappiness with Jimmy Carter and Ronald Reagan led to Anderson's independent candidacy.

More than one third (37%) of registered Democrats and those who lean Democratic wish that someone other than Clinton had won their party's presidential nomination. Fewer voters (32%) expressed similar unhappiness with Dukakis four years ago. Now, these dissatisfied Democrats are a major factor behind Perot's success in the polls.

JUNE 11
PRESIDENT BUSH AND THE ENVIRONMENT

Interviewing Date: 6/4–8/92
Survey #GO 222054

As you may know, George Bush will attend the environmental summit in Rio de Janeiro this week. Which concerns you more—that he will not give enough support to worldwide environmental protection measures, or that he will support environmental agreements that may harm U.S. economic interests?

Not give enough support	48%
May harm U.S. interests	35
Both (volunteered)	4
Neither (volunteered)	4
No opinion	9

Do you approve or disapprove of the way George Bush is handling the issue of the environment?

	Total	Pro-environment	Pro-U.S. economy
Approve	29%	23%	35%
Disapprove	58	66	53
No opinion	13	11	12

Selected National Trend

	Approve	Disapprove	No opinion
January 1992	49%	41%	10%
March 1991	52	38	10

October 1990	45	45	10
July 1990	42	46	12
November 1989	46	40	14

Note: A Gallup Poll conducted during the first days of the United Nations' Earth Summit in Brazil in June suggests that George Bush is losing the public relations battle over the environment in the United States. His stated concern for preserving American jobs over signing treaties in Rio de Janeiro and widespread criticism from the environmental community appear to have damaged the president's environmental image. When asked to choose, nearly one half (48%) of U.S. adults is more concerned that Bush will not give enough support to worldwide environmental protection measures than is concerned that he will support environmental agreements harmful to U.S. economic interests (35%).

Bush's job approval rating on the environment is down sharply from January: 29% versus 49%. In contrast, the president's overall job approval rating dropped 9 percentage points during the same period, from 46% to 37%. Bush has never received more than 52% approval on the environment in a Gallup Poll.

Ironically, the president's hard line on environmental treaties is not winning him praise in either the pro-environmental or pro-economic development camps. Only two in ten (23%) of those who worry that Bush will not go far enough in supporting environmental protection approve of his overall performance on the issue. He fares only marginally better (35% approval) with those who are concerned that the Rio agreements may harm U.S. economic interests.

JUNE 12
HOMOSEXUALITY AND GAY RIGHTS

Interviewing Date: 6/4–8/92
Survey #GO 222054

Do you feel that homosexuality should be considered an acceptable alternative lifestyle, or not?

Yes	38%
No	57
No opinion	5

	Yes	*No*	*No opinion*
By Sex			
Male	34%	63%	3%
Female	42	52	6
By Ethnic Background			
White	37	58	5
Nonwhite	47	48	5
Black	50	45	5
By Education			
College Graduate	52	43	5
Some College	39	57	4
No College	32	63	5
By Region			
East	39	56	5
Midwest	41	54	5
South	34	61	5
West	40	56	4
By Age			
18–29 Years	46	51	3
30–49 Years	42	55	3
50–64 Years	31	62	7
65 Years and Over	25	65	10
By Household Income			
$50,000 and Over	45	52	3
$30,000–$49,999	38	58	4
$20,000–$29,999	41	56	3
Under $20,000	37	59	4
By Politics			
Republicans	24	70	6
Democrats	45	51	4
Independents	44	51	5
By Religion			
Protestants	44	53	3
Catholics	31	63	6
By Political Ideology			
Liberal	56	40	4
Moderate	43	53	4
Conservative	24	72	4

	Yes	No	No opinion
By Bush Approval			
Approve	28	67	5
Disapprove	46	50	4

Selected National Trend

	Yes	No	No opinion
1989	35%	54%	11%
1983	32	58	10
1982	34	51	15

Do you think homosexual relations between consenting adults should be made legal, or not?

Yes	48%
No	44
No opinion	8

	Yes	No	No opinion
By Sex			
Male	51%	44%	5%
Female	47	43	10
By Ethnic Background			
White	49	44	7
Nonwhite	47	43	10
Black	42	49	9
By Education			
College Graduate	69	25	6
Some College	57	38	5
No College	38	53	9
By Region			
East	49	43	8
Midwest	50	43	7
South	43	49	8
West	53	39	8
By Age			
18–29 Years	59	38	3
30–49 Years	55	38	7
50–64 Years	41	50	9
65 Years and Over	30	58	12
By Household Income			
$50,000 and Over	70	26	4
$30,000–$49,999	49	43	8
$20,000–$29,999	46	46	8
Under $20,000	43	51	6
By Politics			
Republicans	41	54	5
Democrats	48	46	6
Independents	55	34	11
By Religion			
Protestants	53	38	9
Catholics	42	52	6
By Political Ideology			
Liberal	65	29	6
Moderate	56	37	7
Conservative	33	60	7
By Bush Approval			
Approve	43	50	7
Disapprove	55	39	6

Selected National Trend

	Yes	No	No opinion
1991	36%	54%	10%
1987	33	55	12
1986	33	54	13
1985	44	47	9
1982	45	39	16
1977	43	43	14

As you know, there has been considerable discussion in the news lately regarding the rights of homosexual men and women. In general, do you think homosexuals should or should not have equal rights in terms of job opportunities?

Should	74%
Should not	18
No opinion	8

Selected National Trend

	Should	Should not	No opinion
1989	71%	18%	11%
1982	59	28	13
1977	56	33	11

Do you think homosexuals should or should not be hired for each of the following occupations:

Salespersons?

Should	82%
Should not	13
It depends (volunteered)	3
No opinion	2

Selected National Trend

	Those replying "should"
1989	79%
1987	72
1985	71
1982	70
1977	68

Members of the armed forces?

Should	57%
Should not	37
It depends (volunteered)	2
No opinion	4

Selected National Trend

	Those replying "should"
1989	60%
1987	55
1985	55
1982	52
1977	51

Members of the president's cabinet?

Should	54%
Should not	39
It depends (volunteered)	3
No opinion	4

Doctors?

Should	53%
Should not	42
It depends (volunteered)	2
No opinion	3

Selected National Trend

	Those replying "should"
1989	56%
1987	49
1985	52
1982	50
1977	44

High-school teachers?

Should	47%
Should not	49
It depends (volunteered)	2
No opinion	2

Clergy?

Should	43%
Should not	50
It depends (volunteered)	2
No opinion	5

Selected National Trend

	Those replying "should"
1989	44%
1987	42
1985	41
1982	38
1977	36

Elementary-school teachers?

Should	41%
Should not	54
It depends (volunteered)	3
No opinion	2

Selected National Trend

	Those replying "should"
1989	42%
1987	33
1985	36
1982	32
1977	27

Note: Public support for gay rights has increased over the past two decades, but the issue continues to divide the country. In a new Gallup Poll, three quarters of adults (74%) endorse the concept that homosexuals should have equal rights in terms of job opportunities. In 1977 this support was more tenuous: only 56% supported gay rights in the workplace.

Although there is now a consensus that gays, like other minorities, deserve protection from job discrimination, they are still viewed as being outside of the mainstream. A majority of respondents (57%) finds homosexuality unacceptable as an alternative life-style. In fact, despite a 15-percentage point increase since 1982 in public support for giving gays equal protection on the job (from 59% to 74%), over the same period acceptance of homosexuality as a life-style has increased only marginally (from 34% to 38%).

Most likely to reject the idea of an acceptable life-style are conservatives (72%), Republicans (70%), people aged 50 and over (64%), men (63%), and people with no college training (63%). Even among the groups most supportive of gay rights, significant proportions would not go so far as to approve the life-style. Roughly one half of women (52%), people under 30 (51%), and Democrats (51%) as well as four in ten college graduates (43%) and liberals (40%) do not think that homosexuality should be regarded as an acceptable life-style.

Many states continue to have laws making homosexual relations a crime. Support for legalizing homosexual relations is up, but it is still less than a majority. About one half of Americans (48%) says that homosexual relations between consenting adults should be legal, but nearly as many (44%) think that such sex should be illegal. The latest survey does suggest, however, that the backlash toward gays seen in public opinion polls has subsided. Support for legalizing homosexual relations dropped sharply from 44% to 33% between 1985 and 1986, when concern about AIDS as a health threat was on the increase. Last year's poll, taken before Magic Johnson announced that he was HIV-positive, showed only a marginal increase (to 36%) from the 1986 figures.

Moral considerations seem to affect opinions toward allowing gays in specific occupations. Eight in ten (82%) say that they may be hired as salespersons, but this support decreases in professions which might serve as role models. Fewer respondents say that homosexuals should be allowed to become doctors (53%), high-school teachers (47%), clergy members (43%), and elementary-school teachers (41%). Women, young people, liberals, college graduates, and upper-income people are willing to go further than their demographic counterparts—men, older people, conservatives, the less well-educated, and lower-income people—in protecting gays from job discrimination.

In his recent interview with Barbara Walters on ABC's "20/20," unannounced presidential candidate H. Ross Perot said that he would not be inclined to appoint a homosexual to certain cabinet positions because it might create undue controversy. The poll shows some division of opinion on this issue, but a majority of the public (54%) say that they would not bar homosexuals from the cabinet.

In the Walters interview, Perot also said that it was not practical to allow gays into the military at this time. Most Americans, however, would look favorably on changing the military's policy of exclusion: 57% say that the armed forces should accept homosexuals, while 37% disagree.

JUNE 14
TRUST IN GOVERNMENT

Interviewing Date: 6/4–8/92*
Survey #GO 222054

How much of the time do you think you can trust the government in Washington to do what is right—always, most of the time, or only some of the time?

Always	2%
Most of the time	21
Some of the time	71
Never (volunteered)	4
No opinion	2

*Gallup survey for CNN/*USA Today*

	Always/ most of the time	Some of the time/ never
By Candidates' Supporters		
Bush voters	56%	26%
Clinton voters	19	24
Perot voters	22	42
Undecided; other	3	8

Selected National Trend*

	Always	Most of the time	Some of the time	Never**
1990	3%	25%	68%	2%
1988	4	37	56	2
1986	3	35	58	2
1984	4	40	53	1
1982	2	31	62	2
1980	2	23	69	4
1978	2	27	64	4
1976	3	30	62	1
1974	2	34	61	1
1972	5	48	44	1
1970	7	47	44	†
1968	7	54	37	†
1966	17	48	28	3
1964	14	62	22	†
1958	16	57	23	†

*Trend based on American National Election Study conducted by the University of Michigan
**"No opinion"—at 4% or less—is omitted.
†Less than 1%

Some people think that the government is trying to do too many things that should be left to individuals and businesses. Others think that the government should do more to solve our country's problems. Which view comes closer to your own?

Government does too much	39%
Government should do more	52
No opinion	9

	Does too much	Should do more	No opinion
By Candidates' Supporters			
Bush voters	40%	27%	35%
Clinton voters	13	32	19
Perot voters	41	34	35
Undecided; other	6	7	11

Note: Independent presidential contender H. Ross Perot surpassed George Bush for the first time in the most recent Gallup test election, 39% versus 31%. Although Perot supporters have no distinctive demographic or ideological profile, they are united by disillusionment with the government in Washington.

This disaffection with government, rather than the candidate himself, is holding Perot's constituency together. As a political outsider, he is well positioned to tap the voter distrust that is now at a historically high level. Three quarters (75%) of the public now say that they trust Washington to do what is right only some of the time or never.

Since the University of Michigan began this measurement in 1958, only once has trust in government been as low as it is today. In 1980, after a period of economic stagflation and a loss of morale from the Iran hostage crisis, only 25% rated government positively.

Since 1990 skepticism toward government has been on the increase. The anti-Washington mood could be Perot's trump card. The Texas entrepreneur wins big among the three quarters of the electorate now turned off by Washington, receiving 42% of their support. Bush and Bill Clinton split the remainder, drawing 26% and 24%, respectively. Unless Clinton or Bush is able to turn voter disaffection to his own advantage, Perot could gain much of this vote by default.

While Perot has a big edge among government's critics, Bush is a strong favorite among those with a more positive view of Washington. Of those who say that they can trust government most of the time or always, 56% support the president for reelection. Only 22% would vote for Perot and 19% for Clinton.

The survey shows that a majority (52%) thinks the government should do more to solve the country's problems, while 39% think that the government is trying to do too many things that should be left to individuals and businesses. The "should do more" bloc currently splits three ways: Perot, 34%; Clinton, 32%; and Bush, 27%.

If Clinton can reframe the debate on his terms, he may attract voters frustrated by government gridlock away from Bush and Perot. Clinton's new message, put forth by

New York Governor Mario Cuomo last week, is that he is the "can-do" candidate. Backed by a likely Democratic majority in Congress, Clinton will portray himself as the only presidential candidate who, if elected, can deliver his domestic agenda and end the political gridlock.

JUNE 17
WATERGATE: TWENTY YEARS LATER

Interviewing Date: 6/4–8/92*
Survey #GO 222054

It has now been twenty years since the break-in at the Watergate. Which of these two statements comes closer to your own point of view about Watergate—it was a very serious matter because it revealed corruption in the Nixon administration, or it was just politics, the kind of thing both parties engage in?

Very serious	49%
Just politics	46
No opinion	5

	Very serious	*Just politics*	*No opinion*
By Age			
18–29 Years	52%	41%	7%
30–49 Years	48	48	4
50–64 Years	52	46	2
65 Years and Over	46	49	5
By Politics			
Republicans	45	50	5
Democrats	55	41	4
Independents	48	46	6

Thinking back to Watergate, do you think that Nixon's actions regarding Watergate were serious enough to warrant his resignation, or not?

Yes	70%
No	21
No opinion	9

Selected National Trend

	Yes	*No*	*No opinion*
May 1986	71%	24%	5%
June 1982	75	19	6
August 1974	65	32	3

Do you think Richard Nixon has regained a position of prominence in public life, or do you think he is still considered an outcast because of Watergate?

Regained prominence	42%
Still an outcast	50
No opinion	8

	Regained prominence	*Still an outcast*	*No opinion*
By Age			
18–29 Years	32%	61%	7%
30–49 Years	45	50	5
50–64 Years	44	49	7
65 Years and Over	49	39	12
By Politics			
Republicans	50	43	7
Democrats	36	58	6
Independents	40	51	9

From what you have heard, read, or remember about some of our past presidents, please tell me whether you approve or disapprove of the way they handled their job as president:

Richard Nixon?

	June 1992	*November 1990*
Approve	35%	32%
Disapprove	59	62
No opinion	6	6

John F. Kennedy?

*Gallup survey for CNN/*USA Today*

	June 1992	November 1990
Approve	76%	84%
Disapprove	14	9
No opinion	10	7

Gerald Ford?

	June 1992	November 1990
Approve	56%	55%
Disapprove	29	34
No opinion	15	11

Ronald Reagan?

	June 1992	November 1990
Approve	50%	54%
Disapprove	47	44
No opinion	3	2

Jimmy Carter?

	June 1992	November 1990
Approve	48%	45%
Disapprove	46	52
No opinion	6	3

Lyndon Johnson?

	June 1992	November 1990
Approve	35%	40%
Disapprove	45	43
No opinion	20	17

Now, thinking about the four living past presidents, would you say you approve or disapprove of their performance since they left office:

Richard Nixon?

	June 1992	November 1990
Approve	51%	54%
Disapprove	34	33
No opinion	15	13

Jimmy Carter?

	June 1992	November 1990
Approve	70%	74%
Disapprove	16	17
No opinion	14	9

Ronald Reagan?

	June 1992	November 1990
Approve	52%	58%
Disapprove	36	32
No opinion	12	10

Gerald Ford?

	June 1992	November 1990
Approve	61%	67%
Disapprove	18	15
No opinion	21	18

Note: Twenty years after the "third-rate burglary" at the Watergate drove him from power, Richard Nixon's elder-statesman efforts are proving only marginally successful in revamping his image. In the latest Gallup Poll, one half of the respondents (50%) still considers Nixon an outcast because of Watergate; 42% now think that he has regained a position of prominence in public life, up 7 percentage points since Gallup first asked this question for *Newsweek* in May 1986. However, Nixon still finishes last in the current assessment of how our four living former presidents have conducted themselves since leaving office.

Nixon's retrospective approval rating (that is, how well Americans now think he did while in office) has improved slightly in the past eighteen months (from 32% to 35%) but still lags well behind the average actual rating (48%) given him during his incumbency. In this he has fared better than three other recent presidents: Ronald Reagan's retrospective rating is down 4 points (from 54% to 50%); Lyndon Johnson's has dropped 5 points, to match Nixon's 35%; and John F. Kennedy's retrospective rating has fallen 8 points although, at the current 76%, he still ranks at least 20 points higher than any of his successors.

There is only one significant difference by age in current views on the impact of the break-in and subsequent coverup: young people judge the "new" Nixon most harshly, with 61% saying that he is still an outcast, compared with only 39% of those over age 65.

Opinion on the seriousness of Watergate has changed very little over the last decade. A 1982 Gallup survey for *Newsweek* found that 52% thought it a very serious matter, while 45% classified it as just politics. In 1992, 49% call it serious and 46% politics.

An interesting side effect of this year's widespread disaffection with candidates and federal officeholders can be noted in respondents' evaluation of the performance of our four living former presidents since they left office. Although the relative ranking has not changed in the eighteen months since Gallup first asked the question, each one has lost approval points. Jimmy Carter still receives the highest marks but is down 4 points, from 74% to 70%; Gerald Ford has slipped 6 points (67% to 61%), as has Reagan (58% to 52%); Nixon is down 3 points, from 54% to 51%.

JUNE 21
PRESIDENTIAL CANDIDATES

Interviewing Date: 6/12–14/92*
Survey #GO 322001

Asked of registered voters: In your opinion, which presidential candidate would do the best job of handling the economy—George Bush, Bill Clinton, or H. Ross Perot?

Perot	39%
Bush	23
Clinton	22
No opinion	16

Also asked of registered voters: I'm going to read off some personal characteristics and qualities. As I read each one, tell me whether you think it applies most to George Bush, Bill Clinton, or Ross Perot:

*Gallup survey for CNN/*USA Today*

Puts the country's interests ahead of politics?

Perot	41%
Bush	23
Clinton	15
None (volunteered)	13
No opinion	8

Can bring about the changes this country needs?

Perot	38%
Bush	20
Clinton	24
None (volunteered)	10
No opinion	8

Can get things done?

Perot	36%
Bush	28
Clinton	18
None (volunteered)	7
No opinion	11

Cares about the needs of people like you?

Perot	31%
Bush	22
Clinton	26
None (volunteered)	12
No opinion	9

Is honest and trustworthy?

Perot	25%
Bush	34
Clinton	15
None (volunteered)	14
No opinion	12

Has a clear plan for solving the country's problems?

Perot	25%
Bush	19
Clinton	21
None (volunteered)	28
No opinion	7

Has a clear understanding of the issues?

Perot	21%
Bush	41
Clinton	23
None (volunteered)	6
No opinion	9

Would display good judgment in a crisis?

Perot	20%
Bush	49
Clinton	17
None (volunteered)	3
No opinion	11

Positive Characteristics as Predictors of Voter Preference

	Best describes preferred candidate	*Best describes another candidate*	*Index value**
Would best handle the economy	74%	15%	+59
Can bring about the changes this country needs	72	13	+59
Cares about the needs of people like you	69	14	+55
Can get things done	68	16	+52
Is honest and trustworthy	64	14	+50
Puts the country's interests ahead of politics	64	17	+47
Would display good judgment in a crisis	67	23	+44
Has a clear understanding of the issues	65	23	+42
Has a clear plan for solving the country's problems	53	14	+39

**How to read this table:* The first column displays the percentage of all voters who now support or lean toward a candidate (Bush, Clinton, or Perot) and associate each characteristic with their preferred candidate. The second column displays the percentage who associate the characteristic with one of the other candidates whom they are not now supporting. The index value, a measure of how strongly each relates to candidate preference, is derived by subtracting the percentage in the second column from the percentage in the first column. (The analysis is based on registered voters who now favor one of the candidates.)

Note: As a businessman and a Washington outsider, H. Ross Perot seems to be the kind of candidate most voters are looking for this year: someone who can bring about change in this country and jump-start the stalled economy. The Texas entrepreneur now holds a big advantage over his opponents on the economy, the key election issue. When asked which candidate is best able to handle the economy, four in ten voters (39%) name Perot, while less than one quarter names George Bush (23%) or Bill Clinton (22%).

Perot also enjoys a clear edge as the candidate of change. Thirty-eight percent of voters name him as the candidate most able to bring about the changes the country needs, while 24% name Clinton and 20% name Bush.

In addition to this image of change, Perot is most likely to be seen as the candidate who puts the country's interests ahead of politics (41%), can get things done (36%), and cares about "people like you" (31%). Bush is most often seen as the candidate who would display good judgment in a crisis (49%), has a clear understanding of the issues (41%), and is honest and trustworthy (34%). None of the three has an advantage as the candidate with a clear plan for solving the country's problems (Perot at 25%; Clinton, 21%; and Bush, 19%).

In the year of the angry voter, Gallup analysis shows that Perot's image as the candidate of change is as valuable an asset as his high rating on the economy. Overall, over seven in ten (72%) voters who now support a candidate say that their choice represents change—similar to the percentage who say that their candidate would best handle the economy (74%). No other positive characteristic tested is as strongly related to candidate preference.

Supporters of each candidate tend to rate their man higher than the opposition on all positive characteristics. Even so, response to the different questions is anything but uniform and provides insight into voter perceptions of the strengths and weaknesses of each candidate.

JUNE 24
SATISFACTION INDEX/ECONOMY

Interviewing Date: 6/12–14/92*
Survey #GO 322001

Asked of registered voters: In general, are you satisfied or dissatisfied with the way things are going in the United States at this time?

Satisfied..14%
Dissatisfied....................................84
No opinion.....................................2

	Satisfied	*Dis-satisfied*	*No opinion*
By Sex			
Male	14%	84%	2%
Female	14	84	2
By Ethnic Background			
White	15	83	2
Nonwhite	9	89	2
Black	4	93	3
By Education			
College Graduate	14	85	1
College Incomplete	16	82	2
No College	14	84	2
By Region			
East	13	84	3
Midwest	14	85	1
South	16	83	1
West	14	85	1
By Age			
18–29 Years	18	81	1
30–49 Years	15	84	1
50 Years and Over	12	85	3
By Household Income			
$50,000 and Over	17	82	1
$30,000–$49,999	12	86	2
$20,000–$29,999	13	86	1
Under $20,000	14	83	3
By Politics			
Republicans	27	71	2
Democrats	9	89	2
Independents	10	90	*
By Political Ideology			
Liberal	7	91	2
Moderate	13	85	2
Conservative	19	80	1
By Bush Approval			
Approve	31	66	3
Disapprove	4	96	*

*Gallup survey for CNN/*USA Today*

*Less than 1%

Asked of registered voters: Are you satisfied or dissatisfied with the way democracy is working in this country?

Satisfied..36%
Dissatisfied....................................60
No opinion.....................................4

Selected National Trend

	Satisfied	*Dis-satisfied*	*No opinion*
January 1992	48%	48%	4%
May 1991	60	36	4

Asked of registered voters: Are you satisfied or dissatisfied with the opportunity for the next generation of Americans to live better than their parents?

Satisfied..22%
Dissatisfied....................................74
No opinion.....................................4

Asked of registered voters: How would you rate economic conditions in this country today—excellent, good, only fair, or poor?

Excellent..1%
Good..11
Fair..47
Poor...41
No opinion.....................................*

*Less than 1%

Selected National Trend

	Excellent	Good	Fair	Poor*
1992				
April 9–12	1%	11%	40%	48%
January 3–6	**	12	46	41

*"No opinion"—at 1% or less—is omitted.
**Less than 1%

Also asked of registered voters: Right now, do you think that economic conditions in the country as a whole are getting better or getting worse?

Better	28%
Worse	61
Same (volunteered)	9
No opinion	2

Selected National Trend

	Better	Worse	Same	No opinion
1992				
April 20–22	40%	45%	13%	2%
March 20–22	37	51	11	1
January 31–February 1	22	70	7	1
January 1–3*	22	71	6	1
1991				
December*	19	69	9	3
October*	25	64	8	3
September*	27	60	10	3
July*	34	51	9	6

*Based on all national adults

Note: Not since Jimmy Carter's presidency has the public been so dissatisfied with the state of the nation. According to a new Gallup Poll, only 14% of registered voters now claim to be satisfied with the way things are going in the United States at this time. More than eight in ten (84%) say that they are dissatisfied, while 2% offer no opinion.

These results closely parallel the findings of a Gallup survey taken in July 1979, when President Carter told a national television audience that the country was in a period of malaise. At that time, 12% were satisfied and 84% dissatisfied with the direction of the country.

George Bush's presidential approval ratings have risen and fallen in concert with public evaluations of the state of the nation. Both approval of his job performance and positive evaluations of the country increased sharply during the Gulf War. Bush approval peaked at 89% at the close of the war in March 1991; satisfaction with the state of the nation peaked at 62% when the United States began air strikes against Iraq in January of that same year.

Both measures have shown a steady downward trend since that time. At 37%, Bush approval has fallen to its lowest level and is statistically similar to former President Ronald Reagan's lowest rating. (Reagan approval fell to 35% in January 1983, a time of economic recession.) Unless he can restore the public's faith in his ability to lead the country, Bush's ratings could decline further. Carter had only a 29% approval rating in July 1979 at the time of his "malaise" speech.

Pessimism about the national economy is a key factor behind the public's dissatisfied mood. Currently, only 12% would rate the state of the economy as good or excellent, identical to the percentage who expressed such positive views back in January. The overwhelming majority continues to rate conditions as only fair (47%) or poor (41%).

Earlier this year there were signs that Americans were beginning to see improvement in the national economy. The percentage who said that the economy was getting better increased from 22% to 40% between January and April. The Los Angeles riots, however, may have been a serious setback to improving economic attitudes; the percentage who believe that the economy is getting better has fallen back to 28%. A clear majority (61%) now says that it is getting worse.

While unhappiness with the economy has much to do with the voters' angry mood, short-term economic concerns are not the only factor. Previous Gallup surveys have shown that dissatisfaction with the political system is at a historic high. The latest poll finds only 36% expressing satisfaction with the way democracy is working in this country, down from 48% in January of this year and 60% in May 1991, after the Gulf War victory.

The American dream of a better life for one's children also seems less attainable to many voters. Fewer than one quarter (22%) now say that they are satisfied with the opportunity for the next generation to live better than their parents, down from 36% in January.

JUNE 24
PUBLIC SCHOOLS

Interviewing Date: 6/4–8/92
Survey #GO 222054

Now, in general, do you think the American system of public schools does a satisfactory job educating children, or do you think the system has failed?

Satisfactory	23%
Failed	68
Mixed (volunteered)	7
No opinion	2

Recently, a company has proposed to develop a private system of schools which are run for profit. Some people feel a for-profit private system will provide healthy competition for the public schools and in the long run will improve the public-school system. Others feel the new schools will attract many of the best students and therefore hurt the public-school system. Generally speaking, how do you feel—will the competition from a new system of for-profit private schools be a good thing or a bad thing for American education?

Good	44%
Bad	46
No opinion	10

Would you consider sending a son or daughter to a for-profit private school if the tuition were $5,500 per year, or not?

Yes	33%
No	58
It depends (volunteered)	6
No opinion	3

Note: A new Gallup Poll shows that 68% of Americans believe that our public schools have failed; only 23% will agree that the public-school system does a satisfactory job of educating children. This perception of failure extends across all demographic and socioeconomic segments and is as high among those who currently have children in public schools as among those who do not.

Entrepreneur Chris Whittle, motivated in part, he says, by the need to provide a competitive stimulus to the public schools, has proposed a new system of private, for-profit schools. Whittle's plans were given additional publicity recently when Yale President Benno Schmidt announced his resignation from the university in order to head the venture.

Respondents show mixed reactions toward this for-profit school idea. When given a choice between two alternatives—the for-profit private system would provide healthy competition and thus, in the long run, improve the public schools, or the for-profit schools would siphon off the best students and hurt the public-school system—Americans split down the middle. Forty-four percent say that the competition provided by the for-profit system would be good for education, but 46% say that it would not.

Only about one third (33%) say that they would consider sending a son or daughter to a for-profit private school if the tuition were $5,500 per year, the figure most often mentioned in discussions of Whittle's idea. Reluctance to send a son or daughter to such a school is somewhat higher among those parents who currently have a child in the public-school system: only one in four (24%) would consider it.

The poll suggests that objections to the for-profit idea may be based as much on economic as philosophic grounds. Those with the lowest incomes and the lowest levels of education are least likely to say that they would consider sending a child to such a for-profit private school.

JULY 2
PRESIDENTIAL TRIAL HEAT/H. ROSS PEROT

Interviewing Date: 6/26–30/92
Survey #GO 322002

Asked of registered voters: Suppose the 1992 presidential election were being held today. If George Bush were the Republican candidate and Bill Clinton were the Democratic candidate and H. Ross Perot were an independent candidate, whom would you vote for? [Those who were undecided were asked: As of today, do you lean more to Bush, the Republican; to Clinton, the Democrat; or to Perot, the independent?]

Bush....................................33%
Clinton....................................27
Perot....................................32
Undecided; other....................................8

	Bush	Clinton	Perot	Undecided; other
By Sex				
Male	31%	25%	38%	6%
Female	34	28	28	10
By Ethnic Background				
White	35	24	34	7
Nonwhite	15	49	24	12
Black	14	51	25	10
By Education				
College Graduate	37	25	30	8
College Incomplete	28	29	35	8
No College	32	26	33	9
By Region				
East	29	30	29	12
Midwest	33	24	35	8
South	35	28	31	6
West	33	24	36	7
By Age				
18–29 Years	36	19	37	8
30–49 Years	32	27	32	9
50 Years and Over	32	29	31	8
By Household Income				
$50,000 and Over	34	21	38	7
$30,000–$49,999	30	25	38	7
$20,000–$29,999	33	37	25	5
Under $20,000	33	28	28	11
By Politics				
Republicans	67	6	22	5
Democrats	10	54	28	8
Independents	25	19	44	12
By Political Ideology				
Liberal	23	40	25	12
Moderate	25	31	37	7
Conservative	46	16	32	6
By Bush Approval				
Approve	66	8	19	7
Disapprove	9	39	43	9

Selected National Trend

	Bush	Clinton	Perot	Undecided; other
1992				
June 12–14	32%	24%	34%	10%
June 4–8	31	25	39	5
May 18–20	35	25	35	5
May 7–10	35	29	30	6
April 20–22	41	26	25	8
April 14–16	42	27	20	11
March 31–April 1	44	25	24	7

Also asked of registered voters: Please tell me whether you have a favorable or unfavorable opinion of each of the following presidential candidates:

George Bush?

Favorable....................................44%
Unfavorable....................................50
Heard of; no opinion....................................6
Never heard of....................................*

*Less than 1%

Selected National Trend

	Favorable	Unfavorable	Heard of; no opinion*
1992			
June 12–14	44%	51%	5%
May 18–20	48	47	5

April 20–22	55	41	4
April 9–12	48	44	8
March 26–29	49	44	7

*"Never heard of"—at less than 1%—is omitted.

Bill Clinton?

Favorable....................45%
Unfavorable....................43
Heard of; no opinion....................11
Never heard of....................1

Selected National Trend

	Favorable	Unfavorable	Heard of; no opinion*
1992			
June 12–14	41%	47%	12%
May 18–20	42	48	9
April 20–22	42	49	9
April 9–12	34	47	19
March 26–29	37	40	23

*"Never heard of"—at 1% or less—is omitted.

H. Ross Perot?

Favorable....................48%
Unfavorable....................34
Heard of; no opinion....................16
Never heard of....................2

Selected National Trend

	Favorable	Unfavorable	Heard of; no opinion*
1992			
June 12–14	52%	30%	17%
May 18–20	50	25	18
April 20–22	41	23	25

*"Never heard of"—from 1% to 11%—is omitted.

Asked of the 48% of the sample who have a favorable opinion of Ross Perot: Why do you have a favorable opinion of Perot?

Characteristics....................31%
A man of action....................9
He can run the country as a business....................8
Honest and trustworthy....................6
Courageous and tough....................3
Independent....................2
He has nothing to gain....................2
A leader....................1

Change....................23
Need a change....................15
He offers a choice....................5
Not a politician....................3

Ideas....................14
He makes sense....................9
He understands people....................5

Nonspecific....................17
Just like him....................14
Have heard nothing unfavorable about him..3

Other....................7
No opinion....................8

Asked of the 34% of the sample who have an unfavorable opinion of Ross Perot: Why do you have an unfavorable opinion of Perot?

Don't know where he stands....................38%
Don't know where he stands on issues....................13
Don't know enough about him....................12
He beats around the bush....................7
Don't like his plans....................6

Characteristics....................24
Untruthful....................8
He's rich....................5
Possible dictator....................4
Arrogant....................2
Sneaky....................2
He's trying to buy the White House....................1
Liberal....................1
Independent....................1

Lack of Experience....................18
Politically inexperienced....................8
He wouldn't make a good president....................3
He can't follow through on promises....................2
He can't run the country like a business....................2
He can't solve everything....................2
He's out of touch with Americans....................1

Just don't like him...............................6
Other..7
No opinion.......................................7

Asked of registered voters: Which of the candidates do you think has offered the most specific plan for improving the economy—George Bush, Bill Clinton, or Ross Perot?

Clinton...36%
Bush...22
Perot..20
None (volunteered)............................14
No opinion.......................................8

As you may know, Bill Clinton presented an economic plan for the country this past week. From what you know about Clinton's plan, do you think it would help the economy, hurt the economy, or not have much effect either way?

Help...34%
Hurt...5
Not much effect.................................36
Don't know enough;
haven't heard about it.......................22
No opinion.......................................3

Asked of registered voters: How worried are you that, as president, Ross Perot would not respect the constitutional limits on his office and would try to take too much power into his own hands?

Very worried.....................................17%
Somewhat worried..............................26
Not too worried.................................28
Not at all worried...............................25
No opinion.......................................4

Note: A new Gallup Poll shows George Bush with 33% of the presidential vote, H. Ross Perot with 32%, and Bill Clinton close behind at 27%. These findings do not constitute a statistically significant shift from Gallup's last survey two weeks ago, but they reinforce the conclusion that Perot's rapid ascent to front-runner status has been halted and may actually be in decline. There are also signs that soon-to-be Democratic nominee Clinton's image has begun to improve in the minds of voters as Perot's becomes increasingly more negative.

Clinton's percentage of the trial heat vote in the latest poll tracked upward at the same time that Perot's was declining. If this trend continues, and if events follow those of previous election years, Clinton can be expected to do well in presidential trial heats over the next several weeks, as the Democratic party's national convention in New York captures the public's attention.

For the first time since March, Clinton is now viewed favorably by as many voters as view him unfavorably. In early June his rating of favorable to unfavorable opinions was 41% to 47%. In the latest poll the replies are positive: 45% have favorable opinions of Clinton, 43% unfavorable.

In addition, Clinton's recent emphasis on specific issues appears to be paying off. Voters give Clinton (36%) more credit than either Bush (22%) or Perot (20%) for having proposed the most specific plan for improving the economy. Thirty-four percent say that Clinton's plan will help the economy, 36% say that it will not have much effect, and 25% do not know enough about it to comment.

The new poll spotlights a troubling trend for Perot; as voters come to know more about him, they are forming more unfavorable than favorable opinions of the Texas billionaire. The percentage of voters with unfavorable attitudes toward Perot has climbed from 25% to 34% since mid-May; his favorability ratings have dropped slightly from 50% to 48%. Although Perot is seen more positively than either Bush or Clinton, his image increasingly resembles that of his two more battle-scarred, politically exposed opponents.

What appears to be hurting Perot most is his lack of specificity on the issues. Voters with an unfavorable opinion of him were asked to explain this attitude in their own words. The number one response, given by 38%, is Perot's vagueness and refusal to take specific positions on issues ("don't know where he stands on issues," "he beats around the bush").

Moreover, about four out of ten (43%) say that they are worried that Perot would not respect the constitutional limits of his office if elected president and would try to take too much power into his own hands. Despite Perot's recent press attention and critical attacks by Republicans, this number is unchanged from two weeks ago.

About one quarter of those with unfavorable opinions of Perot (24%) talk about his personal characteristics: "untruthful," "possible dictator," "arrogant," "sneaky," and so forth. A slightly lower number (18%) say that their unfavorable opinion is based on his lack of experience or lack of training for the presidency.

Favorable opinions of Perot are being driven by specific aspects of his personality or style; 31% of those with a favorable opinion say that it is because "he can run the country like a business," because he is "tough" and "a man of action." Twenty-three percent of those who like Perot say it is because he would represent change, while 14% say it is because of his ideas.

JULY 5
ABORTION

Interviewing Date: 6/29/92
Special Survey

Do you think abortions should be legal under any circumstances, legal only under certain circumstances, or illegal in all circumstances?

Legal, any circumstances........................34%
Legal, certain circumstances...................48
Illegal, all circumstances.......................13
No opinion...5

Selected National Trend

	Legal, any	Legal, certain	Illegal, all*
January 1992	31%	53%	14%
September 1991	33	49	14
May 1991	32	50	17
1990	31	53	12
July 1989	29	51	17
April 1989	27	50	18
1988	24	57	17
1983	23	58	16
1981	23	52	21
1980	25	53	18
1979	22	54	19
1977	22	55	19
1975	21	54	22

*"No opinion" is omitted.

As you may know, in its decision today the Supreme Court approved some abortion restrictions in a Pennsylvania law but said that states cannot make abortion illegal in most cases. All in all, do you think this decision went too far in restricting access to abortions, not far enough in restricting access to abortions, or was it about right?

Too far...31%
Not far enough...................................15
About right..37
No opinion...17

	Too far	Not far enough	About right	No opinion
By Position on Abortion				
Legal, Any	50%	7%	27%	16%
Legal, Certain	24	12	48	16
Illegal, All	14	48	24	14

Thinking about how the abortion issue might affect your vote for major offices, would you:

Only vote for candidates who share your views on abortion?.....................13%
Consider a candidate's position on abortion as just one of many important factors when voting?...........46
Not see abortion as a major issue?...........36
No opinion...5

	Candidate must share my view	Just one factor	Not a major issue
By Position on Abortion			
Legal, Any	41%	31%	36%
Legal, Certain	32	56	46
Illegal, All	25	10	12
No Opinion	2	3	6

Asked of potential Bush voters: As a result of the Supreme Court abortion decision, are you more likely or less likely to vote for George Bush, or will the decision not much affect your chances of voting for him?

More likely	14%
Less likely	10
Not much affect chances	59
No opinion	17

Looking ahead, do you think a woman's legal right to an abortion in this country is very secure, somewhat secure, not too secure, or not at all secure?

Very secure	10%
Somewhat secure	34
Not too secure	35
Not at all secure	14
No opinion	7

Note: The mixed signals now sent out by the Supreme Court in resolving the *Planned Parenthood v. Casey* abortion case coincide with the ambivalent views held by the public. Most Americans do not want *Roe v. Wade* overturned but favor the restrictions imposed by the Pennsylvania law and upheld by the Court, and yet nearly one third thinks that the Court has become too restrictive.

Recent Gallup Polls show that only 14% think abortion should always be illegal. About one half (48%) says that abortion should be legal only under certain circumstances, and one third (34%) opts for the always-legal position.

A substantial number (31%) of those surveyed immediately after the decision thinks that the ruling on the Pennsylvania law goes too far in restricting access to abortion, more than twice as many as those who think that the Court has not gone far enough (15%). Thirty-seven percent call it about right, while 17% have no opinion.

These percentages reflect Americans' overall attitudes about abortion. Of the 34% who favor always-legal abortions, the largest number (50%) believes that the ruling goes too far; conversely, a large plurality (48%) of the 13% who support "illegal under all circumstances" says that it does not go far enough; and a similar plurality (48%) of the 48% who support "legal under certain circumstances" replies that the decision is about right.

The fact that the Supreme Court did not overturn *Roe v. Wade* may have helped George Bush. In January, Gallup asked voters how they would view the president if the Court were to overturn the landmark decision: 19% said that they would be less likely to vote for him, while only 9% thought it more likely (70% replied that it would have no bearing on their vote). In the wake of the current decision (curtailing *Roe v. Wade* without actually overturning it) Bush seems to have benefited: among those who do not support him now but who might be persuaded to do so—one fourth of the voters—14% say that they are more likely to vote for Bush as a result of the Court's decision, while only 10% are less likely. And nearly as many (44%) think that a woman's legal right to an abortion is at least somewhat secure as think it is either not too or not at all secure (49%).

However, President Bush still faces the possibility of a divisive fight over abortion at the Republican national convention. And strategists for Bill Clinton and H. Ross Perot may try to convince the voters that *Roe v. Wade* still is imperiled; that, as its 83-year-old author Justice Harry A. Blackmun has pointed out, it is only one Court appointment away from being overturned.

A majority of voters (59%) now say that a candidate's position on abortion is an important factor in determining how they will vote, and more than one in ten (13%) will vote only for a candidate who shares their views on abortion. This hard-core group of abortion activists now includes many more pro-choice (41%) than pro-life (25%) advocates.

JULY 5
PRESIDENTIAL TRIAL HEAT: YOUNG VOTERS

Interviewing Date: 6/4–8; 12–14/92
Survey #GO 222054; 322001

Asked of registered voters, aged 18–29 years: As of today, do you lean more to George Bush, the Republican; to Bill Clinton, the Democrat; or to H. Ross Perot, the independent?

Bush	34%
Clinton	24
Perot	37
Undecided; other	5

Selected National Trend
(18–29 Years)

	Bush	Clinton	Perot	Undecided; other
1992				
May	40%	29%	26%	5%
March–April	48	27	19	6

Note: George Bush may have lost his grip on the youth vote, which in recent years has leaned Republican. The Gallup Poll shows support for the president among voters aged 18 to 29 slipping from 48% to 34% since the early spring—the largest decline in Bush's standing within any age group. Thus far, Bush's losses have been H. Ross Perot's gains, as support among young voters for the still-undeclared independent candidate almost doubled over the same time period. Based on interviewing conducted in March and April, 19% of voters under age 30 backed Perot; his support level increased to 37% in June.

While Bill Clinton has failed to gain ground among young people in recent months, his efforts to court the "twenty-something" vote may bear fruit as his positions on issues become better known and, especially, if the Perot phenomenon begins to fade. Gallup surveys conducted this year have found many young voters feeling closer to the Democrats than to the Republicans on issues of particular concern to their generation: abortion, AIDS, the environment, and race relations.

Before the 1984 presidential election, young voters were generally regarded as another Democratic constituency, along with such groups as blacks, labor union members, and big-city residents. Gallup's final preelection polls in presidential elections that took place from 1952 to 1980 found Democratic candidates consistently running stronger among the youngest segment of the electorate. In 1984, however, that pattern was broken when Ronald Reagan won a landslide victory over Walter Mondale. With an economic recovery under way, soothing Reagan television commercials told voters that it was "morning in America." Democrat Mondale's support level among young voters (40%) was no higher than his support level among voters of all ages (41%).

In 1988 the direction of the youth vote turned around completely. For the first time, Gallup's final preelection poll showed the Republican candidate's share of the under-30 vote (63% for Bush) significantly exceeding his share of the overall vote (54%).

Today's twenty-something voters entered adulthood in a very different political climate than the previous generation, the so-called baby boomers. The leading edge of this new generation reached maturity around 1980, the year of the Iran hostage crisis and Reagan's election victory over an unpopular Democratic president, Jimmy Carter. It was a time of Republican resurgence after the GOP's fall from grace in the post-Watergate era. Since the early 1980s identification with the Democratic party has fallen to near-record lows, while Republican identification is at a three-decade high point.

Members of the twenty-something generation are somewhat less likely than other Americans to consider themselves Democrats and are more likely to call themselves independents. The latest Gallup Poll figures, based on personal interviews collected during the first quarter of 1992, show equal proportions of 18-to-29 year olds identifying themselves as Democrats (35%) and independents (36%); 29% say that they are Republicans. These party identifications are quite different from those of previous generations of young adults. Both the baby boomers and the purportedly more placid youth of the 1950s had a much greater Democratic orientation than the young voters of the 1990s.

Young Americans shifted toward the Republican party in the mid-1980s, when Reagan's popularity was at a high point. President Reagan's conviction that the best way to improve the economy was to unleash U.S. business probably struck a responsive chord among the young. College students of the 1980s made business the most popular major. While baby boomers viewed corporations as the enemy, the new generation is distinguished by its favorable attitudes toward business. As long as the economy remains sluggish, Clinton and Perot will have a good opportunity to contend for the youth vote. But if young Americans see significant improvement in the economy, then Bush becomes a heavy favorite to win their vote.

JULY 10
HONESTY AND ETHICAL STANDARDS

Interviewing Date: 6/26–30/92
Survey #GO 322002

How would you rate the honesty and ethical standards of the people in these different fields—very high, high, average, low, or very low?

	Very high, high	*Average*	*Low, very low*	*No opinion*
Druggists, pharmacists	66%	28%	4%	2%
Clergy	54	33	9	4
Medical doctors	52	38	9	1
College teachers	50	38	5	7
Dentists	50	42	5	3
Engineers	48	40	3	9
Policemen	42	42	14	2
Funeral directors	35	46	10	9
Television reporters, commentators	31	50	17	2
Journalists	27	54	15	4
Bankers	27	53	17	3
Newspaper reporters	25	53	18	4
Building contractors	19	53	21	7
Lawyers	18	43	36	3
Business executives	18	60	17	5
Local political officeholders	15	56	26	3
Real estate agents	14	55	26	5
Labor union leaders	14	41	38	7
Stockbrokers	13	52	23	12
Senators	13	44	40	3
State political officeholders	11	50	35	4
Congressmen	11	43	43	3
Advertising practitioners	10	49	33	8
Insurance salesmen	9	46	41	4
Car salesmen	5	32	59	4

Note: The public continues to hold pharmacists in high regard for their honesty and ethical standards. Two thirds of Americans say that pharmacists demonstrate high or very high standards, thus giving that profession the top score in Gallup's annual poll on honesty and ethics in twenty-five professions.

In the year of the angry voter, the public's disdain for political officeholders is starkly evident. Elected officials at federal and state levels receive their lowest ratings in sixteen years of polling on the topic. Members of Congress have suffered the sharpest decline: only 13% think that U.S. senators have high standards, compared with 24% in 1990 and 19% last year. Barely one in ten (11%) rates members of the House highly, an 8-point decline from 1991. In fact, only the much-maligned salesmen—of insurance, advertising, and cars—rate lower than U.S. congressmen.

For the fourth consecutive time, respondents designate pharmacy as the most honorable profession (66%), besting the former front-runners, the clergy (54%). The 12-point margin is the highest in the poll's history. It is evident that the clergy have never recovered from the ethical battering sustained during the Bakker and Swaggart televangelist scandals; their ratings have steadily declined from a high of 67% in 1985. Policemen took a similar whipping last year, after the Rodney King beating, with positive ratings (43%) dropping 6 points from 1990. Unlike the clergy, their ratings have stabilized this year (42%).

The widespread cynicism noted in last year's poll is even more pronounced in 1992. While only two groups, pharmacists (up 6) and college teachers (up 5), receive substantially higher positive ratings, no less than six professions see large increases in the number of Americans who judge their honesty and ethical standards to be low or very low: state officeholders (35%, an increase of 7 percentage points); lawyers (36%, up 6); U.S. senators (40%, up 10); insurance salesmen (41%, up 8); U.S. representatives (43%, up 11); and car salesmen (59%, up 10).

JULY 12
PRESIDENTIAL TRIAL HEATS

Interviewing Date: 7/6–8/92*
Survey #GO 322004

Asked of registered voters: Suppose the 1992 presidential election were being held today. If George Bush were the Republican candidate and Bill Clinton were the Democratic candidate and H. Ross Perot were an independent candidate, whom would you vote for? [Those who were undecided were asked: As of today, do you lean more to Bush, the Republican; to Clinton, the Democrat; or to Perot, the independent?]

Bush	35%
Clinton	28
Perot	30
Undecided; other	7

Selected National Trend

	Bush	Clinton	Perot	Undecided; other
1992				
June 26–30	33%	27%	32%	8%
June 12–14	32	24	34	10
June 4–8	31	25	39	5
May 18–20	35	25	35	5
May 7–10	35	29	30	6
April 20–22	41	26	25	8
March 31–April 1	44	25	24	7

Trend in Bush Support

	July 6–8	June 26–30	June 12–14
By Sex			
Male	32%	31%	30%
Female	37	34	34
By Ethnic Background			
White	38	35	34
Nonwhite	11	15	21
By Education			
College Graduate	35	37	32
Some College	38	28	35
No College	33	32	32
By Region			
East	31	29	29
Midwest	42	33	33
South	35	35	36
West	30	33	30
By Age			
18–29 Years	34	36	36
30–49 Years	36	32	32
50 Years and Over	33	32	31
By Household Income			
$50,000 and Over	35	34	37
$30,000–$49,999	38	30	33
$20,000–$29,999	32	33	33
Under $20,000	32	33	29
By Politics			
Republicans	68	67	70
Democrats	10	10	13
Independents	26	25	21
By Political Ideology			
Liberal	17	23	11
Moderate	31	25	25
Conservative	48	46	52

*Gallup survey for CNN/*USA Today*

Trend in Clinton Support

	July 6–8	June 26–30	June 12–14
By Sex			
Male	27%	25%	22%
Female	29	28	25
By Ethnic Background			
White	25	24	21
Nonwhite	56	49	42
By Education			
College Graduate	28	25	25

Some College	25	29	22
No College	30	26	24
By Region			
East	36	30	27
Midwest	23	24	20
South	30	28	24
West	24	24	25
By Age			
18–29 Years	29	19	22
30–49 Years	29	27	25
50 Years and Over	27	31	24
By Household Income			
$50,000 and Over	25	21	20
$30,000–$49,999	25	25	24
$20,000–$29,999	28	37	27
Under $20,000	36	28	24
By Politics			
Republicans	5	6	5
Democrats	57	54	49
Independents	23	19	16
By Political Ideology			
Liberal	49	40	49
Moderate	31	31	23
Conservative	17	16	12

Trend in Perot Support

	July 6–8	*June 26–30*	*June 12–14*
By Sex			
Male	34%	38%	37%
Female	26	28	31
By Ethnic Background			
White	31	34	35
Nonwhite	19	24	24
By Education			
College Graduate	33	30	38
Some College	30	35	36
No College	29	33	31
By Region			
East	28	29	31
Midwest	26	35	36
South	28	31	33
West	40	36	34
By Age			
18–29 Years	30	37	36
30–49 Years	30	32	36
50 Years and Over	31	29	30
By Household Income			
$50,000 and Over	37	38	34
$30,000–$49,999	31	38	38
$20,000–$29,999	31	25	32
Under $20,000	24	28	32
By Politics			
Republicans	23	22	21
Democrats	26	28	28
Independents	41	44	52
By Political Ideology			
Liberal	26	25	31
Moderate	33	37	42
Conservative	29	32	27

Also asked of registered voters: Regardless of which presidential candidate you support, please tell me whether you think George Bush, Bill Clinton, or Ross Perot would best handle each of the following issues:

Economy?

Bush	24%
Clinton	22
Perot	41
No difference; no opinion	13

Health care?

Bush	23%
Clinton	33
Perot	25
No difference; no opinion	19

Education?

Bush	29%
Clinton	33
Perot	25
No difference; no opinion	13

Abortion?

Bush	29%
Clinton	30
Perot	16
No difference; no opinion	25

Foreign affairs?

Bush	63%
Clinton	14
Perot	14
No difference; no opinion	9

Unemployment?

Bush	22%
Clinton	28
Perot	35
No difference; no opinion	15

Environment?

Bush	29%
Clinton	33
Perot	19
No difference; no opinion	19

Also asked of registered voters: Please tell me whether you have a favorable or unfavorable opinion of Senator Al Gore of Tennessee:

Favorable	39%
Unfavorable	17
Heard of; no opinion	25
Never heard of	19

	Favorable	*Unfavor-able*	*Heard of; no opinion*	*Never heard of*
By Democrats				
Total	44%	12%	22%	22%
Clinton Supporters	44	13	20	23
Clinton Non-supporters	44	12	24	20

Note: On the eve of the Democratic party's national convention, Bill Clinton's once-stalled campaign has regained momentum. Now, 28% of registered voters support the Arkansas governor, putting him in a statistical tie for second place with undeclared independent candidate H. Ross Perot (30%) and within striking distance of President George Bush, now the leader with 35%.

In mid-June, before Perot's support began to erode, Clinton was entrenched in third place, trailing the Texas businessman by 10 percentage points (24% to 34%) and the president by 8 points (24% to 32%). Clinton last held a share of second place in early May, in the aftermath of the Rodney King verdict and the Los Angeles riots.

After this week's convention, Clinton can expect his standing in the polls to improve further, at least temporarily. History shows that presidential candidates usually gain 5 or more points in voter support after their party's national convention. Four years ago, Michael Dukakis's support increased by 7 points after the Democratic convention in Atlanta, giving him a 17-percentage point advantage (54% versus 37%) over George Bush in the Gallup Poll. The postconvention boost, however, can be short-lived. Candidate standings in 1988 reverted to preconvention levels within two weeks.

In selecting Tennessee Senator Al Gore as his running mate, Clinton appears to have succeeded in doing himself no harm—a cardinal rule in the vice presidential selection process. Among all voters with an opinion of Gore, twice as many express a favorable (39%) as an unfavorable one (17%). Although Gore has been described as a Clinton clone, his voter appeal may not be identical to Clinton's and thus might help draw votes among disaffected Democrats.

Even before the Gore announcement, Clinton appeared to be gaining ground among some key voter groups likely to look positively on his new running mate. Since mid-June, Clinton's support has increased significantly among voters in the East and South and among political moderates. The Arkansas governor's gains have come almost exclusively from voters who identify with the Democratic party. His support among those who identify with the GOP is unchanged; 5% of Republican and Republican-leaning voters favor Clinton.

As Perot's independent candidacy has lost some of its luster, Clinton is not the only candidate to gain support. President Bush also appears to have won back some voters who had been attracted to Perot's candidacy. In the past month, Bush support has increased among independents, moderates, and liberals—all groups whose support for Perot has dropped significantly since June.

Despite some erosion of support, Perot remains competitive in this race because a plurality (41%) sees the Texas entrepreneur as best able to handle the key issue of 1992: the economy. Only about one half as many names Bush (24%) or Clinton (22%) as the best candidate for the economy. Perot also has a lead on the unemployment issue, traditionally the province of the Democrats. More than one third (35%) see Perot as best equipped to deal with joblessness, compared with 28% for Clinton and 22% for Bush.

The president has little competition in the area of foreign policy. Six in ten (63%) trust Bush to handle foreign affairs best. No candidate has a big edge on domestic issues, which Clinton clearly has to change to have a chance to win in November. No more than one third of the voters now sees Clinton as best able to handle health care (33%), education (33%), the environment (33%), and abortion (30%).

JULY 14
PARTY BETTER FOR PEACE AND PROSPERITY

Interviewing Date: 7/6–8/92
Survey #GO 322004

Asked of registered voters: Looking ahead for the next few years, which political party do you think would be more likely to keep the United States out of war—the Republican or the Democratic party?

Republican	33%
Democratic	45
No difference; no opinion	22

Selected National Trend

	Republican	*Democratic*	*No difference; no opinion*
February 1992	39%	39%	22%
October 1991	45	38	17
July 1991	42	33	25
October 1990	34	36	30
August 1990*	36	34	30
September 1988*	43	33	24
July 1988*	39	36	25
May 1988*	31	39	30
January 1988*	36	35	29
August 1984	36	40	24
April 1984	30	42	28
September 1983	26	39	35
October 1982	29	38	33
April 1981	29	34	37
September 1980	25	42	33
August 1976	29	32	39
September 1972	32	28	40
October 1968	37	24	39
October 1964	22	45	33
October 1960	40	25	35
October 1956	46	16	38
January 1952	36	15	49
September 1951	28	21	51

*Asked of registered voters

Also asked of registered voters: Which political party—the Republican or the Democratic—will do a better job of keeping the country prosperous?

Republican	42%
Democratic	38
No difference; no opinion	20

Selected National Trend

	Republican	*Democratic*	*No difference; no opinion*
February 1992	41%	43%	16%
October 1991	44	41	15
July 1991	49	32	19
October 1990	37	35	28
August 1990*	45	30	25
September 1988*	52	34	14

July 1988*	46	39	15
May 1988*	41	39	20
January 1988*	42	35	23
August 1984	48	36	16
April 1984	44	36	20
September 1983	33	40	27
October 1982	34	43	23
April 1981	41	28	31
September 1980	35	36	29
August 1976	23	47	30
September 1972	38	35	27
October 1968	34	37	29
October 1964	21	53	26
October 1960	31	46	23
October 1956	39	39	22
January 1952	31	35	34
September 1951	29	37	34

*Asked of registered voters

Note: The Democrats have lost ground on Gallup's party-of-prosperity measure, a critical indicator of party strength. By a margin of 42% to 38%, voters now see the Republicans as better able than the Democrats to keep the country prosperous. One in five (20%) sees no difference in the two parties' abilities to bring about prosperity. February poll results on this question were somewhat more favorable for the Democrats (43%) than for the Republicans (41%).

It has been almost a decade since the Democrats last held a significant advantage on the prosperity measure. In September 1983, when political fallout from a recession continued to hurt the GOP's image, the Democrats held a 40%-to-33% edge. Since that time the parties have been rated about evenly or the Republicans have led.

If the Clinton-Gore ticket is to be successful, the Democrats must convince more voters that they, not the Republicans or H. Ross Perot, can best improve the economy. Since Gallup began asking these party-strength questions in 1951, the prosperity measure has proved a reliable barometer of the parties' presidential prospects. Over the past forty years, Democratic candidates have won only three presidential elections. Each time the party has held a clear advantage on economic issues. When Jimmy Carter last won the White House for the Democrats in 1976, his party outpolled the GOP by 47% to 23% on the prosperity measure.

For the first time since George Bush took office, the Democratic party now tops the Republican as the party of peace in the Gallup Poll. Close to one half (45%) of the voters names the Democratic party as the one better able to keep the country out of war, while one third (33%) names the GOP.

Evaluations of the parties' abilities to keep the peace have shifted over the past two years. Last February, the two parties were essentially tied on the party-of-peace question (39% each). Boosted by the Gulf War victory, the GOP held an advantage on war and peace issues in 1991. A Gallup Poll taken in July of last year showed the Republicans ahead by 42% to 33% as the party better trusted to keep the peace.

JULY 15
BILL CLINTON

Interviewing Date: 7/6–8/92*
Survey #GO 322004

Asked of registered voters: Please tell me whether you have a favorable or unfavorable opinion of Bill Clinton:

Favorable	41%
Unfavorable	49
No opinion	10

Selected National Trend

	Favorable	*Unfavorable*	*No opinion***
1992			
June 26–30	45%	43%	11%
June 12–14	41	47	12
May 18–20	42	48	9
April 20–22	42	49	9
April 9–12	34	47	19
March 26–29	37	40	23

*Gallup survey for CNN/*USA Today*
**"Never heard of"—at 1% or less—is omitted.

Also asked of registered voters: Please tell me whether you have a favorable or unfavorable opinion of Hillary Clinton:

Favorable..45%
Unfavorable......................................30
Heard of; no opinion 17
Never heard of (volunteered) 8

Selected National Trend

	Favor-able	Unfavor-able	Heard of; no opinion	Never heard of
1992				
April 20–22	38%	39%	17%	6%
March 20–22	39	26	17	18

Also asked of registered voters: As I read some phrases, please tell me whether you think each one applies or does not apply to Bill Clinton:

Would display good judgment in a crisis?

Yes, applies......................................52%
No, does not apply..............................35
No opinion..13

Has a clear understanding of the issues?

Yes, applies......................................71%
No, does not apply..............................24
No opinion.. 5

Can bring about the changes this country needs?

Yes, applies......................................44%
No, does not apply..............................48
No opinion.. 8

Has a clear plan for solving the country's problems?

Yes, applies......................................38%
No, does not apply..............................53
No opinion.. 9

Also asked of registered voters: Do you think Bill Clinton has the honesty and integrity to serve as president, or not?

Yes..56%
No...36
No opinion.. 8

Also asked of registered voters: How confident are you—very confident, somewhat confident, not too confident, or not at all confident—that Bill Clinton would do each of the following if he is elected:

Improve the economy?

Very confident....................................13%
Somewhat confident.............................40
Not too confident 23
Not at all confident 19
No opinion.. 5

Reduce the federal budget deficit?

Very confident..................................... 7%
Somewhat confident.............................28
Not too confident 29
Not at all confident 30
No opinion.. 6

Improve race relations?

Very confident....................................16%
Somewhat confident.............................47
Not too confident 20
Not at all confident 12
No opinion.. 5

Defend U.S. interests abroad?

Very confident....................................17%
Somewhat confident.............................45
Not too confident 19
Not at all confident 12
No opinion.. 7

Note: Bill Clinton's surge in the polls prior to this week's Democratic national convention has given his campaign a new sense of optimism. Mired in third place only one month ago, Clinton now has a share of the lead. Gallup's most recent survey, conducted for *Newsweek* after Al Gore joined the Democratic ticket, shows a virtual three-way tie: 32% for

George Bush, 31% for Clinton, and 28% for H. Ross Perot.

Despite his improved standing in the polls, Clinton's image problems with the voters persist. The Arkansas governor's favorability ratings, which began tilting negatively in April, show no signs of turning around. The current Gallup Poll shows one half of the voters (49%) with unfavorable views of Clinton, and 41% favorable.

Gallup Poll results continue to suggest that the charges of adultery, draft dodging, and marijuana use leveled against Clinton earlier in the campaign have contributed to his negative image. These so-called character issues, however, may be less relevant now than they were in the spring. A majority of the voters (56%) now says that Clinton has the honesty and integrity to serve as president, while 36% disagree. When Gallup asked a similar question in April, opinion was about evenly split (45% positive versus 47% negative).

Clinton's youth and his lack of experience in foreign affairs do not seem to be major liabilities, at least so far. By a margin of 52% to 35%, voters say that Clinton would display good judgment in a crisis. A majority (62%) is also very or somewhat confident that Clinton would defend U.S. interests abroad.

To win the election, Clinton must do more than overcome doubts about his personal character. Equally important is his ability to persuade voters, many of whom have been attracted to the Perot candidacy, that he can be the agent of change whom they are looking for in this year of political and economic discontent. While more than two thirds (71%) of voters credit Clinton with having a clear understanding of the issues, over one half (53%) is not convinced that he has a clear plan to solve the country's problems. And a plurality (48%) disagrees that Clinton can bring about the changes this country needs.

Hillary Clinton's lower profile over the past few months has been good for her image and, presumably, for her husband's election prospects. The current poll finds more voters expressing favorable views of her than unfavorable ones (45% versus 30%). In April, voter opinion of Mrs. Clinton was about equally divided (38% favorable versus 39% unfavorable).

JULY 22
PRESIDENTIAL TRIAL HEAT

Interviewing Date: 7/17–18/92*
Survey #GO 322005

Asked of registered voters: Suppose the 1992 presidential election were being held today. If George Bush were the Republican candidate and Bill Clinton were the Democratic candidate, whom would you vote for? [Those who were undecided were asked: As of today, do you lean more to Bush, the Republican, or to Clinton, the Democrat?]

Bush	34%
Clinton	56
Undecided; other	10

	Bush	*Clinton*	*Undecided; other*
By Politics			
Republicans	82%	14%	4%
Democrats	4	91	5
Independents	28	51	21
Potential Perot Voters	26	62	12

Selected National Trend

	Bush	*Clinton*	*Undecided; other*
1992			
July 6–8**	48%	40%	12%
June 26–30**	44	41	14
June 12–14**	45	37	18
June 4–8	46	40	14
May 18–20	50	39	11
May 7–10	45	40	15
April 20–22	50	34	16
April 9–12	48	41	11
March 31–April 1	54	34	12
March 26–29	54	38	8

*Gallup survey for CNN/*USA Today*

March 20–22	52	43	5
March 11–12	50	44	6
February 19–20	53	43	4
February 6–9	53	38	9

**Perot voters assigned to the candidate named as their second choice

Also asked of registered voters: Is there any chance that you will vote for George Bush [or Bill Clinton] in November, or is there no chance whatsoever that you will vote for him?

Current Strength of Support*

	Bush	Clinton
Core supporters	22%	44%
Soft supporters	12	13
Potential voters	20	19
No chance	46	24

*Core supporters: those who will not vote for other candidates. Soft supporters: those who might vote for another candidate. Potential voters: nonsupporters who say there is a chance they will vote for the candidate.

Selected National Trend
(George Bush)

	Core supporters	Soft supporters	Potential voters	No chance
1992				
July 6–8	17%	18%	25%	40%
June 26–30	11	16	30	43
June 12–14	10	14	31	45
May 18–20	11	14	27	48

(Bill Clinton)

	Core supporters	Soft supporters	Potential voters	No chance
1992				
July 6–8	13%	15%	26%	46%
June 26–30	11	16	30	43
June 12–14	10	14	31	45
May 18–20	11	14	27	48

Also asked of registered voters: Please tell me whether you have a favorable or unfavorable opinion of each of the following presidential candidates:

George Bush?

Favorable	40%
Unfavorable	53
No opinion	7

Selected National Trend

	Favorable	Unfavorable	No opinion
1992			
July 6–8	49%	45%	6%
June 26–30	44	50	6
June 12–14	44	51	5
May 18–20	48	47	5
April 20–22	55	41	4
April 9–12	48	44	8
March 26–29	49	44	7

Bill Clinton?

Favorable	63%
Unfavorable	25
No opinion	12

Selected National Trend

	Favorable	Unfavorable	No opinion*
1992			
July 6–8	41%	49%	10%
June 26–30	45	43	11
June 12–14	41	47	12
May 18–20	42	48	9
April 20–22	42	49	9
April 9–12	34	47	19
March 26–29	37	40	23

*"Never heard of"—at 1% or less—is omitted.

Also asked of registered voters: Thinking back, which of these statements best describes your voting intentions before Ross Perot's decision not to run for president?

You planned to vote for Perot (core supporter)	9%

You were considering voting for Perot (soft supporter) 30
You definitely were not going to vote for Perot 57
No opinion 4

Also asked of registered voters: From what you have seen or heard about the Democratic convention and the Clinton-Gore ticket, do you think the Democratic party has changed for the better, changed for the worse, or not changed much at all?

Better 61%
Worse 2
Not changed much 32
No opinion 5

Also asked of registered voters: Please tell me whether each of the following makes you more likely or less likely to vote for Bill Clinton:

What you saw or read of this week's Democratic convention?

More likely 60%
Less likely 15
No difference (volunteered) 17
No opinion 8

Selected National Trend

	More likely	*Less likely*	*No difference*	*No opinion*
Postconvention 1988 (Dukakis)	56%	21%	9%	14%
Postconvention 1984 (Mondale)	45	29	12	14

Clinton's choice of Al Gore as his running mate?

More likely 73%
Less likely 10
No difference (volunteered) 13
No opinion 4

Selected National Trend

	More likely	*Less likely*	*No difference*	*No opinion*
Postconvention 1988 (Bentsen)	48%	28%	10%	14%
Postconvention 1984 (Ferraro)	52	26	18	4

Note: Governor Bill Clinton emerges from the Democratic party's national convention with a dramatic lead over George Bush (56% versus 34%), after trailing the president 40% to 48% the previous week. In light of comparable Gallup election polls taken over the last twenty years, this 16-point postconvention "bounce" is extraordinary, although history suggests that it will not last. However, Clinton's ability to sustain his lead may be helped by a recent increase in the number of voters who now say that there is no chance they will vote for Bush. Also ominous for the Bush camp are his high unfavorability ratings, at 53%.

The new Gallup Poll shows that Clinton has succeeded in consolidating his own Democratic base of voters in the new two-way race for president; his biggest vote gains are among Democrats and people describing their political views as liberal. Clinton now receives nine out of every ten Democratic votes (91%), compared with just 74% prior to the convention. Clinton also forges a lead among independents, receiving 51% of their support; only 28% back Bush.

Voters of all political stripes warmed to the Democratic party as a result of the convention and moved to a significantly more favorable view of the party's southern candidate. Based on the convention itself and the Clinton-Gore ticket, a clear majority (61%) believes that the Democratic party has changed for the better. The convention also served to improve Clinton's image: 63% now hold a favorable view of him, compared with 41% in early July. Only 25% now hold an unfavorable view of him.

The poll shows that Clinton is the immediate beneficiary of H. Ross Perot's recent departure from the race. Nearly four in ten (39%) voters say that they were backing, or considering backing, Perot when he announced his decision not to run. Perot backers now prefer Clinton over Bush by a wide margin (62% versus 26%).

Clinton's 22-percentage point postconvention lead over Bush is not without precedent. Michael Dukakis left the 1988 Democratic convention in Atlanta 17 points ahead of Bush, but he sank to a 4-point deficit after the Republican convention one month later. Jimmy Carter had an even larger lead over incumbent Gerald Ford in 1976: 33 points. Yet Carter lost nearly all of that lead during the fall campaign and won by only 2 percentage points.

The size of Clinton's bounce is truly historic. His 16-point increase in support is more than double the average postconvention bounce of 6 points (based on an analysis of Gallup presidential election polls since 1968). By comparison, Dukakis registered a 7-point gain after the Democratic convention four years ago. The largest previous postconvention bounce measured was a 10-point gain for Carter in 1980.

Al Gore appears to be a bigger asset than either of his two most recent Democratic predecessors, Lloyd Bentsen in 1988 and Geraldine Ferraro in 1984. Three quarters (73%) of voters say that Clinton's choice of Gore makes them more likely to vote for Clinton, while only 10% say that it makes them less likely. By comparison, only one half of voters was more likely to support the Democratic ticket due to the vice presidential choices in either of the two previous elections, while roughly one quarter was less likely.

JULY 26
PRESIDENTIAL CANDIDATES

Interviewing Date: 7/17–18/92*
Survey #GO 322005

Asked of registered voters: How much, if any, of the Democratic convention did you watch on television this week? Did you happen to see, hear, or read any news coverage of the Democratic convention?

*Gallup survey for CNN/*USA Today*

Followed convention..........................95%
  Television viewers......................89
  Other coverage...........................6
Did not follow convention......................5

Also asked of registered voters: Regardless of which presidential candidate you support, please tell me whether you think George Bush or Bill Clinton would better handle each of the following issues:

Abortion?

Bush 26%
Clinton..56
Same; neither (volunteered).....................4
No opinion.......................................14

Economy?

Bush 24%
Clinton..58
Same; neither (volunteered).....................9
No opinion...9

Education?

Bush 25%
Clinton..60
Same; neither (volunteered).....................6
No opinion...9

Environment?

Bush 24%
Clinton..59
Same; neither (volunteered).....................6
No opinion.......................................11

Family values?

Bush 37%
Clinton..46
Same; neither (volunteered).....................9
No opinion...8

Foreign affairs?

Bush 64%
Clinton..25
Same; neither (volunteered).....................3
No opinion...8

Health care?

Bush	20%
Clinton	62
Same; neither (volunteered)	6
No opinion	12

National defense?

Bush	57%
Clinton	28
Same; neither (volunteered)	4
No opinion	11

Race relations?

Bush	22%
Clinton	58
Same; neither (volunteered)	9
No opinion	11

Taxes?

Bush	30%
Clinton	49
Same; neither (volunteered)	9
No opinion	12

Unemployment?

Bush	20%
Clinton	65
Same; neither (volunteered)	6
No opinion	9

Those Who Choose Clinton *(Pre- and Postconvention)*

	July 6–8	*July 17–18*	*Convention bounce*
Abortion	36%	56%	+20
Race relations	40	58	+18
Education	46	60	+14
Unemployment	54	65	+11
Economy	49	58	+9
Health care	54	62	+8
National defense	21	28	+7
Foreign affairs	22	25	+3
Taxes	47	49	+2

Also asked of registered voters: How would you describe your political views—very conservative, conservative, moderate, liberal, or very liberal?

	July 17–18	*March 20–22*
Very conservative	9%	7%
Conservative	31	36
Moderate	41	42
Liberal	11	10
Very liberal	4	4
No opinion	4	1

Now, using the same categories, how would you describe the political views of Bill Clinton?

	July 17–18	*March 20–22*
Very conservative	4%	4%
Conservative	13	13
Moderate	37	39
Liberal	26	27
Very liberal	6	6
No opinion	14	11

Also asked of registered voters: Please tell me whether you have a favorable or unfavorable opinion of Hillary Clinton:

Favorable	51%
Unfavorable	24
Heard of; no opinion	23
Never heard of	2

Selected National Trend

	Favorable	*Unfavorable*	*Heard of; no opinion*	*Never heard of*
1992				
July 6–8	5%	30%	17%	8%
April 20–22	38	39	17	6
March 20–22	39	26	17	18

Note: The heavy emphasis on domestic issues throughout the Democratic party's national convention in July is reflected in the postconvention increase in public confidence in Bill Clinton's ability to handle social and economic issues. He makes his greatest gains (comparing pre- and postconvention choices of Clinton versus George Bush as better able to handle each issue) on abortion (up 20 points from 36% to 56%), race relations (up 18 points from 40% to 58%), and education (up 14 points from 46% to 60%).

Clinton also strengthens his already significant lead as the candidate better able to deal with unemployment, now the issue which separates the candidates the most in the voters' minds; Clinton is chosen by 65% of voters surveyed, Bush by only 20%. Clinton's percentage also increases on his ability to handle the economy (up 9 points) and health care (up 8 points).

Clinton gains only slightly in terms of foreign affairs (up 3 points) and national defense (up 7 points) during the convention. These areas remain weak for the Democrats; voters still are more likely to choose Bush over Clinton as better able to handle both, by at least 30 percentage points.

Not all the Democrats' problems were erased as a result of the convention, however. An additional hint of weakness in Clinton's growing appeal to voters is his failure to improve his image on taxes. While he leads Bush on this issue (49% versus 30%), his standing as the better candidate on taxes barely improved during the convention (up 2 points).

Clinton may be vulnerable to some degree to Republican attempts to label him as "liberal." While only 15% consider themselves liberal or very liberal, 32% describe Clinton in these terms. The vast majority consider themselves either moderate or conservative (81%), compared with 54% who believe that Clinton's views are in that spectrum.

The Clinton campaign's efforts to improve Hillary Clinton's image after early gaffes earned her high negatives (39% had an unfavorable opinion of her in April) apparently have paid off. A majority of voters now views her favorably (51%), while only 24% view her unfavorably.

JULY 28
PRESIDENT BUSH/PRESIDENTIAL TRIAL HEAT

Interviewing Date: 7/24–26/92
Survey #GO 322010

Do you approve or disapprove of the way George Bush is handling his job as president?

Approve	32%
Disapprove	59
No opinion	9

	Approve	Disapprove	No opinion
By Sex			
Male	33%	60%	7%
Female	30	59	11
By Ethnic Background			
White	34	57	9
Nonwhite	17	74	9
Black	7	82	11
By Education			
College Graduate	40	56	4
College Incomplete	35	60	5
No College	27	61	12
By Region			
East	28	65	7
Midwest	31	60	9
South	30	61	9
West	38	50	12
By Age			
18–29 Years	39	52	9
30–49 Years	31	60	9
50 Years and Over	28	63	9
By Household Income			
$50,000 and Over	37	58	5
$30,000–$49,999	30	61	9
$20,000–$29,999	34	59	7
Under $20,000	27	59	14
By Politics			
Republicans	64	29	7
Democrats	12	82	6
Independents	27	59	14
By Political Ideology			
Liberal	18	74	8
Moderate	29	62	9
Conservative	44	49	7

Selected National Trend

	Approve	Disapprove	No opinion
1992			
June 26–30	38%	55%	7%
June 12–14	37	55	8
June 4–8	37	56	7
May 18–20	41	52	7
May 7–10	40	53	7
April 20–22	42	48	10
April 9–12	39	54	7
March 26–29	42	51	7
March 20–22	41	49	10
March 11–12	41	47	12
February 28–March 1	41	53	6
February 19–20	39	47	14
February 6–9	44	48	8
January 16–19	46	48	6
January 3–6	46	47	7

Low Points in Presidential Approval

	Approve	Year	Chief public concerns
Bush	32%	1992	Economy; unemployment
Reagan	35	1983	Unemployment; recession
Carter	28	1979	Inflation; energy problems
Ford	37	1975	Inflation; unemployment
Nixon	24	1974	Inflation; unemployment; Watergate
Johnson	35	1968	Vietnam; crime
Kennedy	56	1963	Keeping peace; race relations
Eisenhower	48	1958	Unemployment; keeping peace
Truman	23	1951	Korean War; economy
Roosevelt	54	1938	Keeping out of war; unemployment

Asked of registered voters: Suppose the 1992 presidential election were being held today. If George Bush were the Republican candidate and Bill Clinton were the Democratic candidate, whom would you vote for? [Those who were undecided were asked: As of today, do you lean more to Bush, the Republican, or to Clinton, the Democrat?]

Bush	36%
Clinton	56
Undecided; other	8

Note: President George Bush's job approval rating has fallen to 32% in the Gallup Poll, his lowest approval score to date. Only three of the last nine presidents—Jimmy Carter, Richard Nixon, and Harry Truman—have received lower ratings while in office.

One month ago, before the Democratic national convention, Bush approval was significantly higher (38%). With the president's appeal at low ebb, Democratic candidate Bill Clinton now leads Bush by 20 percentage points among registered voters (56% versus 36%). Clinton held a statistically similar lead (56% versus 34%) in a Gallup survey taken immediately after the convention.

For Bush, the 1992 election could not have come at a worse time. Only one previous president—Carter—has faced the prospect of starting a campaign for reelection with approval ratings in the low 30s (33% in July 1980). Bush can ill afford any further erosion in his ratings.

Carter, whose popularity bottomed out at 28% in July 1979, regained enough to secure his party's nomination in 1980, but he lost decisively to Ronald Reagan in November of that year. Nixon and Truman, who had the lowest ratings on record (24% and 23%, respectively), both bowed out at their low points in approval. Nixon resigned under threat of impeachment during the Watergate investigations in August 1974, while Truman decided not to seek another term when the Korean War peace talks broke down in late 1951.

Gerald Ford, the last Republican president to be rejected by the voters, hit his low point in approval (37%) in early 1975 but quickly rebounded. In election year 1976, Ford approval ratings ranged from 45% to 53%, significantly above Bush's 1992 ratings, yet Ford lost the November election by a close margin to Carter.

JULY 29
VICE PRESIDENT QUAYLE

Interviewing Date: 7/24–26/92
Survey #GO 322010

Do you think George Bush should keep Dan Quayle as his vice presidential running mate this year, or should he choose someone else?

	Total	Registered voters only
Keep Quayle	37%	41%
Choose someone else	50	48
No opinion	13	11

	Keep Quayle	Choose someone else	No opinion
By Politics (Registered Voters)			
Republicans	57%	37%	6%
Democrats	30	56	14
Independents	39	49	12

Selected National Trend

	Keep Quayle	Choose someone else	No opinion
1991			
November	43%	46%	11%
August	42	52	6
May	39	52	9
1990			
November	36	55	9
March	35	49	16

Asked of registered voters: If George Bush keeps Dan Quayle as his running mate, would you be more likely or less likely to vote for the Republican ticket in November?

More likely	22%
Less likely	40
No difference (volunteered)	35
No opinion	3

	More likely	Less likely	No difference	No opinion
By Politics				
Republicans	37%	19%	42%	2%
Democrats	11	53	35	1
Independents	22	43	31	4

If George Bush does replace Dan Quayle on the ticket, would you have more respect for Bush, less respect, or would your opinion of Bush not change much?

More respect	21%
Less respect	11
Not change much	65
No opinion	3

Suppose for a moment that George Bush does decide to replace Dan Quayle on the Republican ticket. If Bush selects [Name] as his running mate, would you be more likely or less likely to vote for the Republican ticket in November:

Secretary of State James Baker?

More likely	40%
Less likely	32
Not much difference (volunteered)	22
No opinion	6

Secretary of Defense Dick Cheney?

More likely	28%
Less likely	37
Not much difference (volunteered)	25
No opinion	10

Former Secretary of Labor Elizabeth Dole?

More likely	28%
Less likely	42
Not much difference (volunteered)	21
No opinion	9

Kansas Senator Bob Dole?

More likely	30%
Less likely	36
Not much difference (volunteered)	24
No opinion	10

Secretary of HUD Jack Kemp?

More likely....................................29%
Less likely.....................................36
Not much difference (volunteered)...........22
No opinion.....................................13

General Colin Powell?

More likely....................................40%
Less likely.....................................31
Not much difference (volunteered)...........22
No opinion.....................................7

Based on what you know about Vice President Dan Quayle, do you think he is qualified to serve as president if it becomes necessary, or not?

Yes...32%
No..62
No opinion.....................................6

Selected National Trend

	Yes	*No*	*No opinion*
1992			
January	37%	54%	9%
1991			
November	37	53	10
August	40	54	6
May (late)	39	52	9
May	38	53	9
1990			
November	33	59	8
March	31	54	15
1989			
May	34	52	14
1988			
October	46	42	12
September	34	47	19
August	41	40	19

Based on what you know about the Democratic vice presidential candidate, Al Gore, do you think he is qualified to serve as president if it becomes necessary, or not?

Yes...64%
No..19
No opinion.....................................17

Note: Amid speculation about whether President George Bush will replace Dan Quayle as his vice presidential running mate in this year's election, the latest Gallup Poll shows that 62% of Americans doubt Quayle's fitness for the presidency, up 8 points from Gallup's last survey in January; only 32% think that he is qualified. About one half (50%) thinks that Bush should replace Quayle on the ticket, a percentage that has remained fairly constant over the past two years.

These latest, more negative images of the vice president may reflect the political troubles in which Bush finds himself. Bush now is at his all-time low in presidential approval ratings (32%). In addition, Al Gore's entrance into the vice presidential sweepstakes may account for some of the increased negativity toward Quayle. Gore is seen as qualified to be president by 64% of respondents, while only 19% think that the Tennessee senator is unqualified.

Whatever Bush decides about Quayle may not have much impact on the president's standing with the public; nearly two thirds (65%) say that replacing Quayle would not affect their opinion of Bush (21% would respect him more, 11% less).

If Bush keeps Quayle, only 22% of respondents say that they would be more likely to vote for the Republican ticket, while 40% would be less likely. One of Bush's dilemmas, however, lies in the Republicans' response to this question: by an 18-point margin (37% to 19%) they would be more likely to vote for the Bush-Quayle ticket. Thus, Bush risks alienating some of his most loyal supporters if he decides to replace Quayle.

In past elections, Gallup data have shown that vice presidential concerns have had virtually no effect on the outcome of the race. President Bush now has to decide whether 1992 will be different and whether a change of partners can really help his flagging campaign. The new poll indicates that among the six most often-cited replacements, only two can help. By a margin of 9 points, Chief of Staff General Colin Powell would make people more likely (40%) rather than less likely (31%) to vote for the Republican ticket; with Secretary of State James Baker, the margin is 8 points, 40% more likely and 32% less likely. The other four all receive more negative replies: Senator Bob

Dole (minus 6 points), HUD Secretary Jack Kemp (minus 7), Defense Secretary Dick Cheney (minus 9), and Elizabeth Dole (minus 14).

JULY 29
IRAQI SITUATION

Interviewing Date: 7/24–26/92
Survey #GO 322010

Turning to the situation in the Middle East, if Iraq refuses to allow United Nations inspectors access to Iraqi buildings—as specified by the terms of the UN resolutions which ended the Gulf War—would you favor or oppose the use of military action, including air strikes, against Iraq by the United States and its allies?

Favor 70%
Oppose.......................................24
No opinion...................................6

More generally, would you favor or oppose having U.S. forces resume military action against Iraq to force Saddam Hussein from power?

Favor 67%
Oppose.......................................28
No opinion...................................5

Selected National Trend

	Favor	*Oppose*	*No opinion*
1992			
February 6–9	62%	35%	3%
1991			
April 18–19	51	43	6
March 14–15	57	38	5

Note: Americans solidly support the idea of the resumption of military force against Iraq if terms of the 1991 Gulf War cease-fire are not met. More generally, two thirds support the use of U.S. military action to force Iraqi President Saddam Hussein from power, the highest level of anti-Saddam sentiment measured since the war.

When asked about the possibility of military action against Iraq if that country refuses to allow UN inspectors access to Iraqi buildings, as specified in the terms of the Gulf War cease-fire, seven out of ten (70%) would favor such action if access is not granted; 24% would not. Iraqi officials have announced that they will allow inspectors into the buildings, but questions continue to arise about Iraq's compliance with other aspects of the cease-fire.

President George Bush, concerned with his reelection chances, has been emphasizing his foreign policy background and the Iraqi situation in recent speeches. The poll results suggest that Bush is on firm ground. The high level of support for the removal of Saddam, however, indicates that there is some political risk in calling attention to the Iraqi leader's presence—the unfinished business of the Gulf War.

AUGUST 2
PRESIDENTIAL TRIAL HEAT: THE GENDER GAP

Interviewing Date: 7/24–26/92
Survey #GO 322010

Asked of registered voters: Suppose the 1992 presidential election were being held today. If George Bush were the Republican candidate and Bill Clinton were the Democratic candidate, whom would you vote for? [Those who were undecided were asked: As of today, do you lean more to Bush, the Republican, or to Clinton, the Democrat?]

	Clinton	*Bush*	*Undecided; other*
By Sex			
Male	54%	39%	7%
Female	58	33	9
By Education			
College–Male	46	48	6
College–Female	57	34	9

No College–Male	62	30	8
No College–Female	59	32	9

*Also asked of registered voters: In politics, as of today, do you consider yourself a Republican, a Democrat, or an independent? [Those who were undecided were asked: As of today, do you lean more to the Democratic party or to the Republican party?]**

	Republican/lean Republican	Democratic/lean Democratic
By Sex		
Male	40%	53%
Female	33	55
By Education		
College–Male	51	43
College–Female	39	52
No College–Male	31	62
No College–Female	30	59

*The percentage of those who identify with neither party is omitted.

Interviewing Date: 1/3–6/92
Survey #GO 222034

Asked of registered voters: We'd like to know which issues you think are important for the presidential candidates to discuss and debate in the 1992 campaign. As I read a list of issues, please rate each as very important, somewhat important, not too important, or not at all important:

Those Replying "Very Important"

	College–Male	College–Female	Gender gap
Abortion	24%	44%	+20
Poverty; homelessness	63	78	+15
Race relations	39	52	+13
Health care	68	80	+12
Unemployment	74	85	+11
Crime	66	76	+10
Taxes	58	67	+9
AIDS	59	67	+8
Drugs; drug abuse	68	76	+8
National defense	32	37	+5
Economy	92	95	+3
Education	86	89	+3
Environment	58	61	+3
Foreign affairs	33	34	+1
Federal budget deficit	80	79	-1
Foreign trade	59	47	-12

Interviewing Date: 5/18–20/92
Survey #GO 222053

Asked of registered voters: Please tell me whether you have a favorable or unfavorable opinion of Supreme Court Justice Clarence Thomas:

	Favorable	Unfavorable	Heard of; no opinion*
By Education			
College–Male	55%	26%	17%
College–Female	37	46	14
No College–Male	49	27	17
No College–Female	37	27	25

*"Never heard of" is omitted.

Interviewing date: 7/23–24/92*
Special Survey

Asked of registered voters: Do you think abortions should be legal under any circumstances, legal only under certain circumstances, or illegal in all circumstances?

	Legal, any	Legal, certain	Illegal, all**
By Education			
College–Male	46%	47%	7%
College–Female	47	39	12
No College–Male	22	50	25
No College–Female	26	55	15

*Gallup survey for *Newsweek*
**"No opinion" is omitted.

Note: If the Democrats are to recapture the White House this November, they must maintain an advantage among women. The most recent Gallup Poll, taken one week after the Democratic party's national convention, shows Bill Clinton with a 25-percentage point lead over George Bush among women voters (58% versus 33%). Clinton's margin is cut to 15 points among men (54% versus 39%).

Since 1980, when a so-called gender gap in support for Republican presidential candidate Ronald Reagan was first noted, Democratic presidential candidates have had more success with female voters than male voters. But in the last three elections, Democratic candidates Jimmy Carter, Walter Mondale, and Michael Dukakis failed to exploit the GOP gender gap, and in the end the vote was not close enough for gender differences in candidate support to affect the outcome.

The size of Clinton's margin in postconvention polls, however, does not guarantee that the Democratic ticket will win the female vote in November. Four years ago at this time, Dukakis had as big a lead among women as Clinton does today (58% to 34% in a Gallup Poll taken in July 1988). Gallup's final 1988 preelection poll, however, showed Dukakis losing the women's vote to Bush by a 4-point margin.

A gender gap in political attitudes has only been apparent since the early 1980s. Throughout his presidency, Reagan consistently scored higher approval ratings among men than women. These differences were not evident for Reagan's predecessors, as Gallup approval ratings from Dwight Eisenhower through Carter show little variation in opinion by gender. President Bush, who promised a "kinder, gentler" America during the 1988 campaign, has had a smaller gender gap in his job performance ratings than Reagan. For much of this campaign year, women voters have supported Bush in preelection polls at about the same rate as men.

The gender gap seen in the most recent Gallup Poll occurs only among college-educated voters. Women with at least some college training favor Clinton over Bush by 23 percentage points (57% to 34%), while college men divide their vote about equally between Clinton (46%) and Bush (48%). Among noncollege voters, however, there is little variation in candidate support by gender: Clinton leads by 27 points among women and 32 points among men.

These gender differences in candidate preference reflect underlying partisanship differences. College-educated women call themselves Democrats more often than they identify with the Republican party (52% versus 39%). College-educated men, however, more often report Republican rather than Democratic leanings (51% versus 43%). Men and women without college training do not differ significantly in their party allegiance.

Now that economic issues are no longer working to the Republicans' advantage, the Democrats are in a strong position to win votes from college-educated women on the basis of social issues, including abortion. Like their male counterparts, college women consider the economy to be the key issue in this year's presidential race, but they are much less narrowly focused on that issue than college males. Specifically, a Gallup Poll taken in January found college women rating five issues significantly higher in importance than did college men: abortion (44% versus 24%), poverty and homelessness (78% versus 63%), race relations (52% versus 39%), health care (80% versus 68%), and unemployment (85% versus 74%).

On the issue of abortion, college men and women are equally likely to take a pro-choice position. For example, a Gallup Poll for *Newsweek* in July shows 46% of college men and 47% of college women expressing the view that abortion should be legal under any circumstances. While sharing similar opinions on abortion, college women rate the issue much higher in terms of their presidential vote than do college men.

In their primary campaigns Democratic Senate candidates Carol Moseley Braun in Illinois and Lynn Yeakel in Pennsylvania made an issue of the Clarence Thomas-Anita Hill hearings and no doubt will continue to do so in the fall. At the presidential level, however, the Thomas-Hill hearings do not seem to have energized women voters the way the abortion decision has, although the hearings appear to have affected college women differently than other Americans. A May Gallup survey found a plurality of college women (46%) expressing an unfavorable opinion of Supreme Court Justice Thomas, while men and noncollege-educated women tended to have favorable views of Thomas.

AUGUST 2
ABORTION: BY POLITICS

Interviewing Date: 7/17–18/92
Survey #GO 322005

Asked of registered voters: Regardless of which presidential candidate you support, please tell me whether you think George Bush or Bill Clinton would better handle the abortion issue:

	Republican/lean Republican	*Democrat/lean Democratic*
Bush	50%	9%
Clinton	31	75
Same; neither (volunteered)	4	2
No opinion	15	14

InterviewingDate: 1/6–9/92
Survey #GO 222035

Asked of registered voters: Would you be more likely or less likely to vote for a presidential candidate who favored making abortion illegal, except in cases of rape, incest, and when the woman's life is in danger, or would it not make much difference?

	Republican/lean Republican	*Democrat/lean Democratic*
More likely	49%	40%
Less likely	42	50
Not much difference	7	8
No opinion	2	2

Note: While many Republican voters disagree with George Bush on abortion, 1992 Gallup surveys show that abortion is not so divisive an issue among rank-and-file Republicans that it is likely to cause serious defections from the Bush-Quayle ticket. To the average Republican, abortion is simply not that relevant to his or her presidential vote. A Gallup Poll taken earlier this year found only one third of Republicans saying that abortion should be a very important issue in the presidential campaign, compared with two fifths of Democrats. When presented with a list of sixteen major issues, Republicans rated abortion last in importance.

As this month's GOP national convention approaches, Republican pro-choice activists are seeking to publicize their efforts to change the party's platform from its uncompromising pro-life position of four years ago. When Gallup tested how Republicans respond to the president's own position on the issue—that abortion should be legal only in cases of rape, incest, and when a woman's life is in danger—a larger percentage said that they would be more likely to support a candidate taking Bush's position than said it made their support less likely (49% versus 42%).

This 49% support hardly represents a ringing endorsement of the president's abortion stand within his party. Other Gallup abortion measures indicate that most Republicans are not eager to change the country's laws that have given women access to legal abortion since the 1973 *Roe v. Wade* decision. A June poll found six in ten Republican-oriented voters (58%) saying that they oppose changing the laws in order to make it more difficult for a woman to get an abortion.

While rank-and-file Republicans generally do not embrace the agenda of the pro-life movement, it does not follow that they are in total agreement with GOP pro-choice groups on the issue. Like the public as a whole, Republicans tend to take a middle position on abortion, avoiding the extremes usually associated with activists on both sides of the issue. A Gallup survey in January found 56% of Republicans and GOP leaners saying that abortion should be legal only under certain circumstances. Three in ten (27%) took a strong pro-choice position ("legal under any circumstances"), while one half as many (12%) took a strong pro-life position ("illegal in all circumstances").

By supporting legal abortion in only a few extreme cases, Bush can keep his pro-life supporters content while still attempting to appeal to those with a middle position on abortion. Within his party, it is not women per se who are most likely to have problems with his abortion position. Instead, it is younger and better educated Republicans and those who live in the eastern or western states.

A Gallup Poll taken immediately after the Democratic national convention found that nearly one third of Republican voters (31%) said that Bill Clinton, who is campaigning as a pro-choice candidate, would handle the abortion issue better than Bush. Yet analysis of that same poll does not suggest that abortion is a major factor motivating Republicans to defect to Clinton. What most separates Bush defectors from loyalists within the GOP is their level of unhappiness with the president over the issues of the economy, taxes, and, somewhat surprisingly, family values.

AUGUST 4
FOREIGN POLICY

Interviewing Date: 7/31–8/2/92
Survey #GO 322011

Would you like to see James Baker step down as secretary of state to run George Bush's campaign for reelection, or not?

Yes....................19%
No....................44
No opinion....................37

	Yes	*No*	*No opinion*
By Politics			
Republicans	27%	44%	29%
Democrats	15	47	38
Independents	16	41	43

If Baker were to step down as secretary of state, how serious a setback do you think it would be for U.S. diplomatic efforts in the Middle East—very serious, somewhat serious, not too serious, or not at all serious?

Very serious....................19%
Somewhat serious....................37
Not too serious....................19
Not at all serious....................11
No opinion....................14

	Very, somewhat serious	*Not too, not at all serious*	*No opinion*
By Politics			
Republicans	58%	29%	13%
Democrats	56	31	13
Independents	53	32	15

*Last year, Saddam Hussein withdrew from Kuwait but he remains in power in Iraq. Do you think this was a victory for U.S. and allied forces in the Persian Gulf region, or not?**

Yes....................25%
No....................69
No opinion....................6

Selected National Trend

	Yes	*No*	*No opinion*
1991			
April 18–19	36%	55%	9%
April 4–5	46	45	9
March 14–15	55	38	7
March 1	29	68	3
February 22	29	68	3
February 1	37	60	3

*The wording of the question changes in 1992 from that used in earlier surveys: "Do you agree or disagree with the following statement: If Saddam Hussein withdraws from Kuwait but remains in power in Iraq, that will be a victory for the U.S. and allied forces."

If Saddam Hussein again fails to comply with United Nations cease-fire resolutions, do you think the United States should:

Take no military action?....................14%
Take military action to force Saddam to comply with the resolutions?....................11

Take military action to force Saddam to comply with the resolutions and remove him from power in Iraq?............69
No opinion..6

Have you heard or read about international efforts to provide relief supplies to Sarajevo and other cities in the former Yugoslavian republic of Bosnia?

Yes..62%
No..36
No opinion..2

If Serbian forces continue to block relief efforts to Sarajevo, do you think the United States should take the lead in seeking United Nations-backed air strikes against the Serbians, or not?

Yes..35%
No..45
No opinion......................................20

Note: By holding onto power in Iraq, Saddam Hussein is seriously hampering George Bush's ability to capitalize politically on his administration's major foreign policy triumph: last year's Gulf War victory. A just-completed Gallup Poll finds only one quarter of Americans (25%) saying that the Gulf War's outcome—Iraq driven from Kuwait, but Saddam still in power—should be considered a success for the United States and its allies; seven in ten (69%) say that it should not be regarded as a success.

When Gallup asked this question for *Newsweek* in March 1991, at the end of the Gulf War, a majority (55%) considered the war a success. By April of last year, however, as Saddam crushed the Kurdish rebellion in Iraq, the proportion of those who viewed the outcome as an unqualified success fell to 36%.

If President Bush decides to resume military action against Iraq, there is a clear mandate to oust Saddam from power. If the Iraqi leader again fails to comply with UN resolutions, two thirds of Americans (69%) say that the United States should continue the fighting until he is overthrown.

On another foreign policy front, the current Gallup survey shows that the American public generally does not favor a more aggressive stance by the United States in Yugoslavia, as Bill Clinton and others critical of administration policy have proposed. By a margin of 45% to 35% the public opposes our taking the lead in seeking United Nations-backed air strikes against the Serbians if they continue to block relief efforts to Sarajevo.

With these tensions in foreign policy, the poll indicates that the president risks damaging himself politically if he asks Jim Baker to step down as secretary of state to run the Bush-Quayle campaign. The Baker move, expected by many Washington insiders, would not play well with the public. Only one in five (19%) say that they would like to see Baker leave State to head Bush's reelection effort; 44% oppose this move, while 37% offer no opinion.

Even Republicans, who would seem to have the most at stake, are not inclined to approve of Baker's stepping down from State. By a margin of 44% to 27% self-described Republicans do not favor a switch in posts for Baker. Moreover, American diplomatic efforts in the Middle East are expected to suffer if the Baker move takes place. A majority overall (56%) and a similar majority of Republicans (58%) think that the loss of Baker would be a very or somewhat serious setback for U.S. diplomacy.

AUGUST 4
PRESIDENT BUSH/PRESIDENTIAL TRIAL HEAT/CONGRESS

Interviewing Date: 7/31–8/2/92
Survey #GO 322011

Do you approve or disapprove of the way George Bush is handling his job as president?

Approve..29%
Disapprove......................................60
No opinion......................................11

	Approve	*Dis-approve*	*No opinion*
By Sex			
Male	30%	60%	10%
Female	28	60	12

By Ethnic Background			
White	31	58	11
Nonwhite	16	70	14
Black	12	75	13
By Education			
College Graduate	31	62	7
College Incomplete	35	57	8
No College	26	60	14
By Region			
East	25	66	9
Midwest	29	60	11
South	34	55	11
West	29	59	12
By Age			
18–29 Years	31	56	13
30–49 Years	33	58	9
50 Years and Over	25	63	12
By Household Income			
$50,000 and Over	36	58	6
$30,000–$49,999	32	60	8
$20,000–$29,999	32	57	11
Under $20,000	22	66	12
By Politics			
Republicans	57	32	11
Democrats	12	82	6
Independents	27	57	16
By Political Ideology			
Liberal	16	76	8
Moderate	25	65	10
Conservative	44	47	9

Selected National Trend

	Approve	Dis-approve	No opinion
1992			
July 24–26	32%	59%	9%
June 26–30	38	55	7
June 12–14	37	55	8
June 4–8	37	56	7
May 18–20	41	52	7
May 7–10	40	53	7
April 20–22	42	48	10
April 9–12	39	54	7

Asked of registered voters: Suppose the 1992 presidential election were being held today. If George Bush were the Republican candidate and Bill Clinton were the Democratic candidate, whom would you vote for? [Those who were undecided were asked: As of today, do you lean more to Bush, the Republican, or to Clinton, the Democrat?]

Bush	32%
Clinton	57
Undecided; other	11

Selected National Trend

	Bush	Clinton	Undecided; other
1992			
July 24–26	36%	56%	8%
July 17–18	34	56	10
July 6–8*	48	40	12
June 26–30*	44	41	14
June 12–14*	45	37	18
June 4–8	46	40	14
May 18–20	50	39	11
May 7–10	45	40	15
April 20–22	50	34	16
April 9–12	48	41	11
March 31–April 1	54	34	12
March 26–29	54	38	8
March 20–22	52	43	5
March 11–12	50	44	6
February 19–20	53	43	4
February 6–9	53	38	9

*Perot voters assigned to the candidate named as their second choice

Also asked of registered voters: If the elections for Congress were being held today, which party's candidate would you vote for in your congressional district—the Democratic party's candidate or the Republican party's candidate? [Those who were undecided were asked: As of today, do you lean more to the Democratic party's candidate or to the Republican party's candidate?]

Democratic candidate	56%
Republican candidate	36
Undecided; other	8

Selected National Trend

	Democratic candidate	*Republican candidate*	*Undecided; other*
April 1992	47%	44%	9%
August 1990	47	46	7
May 1988	52	37	11
July 1986	54	40	6
April 1984	52	42	6
September 1982	53	35	12
June 1980	54	39	7
July 1978	50	36	14

Note: George Bush's standing with the American people, already at an all-time low, falls even further in the latest Gallup Poll. Only 29% now approve of the way that he is handling his presidential duties. Since Gallup first asked the public to rate the chief executive's job performance, only three presidents have ever scored below 30%: Jimmy Carter, Richard Nixon, and Harry Truman. None was able to recover politically.

The president's eroding popularity may spell trouble for congressional Republicans as well as for the top of the ticket. Democratic candidates are now preferred over GOP candidates for Congress by a 20-point margin, 56% to 36%. A Gallup Poll taken in April, when Bush approval stood at 42%, had the race for Congress about even: 47% of voters preferred the Democrats, 44% the Republicans.

Despite his campaign's recent offensive, Bush has been unable to cut into Bill Clinton's big lead. The post-Democratic national convention "bounce" shows no signs of fading. Clinton's current 25-point margin (57% versus 32%) is comparable to his 22-point margin (56% versus 34%) in a poll taken two weeks ago, immediately after the convention. Last week's poll showed a 20-point lead for the Arkansas governor.

Should Clinton's lead hold, he is likely to have "coattails" on which other Democratic candidates might ride to victory in November. The Democrats have reason to be optimistic about their chances for maintaining their majority in Congress, despite redistricting changes that are expected to help the Republicans.

The potential for Clinton coattails is strongly evident in the poll results. If the election were held today, 56% of registered voters say that they would support the Democratic candidate for Congress in their district, while 36% would support the Republican. This 20-point advantage in the Gallup survey is the largest lead held by congressional Democrats at this point in the campaign since 1982, when a September poll showed the Democrats with an 18-point advantage (53% to 35%). In that off-year election, the Democrats made major gains in the House of Representatives and won twenty-six seats.

AUGUST 9
BILL CLINTON: A COMPARISON OF HIS LEAD

Size of Leading Candidate's Margin*
(Between the Conventions)

	Lead	*Loss from early lead*	*Election outcome*
Johnson (1964)	+36	-13	Won
Nixon (1972)	+26	-3	Won
Clinton (1992)	+25	?	?
Carter (1976)	+22	-20	Won
Reagan (1980)	+16	-6	Won
Nixon (1968)	+16	-15	Won
Reagan (1984)	+11	-7	Won
Dukakis (1988)	+7	-14	Lost
Kennedy (1960)	+6	-5	Won

*Insufficient data for Truman

Presidential Approval Ratings
(Drop from High to Low Point)

	High point	*Low point*	*Point change*	*Time span*
Truman	87%	23%	-64	6yr5mo
Bush	89	29	-60	1yr5mo
Carter	75	28	-47	3yr3mo
Johnson	79	35	-44	4yr5mo
Nixon	67	24	-43	1yr6mo
Ford	71	37	-34	5mo
Reagan	67	35	-33	1yr8mo
Eisenhower	79	48	-31	2yr4mo
Kennedy	83	56	-27	2yr4mo

Presidential Approval Ratings*
(In Election Year)

	Average	Percent of vote	Election outcome
Johnson (1964)	74%	61%	Won
Eisenhower (1956)	73	57	Won
Nixon (1972)	56	61	Won
Reagan (1984)	55	59	Won
Ford (1976)	48	48	Lost
Carter (1980)	41	41	Lost
Bush (1992)	40**	?	?

*Insufficient data for Truman; not applicable for Kennedy
**Bush average based on January through July 1992

Note: Bill Clinton's 25-point lead over President George Bush is one of the largest on record at this point in a presidential election race. Only one previous candidate—incumbent Lyndon Johnson—enjoyed a significantly larger advantage over his opponent in a Gallup survey taken between the two national party conventions. Johnson led Barry Goldwater, his GOP rival, by 36 points at this time in 1964. Clinton's current 57%-to-32% advantage over Bush is almost identical to incumbent Richard Nixon's 57%-to-31% margin (26 points) over George McGovern in August 1972.

To overcome Clinton's lead, Bush would have to pull off the greatest comeback of any presidential candidate since World War II. The president should benefit from his party's upcoming convention, since Gallup postconvention polls show an average 6-point increase in support for presidential candidates, but Bush will need far more than a typical postconvention bounce to close the gap with Clinton.

Thus far, Gerald Ford's 20-point comeback in 1976 represents the greatest swing in support between the convention and the November election. But Ford's impressive comeback fell short; despite his gains, Jimmy Carter's 22-point lead prior to the Republican convention proved insurmountable.

The only presidential candidate since 1960 who was ahead at this point in a campaign, but failed to win, was Michael Dukakis in 1988. His 17-point lead over George Bush in a Gallup Poll taken immediately after his party's convention is often cited as evidence of the unreliability of convention-period surveys. Two weeks after the convention, however, Bush had already cut the Dukakis lead to 7 points (49% to 42% in an early August poll). Now, Clinton's postconvention lead over the same time frame has remained stable.

Bush's low approval ratings throughout 1992 do much to explain Clinton's huge edge in the polls. Since the 1950s no president with an average approval rating under 50% has been reelected. To date, Bush has a 40% average approval rating for the year. Unless he makes a dramatic recovery, that number is likely to fall further.

Ford, who was able to climb back into contention against Carter, had significantly higher ratings in 1976—averaging 48% for the year—than Bush has today. Ford's average rating mirrored his percentage of the popular vote that year. Since Dwight Eisenhower, no president's share of the popular vote has exceeded his average approval rating during the election year by more than 5 percentage points.

President Bush's loss of popularity since the Gulf War victory is unprecedented. Only Harry Truman had a larger gap between his high and low points of public approval, but Truman's fall from his high of 87% at the end of World War II to 23% during the Korean War occurred over a span of more than six years. Bush's fall to 29% this past weekend, from a high of 89% after the Gulf War, took less than a year and one half.

AUGUST 14
SEXUAL EQUALITY AT THE BEACH

Interviewing Date: 7/31–8/2/92
Survey #GO 322011

Do you think women should be permitted to sunbathe topless on public beaches, if they choose to, or do you think topless sunbathing on public beaches should be banned?

Permitted	33%
Banned	63
No opinion	4

	Permitted	Banned	No opinion
By Sex			
Male	50%	45%	5%
Female	18	79	3

Asked of those who replied "banned": What is the main reason why you think it should be banned:

On moral or religious grounds?................28%
Because it puts women at risk of sexual harassment?........................11
Because families, children, and other people who use public beaches may feel uncomfortable?..........50
Other (volunteered)..............................10
No opinion..1

	Moral grounds	Sexual harass-ment	Feel uncom-fortable*
By Sex			
Male	28%	14%	50%
Female	29	10	50

*"Other" and "no opinion" are omitted.

Some people have proposed designating certain public beaches where women would be permitted to sunbathe topless while banning topless sunbathing on all other public beaches. Would you favor or oppose this proposal that would limit topless sunbathing to certain public beaches?

Favor..58%
Oppose..38
No opinion..4

	Favor	Oppose	No opinion
By Sex			
Male	63%	32%	5%
Female	52	44	4

Asked of women: Would you, yourself, consider sunbathing topless on a public beach if it were allowed?

Yes..6%
No..92
No opinion..2

	Yes	No	No opinion
By Age			
18–29 Years	11%	86%	3%
30–49 Years	10	90	*
50 Years and Over	1	97	2

*Less than 1%

Note: A recent court decision in New York may allow women to go topless on that state's public beaches. However, according to a new Gallup Poll, the women of America do not seem to be clamoring for the right to bare their chests in public.

While their motives may be suspect, men are the strongest proponents of giving women the right to go topless at the beach. The poll finds that 50% of men, compared with only 18% of women, believe that women should be permitted to sunbathe topless in public.

Both men and women who oppose topless beaches say that they do so with the interests of other beachgoers in mind. Fifty percent of opponents think that topless women make others uncomfortable, particularly families and children. Fewer (28%) explain their opposition to this form of public nudity on moral or religious grounds, while one in ten (11%) believes that it puts women at risk of sexual harassment.

For the women challenging New York State's ban on toplessness, the issue is sex discrimination. On this basis they also oppose compromise legislation that would restrict toplessness for women to designated beaches unless, of course, the restriction applies equally to men.

The public at large seems amenable to the compromise proposal. While one third (33%) generally supports legalization of topless sunbathing, many more would do so (58%) if the law confined the practice to designated beaches (52% of women, 63% of men).

Segregation of topless women to certain beaches satisfies most of those whose main objection is the discomfort of others, but it does little to change the minds of those who oppose the practice for religious or moral reasons. Moreover, while going topless may be de rigueur in Europe, it is still anathema to most American women. Only 6% of all women polled (11% of those under age 30) would themselves consider sunbathing topless on a public beach if it were allowed.

AUGUST 16
PRESIDENT BUSH/PRESIDENTIAL TRIAL HEAT/PRESIDENTIAL CANDIDATES

Interviewing Date: 8/10–12/92*
Survey #GO 322012

Asked of registered voters: Do you approve or disapprove of the way George Bush is handling his job as president?

Approve	35%
Disapprove	58
No opinion	7

Selected National Trend

	Approve	Dis-approve	No opinion
1992			
July 31–August 2	29%	60%	11%
July 24–26	32	59	9
June 26–30	38	55	7
June 12–14	37	55	8
June 4–8	37	56	7

Also asked of registered voters: Suppose the 1992 presidential election were being held today. If George Bush were the Republican candidate and Bill Clinton were the Democratic candidate, whom would you vote for? [Those who were undecided were asked: As of today, do you lean more to Bush, the Republican, or to Clinton, the Democrat?]

Bush	37%
Clinton	56
Undecided; other	7

*Gallup survey for CNN/*USA Today*

Selected National Trend

	Bush	Clinton	Undecided; other
1992			
July 31–August 2	32%	57%	11%
July 24–26	36	56	8
July 17–18	34	56	10
July 6–8*	48	40	12

*Perot voters assigned to the candidate named as their second choice

Asked of those who support George Bush or Bill Clinton: Do you support the Bush-Quayle or Clinton-Gore ticket strongly or only moderately?

	Bush-Quayle	Clinton-Gore
Strongly	37%	44%
Moderately	63	56

Asked of registered voters: Please tell me whether you have a favorable or unfavorable opinion of each of the following presidential and vice presidential candidates:

George Bush?

	August 10–12	July 6–8
Favorable	43%	49%
Unfavorable	51	45
No opinion	6	6

Dan Quayle?

	August 10–12	July 17–18
Favorable	32%	33%
Unfavorable	59	58
No opinion	9	9

Bill Clinton?

	August 10–12	July 6–8
Favorable	57%	41%
Unfavorable	34	49
No opinion	9	10

Al Gore?

	August 10–12	July 6–8
Favorable	62%	39%
Unfavorable	20	17
No opinion	18	44*

*Includes "never heard of"

Also asked of registered voters: Is there any chance that you will vote for George Bush in November, or is there no chance whatsoever that you will vote for him?

	No chance
Registered voters	47%

Selected National Trend

	No chance
1992	
July 17–18	46%
July 6–8	46
June 26–30	43
June 12–14	45
May 18–20	48

Also asked of registered voters: If George Bush is reelected in November, do you think the country will be better off or worse off four years from now?

	August 10–12	January
Better	31%	42%
Worse	50	43
Same (volunteered)	8	6
No opinion	11	9

Also asked of registered voters: How do you think our national security has been affected by George Bush's policies—do you think the United States is a lot more secure, somewhat more secure, somewhat less secure, or a lot less secure?

A lot more secure	17%
Somewhat more secure	40
Somewhat less secure	23
A lot less secure	13
No opinion	7

Also asked of registered voters: Does having Dan Quayle as his running mate make you more likely to vote for George Bush in November, less likely, or will it not have much effect on your vote?

More likely	6%
Less likely	25
Not much effect	68
No opinion	1

Selected National Trend

	More likely	Less likely	Not much effect	No opinion
1992				
May 18–20	12%	26%	61%	1%
January	11	19	69	1
1991				
September	9	16	71	4

Also asked of registered voters: Regardless of which presidential candidate you support, please tell me whether you think George Bush or Bill Clinton would better handle each of the following issues:

Foreign affairs?

Bush	62%
Clinton	30
Same; neither (volunteered)	2
No opinion	6

Selected National Trend

	Bush	Clinton	Same; neither	No opinion
1992				
July 17–18	64%	25%	3%	8%
March 20–22	70	22	*	8

*Less than 1%

Family values?

Bush	41%
Clinton	48
Same; neither (volunteered)	3
No opinion	8

Crime and drugs?

Bush	35%
Clinton	51
Same; neither (volunteered)	5
No opinion	9

Economy?

Bush	30%
Clinton	60
Same; neither (volunteered)	3
No opinion	7

Selected National Trend

	Bush	Clinton	Same; neither	No opinion
1992				
July 17–18	24%	58%	9%	9%
March 20–22	37	49	2	12

AIDS?

Bush	24%
Clinton	56
Same; neither (volunteered)	7
No opinion	13

Also asked of registered voters: At its convention later this month, do you think the Republican party should take a position opposed to legal abortion, in favor of legal abortion, or should the party take no position on the abortion issue?

	Total	Republicans voters only
Opposed	25%	38%
In favor	32	22
Take no position	36	36
No opinion	7	4

Also asked of registered voters: Which do you think is the better way to bring about the changes this country needs—change Congress from Democratic to Republican control, or change from a Republican to a Democratic president?

Change Congress	34%
Change president	45
Both (volunteered)	4
No opinion	17

Also asked of registered voters: From what you have heard, read, or remember about the following former presidents, please tell me whether you approve or disapprove of the way each handled his job as president:

Jimmy Carter?

Approve	50%
Disapprove	43
No opinion	7

Selected National Trend

	Approve	Dis-approve	No opinion
June 1992	48%	46%	6%
November 1990	45	52	3

Ronald Reagan?

Approve	48%
Disapprove	49
No opinion	3

Selected National Trend

	Approve	Dis-approve	No opinion
June 1992	50%	47%	3%
November 1990	54	44	2

Note: James Baker takes over President George Bush's reelection campaign faced with a 19-percentage point deficit. A Gallup Poll completed as Baker's move to the White House became official shows Bill Clinton leading Bush by a margin of 56% to 37%

Baker helped to orchestrate Bush's comeback against Michael Dukakis four years ago. Dukakis led by 17 points after the Democratic national convention, but two weeks later his lead already had shrunk to 7 points. This year, Clinton's lead has shown little erosion between the conventions.

The challenge for Baker now is of similar magnitude to the task he faced in 1976 as manager of President Gerald Ford's campaign.

Ford closed the 22-point gap between the conventions to 2 points but nonetheless lost the election to Jimmy Carter.

The new poll provides at least one hopeful sign for Bush and Baker: a modest improvement in the president's approval rating (to 35%), which had fallen below 30% in a Gallup survey released one week ago. If Bush is to win reelection, his approval rating must improve significantly. No president since Harry Truman has won reelection with an approval rating under 50%. For example, at this juncture in 1980, Carter's approval rating had fallen to 32%.

Bush can expect some improvement in his standing against Clinton after the GOP convention. Only twice in recent history has a candidate failed to get a postconvention bounce: Hubert Humphrey in 1968 and George McGovern in 1972. It may be difficult, however, for Bush to achieve a substantial bounce this time. Fewer than one half (43%) say that they have a favorable opinion of Bush, compared with 51% at this point in 1988. Nearly one half (47%) now say that there is no chance they will vote for Bush in November, compared with 38% in a poll between the conventions four years ago. And Clinton's supporters are more likely than Dukakis's voters of four years ago to feel strongly about their choice for president. In other findings from the poll, Dan Quayle is viewed unfavorably by six out of every ten voters (59%), while 25% say that he makes them less likely to vote for the Republican ticket.

The key issue driving this year's election so far has been the economy, and Clinton leads Bush by a 2-to-1 margin as the candidate better able to handle the economy (60% versus 30%). The president now trails Clinton as better able to deal with crime and drugs (35% versus 51%) and on family values (41% versus 48%), both themes that Republicans can be expected to press hard. By contrast, Bush holds a 2-to-1 margin over Clinton as the candidate better able to handle foreign affairs (62% versus 30%), thus making foreign policy the only dimension tested on which Bush beats Clinton. Additionally, 57% say that Bush's policies have made the United States more secure, while 36% say that they have made this country less secure.

One additional finding: President Reagan, who will address the Republican convention on Monday night, now gets a less favorable retrospective job approval rating than Carter, the man he defeated in 1980. Reagan receives 48% approval, 49% disapproval compared with Carter's 50% approval, 43% disapproval.

AUGUST 19
PRESIDENTIAL TRIAL HEAT/ IRAQI SITUATION

Interviewing Date: 8/17/92*
Survey #GO 322016

Asked of registered voters: Suppose the 1992 presidential election were being held today. If George Bush were the Republican candidate and Bill Clinton were the Democratic candidate, whom would you vote for? [Those who were undecided were asked: As of today, do you lean more to Bush, the Republican, or to Clinton, the Democrat?]

Bush	35%
Clinton	58%
Undecided; other	7

Also asked of registered voters: If Saddam Hussein again fails to comply with United Nations cease-fire resolutions, do you think the United States should:

	Aug. 17	*Jul. 31– Aug. 2*
Take no military action?	14%	14%
Take military action to force Saddam to comply with the resolutions?	13	11
Take military action to force Saddam to comply with the resolutions and remove him from power in Iraq?	62	69
No opinion	11	6

*Gallup survey for CNN/*USA Today*

Also asked of registered voters: If George Bush orders military action against Iraq this week, do you think helping his own reelection chances will be:

His main reason for taking military action?	14%
One of his reasons for taking military action?	32
Not one of his reasons for taking military action?	44
No opinion	10

Also asked of registered voters: In general, do you think George Bush would take his own reelection needs into account when making decisions about whether to use force against Iraq, or not?

Yes	48%
No	42
No opinion	10

Also asked of registered voters: If George Bush orders military action that results in Saddam Hussein being removed from power, would you be more likely to vote for Bush, less likely to vote for him, or would it not have much effect on your vote?

More likely	12%
Less likely	6
Not much effect	79
No opinion	3

Also asked of registered voters: If George Bush orders military action that forces Iraq to comply with UN resolutions but does not result in Saddam Hussein being removed from power, would you be more likely to vote for Bush, less likely to vote for him, or would it not have much effect on your vote?

More likely	2%
Less likely	10
Not much effect	83
No opinion	5

Note: If President George Bush orders military action against Iraq, many voters will suspect that his actions are politically motivated. According to a Gallup Poll conducted as the Republican national convention got under way in Houston, nearly one half of voters (46%) would see a new move against Iraq at least partly as an attempt to boost Bush's reelection chances. Overall, 32% think that election-year politics would be one of the factors behind the president's decision, while 14% think that politics would be the major factor.

Voters overwhelmingly say that they would support going back into Iraq militarily, provided that one of the objectives is to remove Saddam Hussein from power. Six in ten (62%) reply that if Iraq again fails to comply with UN resolutions, the United States should take action beyond enforcing the resolutions and overthrow the Iraqi leader. In contrast, only 13% would favor military action that stops short of ousting Saddam; 14% would favor no military action at all.

The poll suggests that the political risks are high if the president decides that new attacks on Iraq are warranted. Even if the military action succeeded in taking out Saddam, only 12% of voters overall say that this would improve their chances of voting for Bush's reelection (6% would be less likely to vote for Bush, while 79% say that it would not affect their vote). And if the military effort did not result in Saddam's ouster, only 2% would be more likely to vote for Bush, while 10% would be less likely to support him.

AUGUST 25
PRESIDENT BUSH/PRESIDENTIAL TRIAL HEAT/PRESIDENTIAL CANDIDATES

Interviewing Date: 8/21–22/92*
Survey #GO 322013

Asked of registered voters: Do you approve or disapprove of the way George Bush is handling his job as president?

*Gallup survey conducted for CNN/*USA Today*

Approve	40%
Disapprove	54
No opinion	6

Selected National Trend

	Approve	Disapprove	No opinion
1992			
August 8–10	35%	58%	7%
July 31–August 2	29	60	11
July 24–26	32	59	9
June 26–30	38	55	7
June 12–14	37	55	8

Also asked of registered voters: Suppose the 1992 presidential election were being held today. If George Bush were the Republican candidate and Bill Clinton were the Democratic candidate, whom would you vote for? [Those who were undecided were asked: As of today, do you lean more to Bush, the Republican, or to Clinton, the Democrat?]

Bush	42%
Clinton	52
Undecided; other	6

Selected National Trend

	Bush	Clinton	Undecided; other
1992			
August 17	35%	58%	7%
August 8–10	37	56	7
July 31–August 2	32	57	11
July 24–26	36	56	8
July 17–18	34	56	10
July 6–8*	48	40	12

*Perot voters assigned to the candidate named as their second choice

Also asked of registered voters: Please tell me whether you have a favorable or unfavorable opinion of each of the following presidential and vice presidential candidates:

George Bush?

	August 21–22	August 10–12
Favorable	50%	43%
Unfavorable	47	51
No opinion	3	6

Dan Quayle?

	August 21–22	August 10–12
Favorable	40%	32%
Unfavorable	52	59
No opinion	8	9

Bill Clinton?

	August 21–22	August 10–12
Favorable	57%	57%
Unfavorable	37	34
No opinion	6	9

Al Gore?

	August 21–22	August 10–12
Favorable	60%	62%
Unfavorable	23	20
No opinion	17	18

Also asked of registered voters: From what you have seen or heard about the wives of the presidential candidates, please tell me whether you have a favorable or an unfavorable opinion of each:

Barbara Bush?

	August 21–22	August 17
Favorable	81%	69%
Unfavorable	12	10
No opinion	7	21

Hillary Clinton?

	August 21–22	July 17–18
Favorable	56%	51%
Unfavorable	26	24
No opinion	18	25

Also asked of registered voters: If the elections for Congress were being held today, which party's candidate would you vote for in your congressional district—the Democratic party's candidate or the Republican party's candidate? [Those who were undecided were asked: As of today, do you lean more to the Democratic party's candidate or to the Republican party's candidate?]

	August 21–22	August 10–12
Democratic candidate	50%	56%
Republican candidate	45	36
Undecided; other	5	8

Also asked of registered voters: Which do you think is the better way to bring about the changes this country needs—change Congress from Democratic to Republican control, or change from a Republican to a Democratic president?

	August 21–22	August 10–12
Change Congress	39%	34%
Change president	41	45
Both (volunteered)	4	4
No opinion	16	17

Also asked of registered voters: From whatever you saw or heard about the Republican convention, is your opinion of the Republican party more favorable or less favorable?

	August 1992	August 1988
More favorable	35%	43%
Less favorable	41	26
No change (volunteered)	18	20
No opinion	6	11

Also asked of registered voters: From what you saw or heard about George Bush's speech at the convention, is your opinion of Bush more favorable or less favorable?

More favorable	39%
Less favorable	35
No change (volunteered)	16
No opinion	10

Also asked of registered voters: Regardless of which presidential candidate you support, please tell me whether you think George Bush or Bill Clinton would better handle each of the following issues:

Foreign affairs?

	August 21–22	August 10–12
Bush	73%	62%
Clinton	19	30
No opinion	8	8

Family values?

	August 21–22	August 10–12
Bush	54%	41%
Clinton	33	48
No opinion	13	11

Taxes?

	August 21–22	July 17–18
Bush	43%	30%
Clinton	46	49
No opinion	11	21

Economy?

	August 21–22	August 10–12
Bush	37%	30%
Clinton	52	60
No opinion	11	10

Federal budget deficit?

Bush	37%
Clinton	47
No opinion	16

Abortion?

	August 21–22	July 17–18
Bush	36%	26%
Clinton	49	56
No opinion	15	18

Health care?

	August 21–22	*July 17–18*
Bush	33%	20%
Clinton	54	62
No opinion	13	18

Note: President George Bush received a 5-point bounce from last week's Republican national convention but still trails Arkansas Governor Bill Clinton by 10 points. A Gallup Poll following the GOP's four days in the media spotlight shows Clinton leading Bush by 52% to 42%. In a Gallup survey completed the week before the convention, Clinton held a 19-point lead, 56% to 37%.

An analysis of Gallup Polls from the last seven presidential elections indicates that candidates almost always register an increase in support immediately after their party's convention. By historical standards, Bush's bounce is about average; the typical postconvention bounce in Gallup surveys taken between 1960 and 1988 is 6 points.

In the aftermath of Houston, the president wins higher ratings on virtually every survey trend measure. His approval rating is up 5 points, to 40%. In addition, more voters now have a favorable than an unfavorable opinion of the president (50% versus 47%), a reversal of his preconvention favorability ratings (43% favorable versus 51% unfavorable). Moreover, Bush has improved his standing relative to Clinton on major campaign issues, ranging from a low of 7 points (the economy) to a high of 13 points (taxes, family values, health care).

Dan Quayle, whose acceptance speech generally received positive marks, now may be less of a liability for Bush. The vice president's favorability ratings are still negative (40% favorable versus 52% unfavorable) but less so than before the convention (32% favorable versus 59% unfavorable).

The new poll suggests that the major themes of the convention made an impact with the voters. Before this week, for example, Clinton had an edge over Bush as the candidate better for family values. Bush now leads by 54% to 33% on this issue.

The Republican attacks on the Democratic Congress also appear to have paid off. A congressional trial heat taken before the convention showed Democratic candidates leading by 20 percentage points; now, that lead has been cut to 5 points. And now as many voters say electing a Republican Congress is the better way to bring about change as say it would be better to elect a Democratic president (39% versus 41%).

The Republicans also regained some ground they had lost on the tax issue, which had been a key to their electoral success over the past two decades. Prior to the convention, voters preferred Clinton over Bush on the issue of taxes by a margin of 49% to 30%. Now the two candidates are in a virtual standoff on taxes (Bush 43%, Clinton 46%). In addition, voters currently are more apt to see Clinton as the candidate likely to raise their taxes.

Despite the gains registered by Bush and the Republicans in the poll, the GOP convention was not all good news for the president. Unlike the Democratic national convention in New York in July, this convention receives mixed reviews at best from the broader electorate. A Gallup/*Newsweek* Poll taken on August 21 finds more voters saying that their image of the GOP was hurt by the convention than say that the convention improved their image of the party (41% versus 35%). The president's acceptance speech, seen as critical going into the convention, also receives lackluster ratings; 39% say that the speech made them feel more favorable toward Bush, while 35% reply less favorable.

After a week of criticism by Republicans, Clinton's image with the voters seems unaffected. The poll finds voters' opinions on Clinton dividing 57% favorable versus 37% unfavorable—almost no change from his preconvention ratings (57% favorable versus 34% unfavorable). Moreover, voters are no more likely to say that they question Clinton's ability to serve as president because of the draft evasion allegations, or to consider Clinton dishonest, than they were one week ago. As for Hillary Clinton, the *Newsweek* Poll found her favorability ratings unchanged (56% favorable, 26% unfavorable), despite several days of "Hillary-bashing."

SEPTEMBER 5
PRESIDENTIAL TRIAL HEAT/PRESIDENTIAL CANDIDATES/PRESIDENT BUSH

Interviewing Date: 8/31–9/2/92*
Survey #GO 322015

Asked of registered voters: Suppose the 1992 presidential election were being held today. If George Bush were the Republican candidate and Bill Clinton were the Democratic candidate, whom would you vote for? [Those who were undecided were asked: As of today, do you lean more to Bush, the Republican, or to Clinton, the Democrat?]

Bush 39%
Clinton 54
Undecided; other 7

	Bush	Clinton	Undecided; other
By Sex			
Male	41%	53%	6%
Female	37	55	8
By Ethnic Background			
White	43	51	6
Nonwhite	13	80	7
Black	8	87	5
By Education			
College Graduate	41	53	6
College Incomplete	45	50	5
No College	36	56	8
By Region			
East	32	59	9
Midwest	41	52	7
South	41	54	5
West	43	49	8
By Age			
18–29 Years	38	58	4
30–49 Years	39	53	8
50 Years and Over	40	53	7
By Household Income			
$50,000 and Over	47	48	5
$30,000–$49,999	43	50	7
$20,000–$29,999	37	55	8
Under $20,000	31	64	5
By Politics			
Republicans	82	14	4
Democrats	9	89	2
Independents	35	51	14
By Political Ideology			
Liberal	15	78	7
Moderate	33	60	7
Conservative	60	35	5

*Gallup survey for CNN/*USA Today*

Selected National Trend

	Bush	Clinton	Undecided; other
1992			
August 21–22	42%	52%	6%
August 17	35	58	7
August 8–10	37	56	7
July 31–August 2	32	57	11
July 24–26	36	56	8
July 17–18	34	56	10
July 6–8*	48	40	12

*Perot voters assigned to the candidate named as their second choice

Also asked of registered voters: Is there any chance that you will vote for George Bush in November, or is there no chance whatsoever that you will vote for him?

Current supporters 39%
Potential voters 15
No chance 46

Also asked of registered voters: Is there any chance that you will vote for Bill Clinton in November, or is there no chance whatsoever that you will vote for him?

Current supporters 54%
Potential voters 14
No chance 32

Also asked of registered voters: Please tell me whether you have a favorable or unfavorable opinion of each of the following presidential candidates:

George Bush?

Favorable	45%
Unfavorable	49
No opinion	6

	Favorable	Unfavorable	No opinion
By Sex			
Male	47%	49%	4%
Female	42	50	8
By Ethnic Background			
White	47	48	5
Nonwhite	22	68	10
Black	14	78	8
By Education			
College Graduate	46	51	3
College Incomplete	47	49	4
No College	43	49	8
By Region			
East	38	53	9
Midwest	46	50	4
South	50	45	5
West	44	51	5
By Age			
18–29 Years	38	54	8
30–49 Years	45	52	3
50 Years and Over	47	46	7
By Household Income			
$50,000 and Over	51	46	3
$30,000–$49,999	48	50	2
$20,000–$29,999	43	51	6
Under $20,000	37	54	9
By Politics			
Republicans	83	13	4
Democrats	18	77	5
Independents	41	51	8
By Political Ideology			
Liberal	18	78	4
Moderate	40	55	5
Conservative	64	31	5

Selected National Trend

	Favorable	Unfavorable	No opinion
1992			
August 21–22	50%	47%	3%
August 10–12	43	51	6
July 17–18	40	53	7
July 6–8	49	45	6
June 26–30	44	50	6
June 12–14	44	51	5
May 18–20	48	47	5
April 20–22	55	41	4
April 9–12	48	44	8
March 26–29	49	44	7
March 20–22	57	40	3
March 11–12	57	38	5
February 28–March 1	53	44	3
January 31–February 2	56	41	3
January 3–6	53	45	2

Bill Clinton?

Favorable	57%
Unfavorable	37
No opinion	6

	Favorable	Unfavorable	No opinion
By Sex			
Male	54%	40%	6%
Female	60	34	6
By Ethnic Background			
White	55	39	6
Nonwhite	72	17	11
Black	79	11	10
By Education			
College Graduate	55	40	5
College Incomplete	54	40	6
No College	59	34	7
By Region			
East	59	33	8
Midwest	59	36	5
South	57	36	7
West	51	44	5

By Age			
18–29 Years	61	34	5
30–49 Years	58	38	4
50 Years and Over	54	37	9
By Household Income			
$50,000 and Over	51	44	5
$30,000–$49,999	53	44	3
$20,000–$29,999	59	33	8
Under $20,000	66	26	8
By Politics			
Republicans	23	70	7
Democrats	84	11	5
Independents	57	36	7
By Political Ideology			
Liberal	73	20	7
Moderate	65	29	6
Conservative	39	56	5

Selected National Trend

	Favorable	*Unfavor-able*	*No opinion*
1992			
August 21–22	57%	37%	6%
August 10–12	57	34	9
July 17–18	63	25	12
July 6–8	41	49	10
June 26–30	45	43	12
June 12–14	41	47	12
May 18–20	42	48	10
April 20–22	42	49	9
April 9–12	34	47	19
March 26–29	37	40	23

Also asked of registered voters: Do you approve or disapprove of the way George Bush is handling his job as president?

Approve....................39%
Disapprove....................54
No opinion....................7

	Approve	*Dis-approve*	*No opinion*
By Sex			
Male	40%	54%	6%
Female	38	54	8
By Ethnic Background			
White	43	51	6
Nonwhite	19	72	9
Black	14	79	7
By Education			
College Graduate	38	59	3
College Incomplete	42	51	7
No College	39	53	8
By Region			
East	33	59	8
Midwest	43	51	6
South	44	51	5
West	38	54	8
By Age			
18–29 Years	39	52	9
30–49 Years	40	55	5
50 Years and Over	39	54	7
By Household Income			
$50,000 and Over	45	54	1
$30,000–$49,999	46	52	2
$20,000–$29,999	42	55	3
Under $20,000	34	61	5
By Politics			
Republicans	79	19	2
Democrats	14	83	3
Independents	37	58	5
By Political Ideology			
Liberal	19	80	1
Moderate	35	62	3
Conservative	59	38	3

Selected National Trend

	Approve	*Dis-approve*	*No opinion*
1992			
August 21–22	40%	54%	6%
August 10–12	35	58	7
July 31–August 2	29	60	11
July 24–26	32	59	9
June 26–30	38	55	7
June 12–14	37	55	8
June 4–8	37	56	7
May 18–20	41	52	7
May 7–10	40	53	7

Presidential Trial Heats
(Labor Day)

	Challenger	*Incumbent*
1992	Clinton 54%	Bush 39%
1984	Mondale 37	Reagan 56
1980	Reagan 39	Carter 39
1976	Carter 51	Ford 36
1972	McGovern 30	Nixon 64
1964	Goldwater 29	Johnson 65
1956	Stevenson 41	Eisenhower 52
1948	Dewey 47	Truman 39
1944	Dewey 49	Roosevelt 51
1940	Willkie 45	Roosevelt 55

Note: At a time when George Bush needs to build momentum, Bill Clinton is picking up votes and securing a formidable lead. A new Gallup Poll shows that Bush's support has actually fallen 3 points since the Republican national convention, thus giving Clinton a 15-point lead, 54% to 39%.

History suggests that Clinton's advantage over Bush will close in the coming weeks, but the president faces an uphill battle in the weeks ahead. Only two sitting presidents have trailed a challenger in a Gallup survey at this time in the election year. In early September 1976, President Gerald Ford was 15 points behind Jimmy Carter. At the same period in 1948, President Harry Truman trailed Thomas Dewey by 8 points.

However, no candidate as far behind as Bush at this stage of the race has ever come back to win. While Truman made a dramatic comeback to defeat Dewey, and Ford rallied from behind to finish within 2 points of Carter, Gallup election trends show that, by September, support for both presidents was on the rise. By contrast, Bush's campaign did not gain momentum during the convention period; he was unable to match Clinton's convention success or parlay his own 5-point convention "bounce" into further gains.

Evidence of Clinton's strength is found in his broad base of support. His double-digit lead over Bush holds up with nearly all groups of voters: men and women, whites (close at 8%), blacks and Hispanics, young and old, and most regions of the country. Bush runs best in the West (43% versus Clinton's 49%) and among people in upper-income households (47% versus 48%).

Nearly one half of the electorate (46%) say that there is no chance they will vote for Bush in November. This leaves only 15% not already committed to voting for Bush who say that there is some chance they will cast their ballots for him. In order to win, Bush needs to convert twelve out of these fifteen potential voters. By contrast, only one in three (32%) say that there is no chance they will vote for Clinton.

Bush's prospects of surmounting the deficit are dimmed by two other poll findings. First, while Clinton enjoys a high ratio of favorable-to-unfavorable ratings (57% versus 37%), Bush's tilt negative (45% favorable, 49% unfavorable). Second, approval of the way that Bush is handling his job as president (39%) is also ominously low. Successful incumbent presidential candidates have had job approval ratings of 50% or more in their year of reelection with just one exception—Harry Truman, who had ratings of 36% and 39% in the only two Gallup approval measures of the 1948 election year.

SEPTEMBER 6
PRESIDENTIAL TRIAL HEAT: OLDER VOTERS

Interviewing Date: January–June 1992
Various Surveys

In politics, as of today, do you consider yourself a Republican, a Democrat, or an independent?

	Total	*Voters age 18–64*	*Voters age 65 and over*
Republican	29%	29%	33%
Democrat	38	37	43
Independent	33	34	24

Interviewing Date: 8/21–28/92
Survey #GO 322014; 322015

Asked of registered voters: If the presidential election were being held today, would you vote for the Republican ticket of George Bush and Dan Quayle or for the Democratic ticket of Bill Clinton and Al Gore? [Those who were undecided were asked: As of today, do you lean more to Bush and Quayle, the Republicans, or to Clinton and Gore, the Democrats?]

	Bush-Quayle	Clinton-Gore	Undecided; other
Total			
Post-GOP Convention	41%	51%	8%
Pre-GOP Convention	35	56	9
By Voters Age 18–64			
Post-GOP Convention	41	51	8
Pre-GOP Convention	37	56	7
By Voters Age 65 and Over			
Post-GOP Convention	38	53	9
Pre-GOP Convention	33	55	12

Interviewing Date: July–August 1992
Five Surveys Conducted between the Democratic and Republican National Conventions

Asked of registered voters: Do you approve or disapprove of the way George Bush is handling his job as president?

	Total	Age 18–64	Age 65 and over
Approve	33%	34%	29%
Disapprove	60	60	62
No opinion	7	6	9

Interviewing Date: 1/3–9/92
Survey #GO 222034

Asked of registered voters: We'd like to know which issues you think are important for the presidential candidates to discuss and debate in the 1992 campaign. As I read a list of issues, please rate each as very important, somewhat important, not too important, or not at all important:

	Those Saying "Very Important" Age 18–64	Age 65 and over
Foreign trade	51%	68%
Crime	75	86
Drugs; drug abuse	75	86
National defense	41	52
Unemployment	82	92
Race relations	46	52
Foreign affairs	35	42
Taxes	69	75
Health care	79	84
Federal budget deficit	78	82
AIDS	66	70
Education	88	84
Environment	60	56
Abortion	37	40
Economy	93	92
Poverty; homelessness	76	76

Note: Arkansas Governor Bill Clinton is the early favorite in the battle for the senior vote. Gallup test elections conducted in late August, after the Republican national convention, show Clinton with a 15-point lead over President George Bush among voters age 65 and over (53% versus 38%). Older voters may prove critical to the Democrats' chances of recapturing the White House, as the same polls show a smaller lead for Clinton (10 points) among voters under 65.

This week, as Clinton campaigned among seniors in the South, he used a familiar Democratic weapon to try to win their votes: raising concern that the Republicans are planning to cut old-age benefits. Based on a University of North Carolina study, the Clinton campaign claims that the Bush health plan would seriously reduce Medicare and Medicaid benefits to the elderly.

The Clinton campaign's broadside against the president's health-care proposals recalls a similar attack on Paul Tsongas's economic plan during the Florida Democratic primary. The charges that Tsongas would target Social Security benefits in an effort to reduce the deficit seemed to have the intended effect. Exit polls showed that solid support among retirees helped Clinton defeat Tsongas in Florida.

For years, seniors have demonstrated political clout beyond their numbers in the population. While low voting rates among young people give political candidates reason to disregard their views, seniors' strong track record of voter participation ensures that their opinions are heard. Indeed, voter turnout among seniors is even higher today than it was twenty years ago, according to the U.S. Bureau of the Census. And in the 1988 presidential election, seven in ten seniors reported voting.

By comparison, fewer than four in ten voting-age adults under age 30 cast their ballots.

The generation of Americans who are now 65 years old or more and who grew up during the Great Depression came of age politically during Franklin Roosevelt's New Deal. Their Democratic roots are evident to this day in their party preferences: the Democrats have a 10-point edge over the GOP among seniors (43% versus 33%).

Four years ago, Gallup's final preelection poll showed Bush and Michael Dukakis dividing the over-65 vote, 50% to 50%. However, given his approval ratings among the elderly, the president will be fortunate to do as well this November. Throughout 1992, Gallup has found Bush approval among seniors to be a few points lower than the overall ratings. In the period between the national political conventions, when Bush approval slipped to 33% overall, it dropped to 29% among voters over age 65.

Like younger voters, seniors put economic concerns at the top of their list of important campaign issues. Nine in ten rate the economy (92%) and unemployment (92%) as very important. Unlike younger voters, however, seniors rate crime (86%) and drugs (86%) second in importance only to economic issues. Also included in their top tier are health care (84%), education (84%), and the federal budget deficit (82%).

The one issue on which senior voters differ most from younger voters is foreign trade. Two thirds of seniors (68%), compared with only one half of those under age 65 (51%), say that foreign trade should be a very important campaign issue. Previous Gallup surveys have shown the older generation to be more protectionist and isolationist. This group also scores high on anti-Japan sentiment, perhaps as a reflection of their memory of that country as a World War II adversary.

SEPTEMBER 13
KEY CAMPAIGN ISSUES

Interviewing Date: 8/31–9/2/92*
Survey #GO 322015

*Gallup survey for CNN/*USA Today*

Asked of registered voters: We'd like to know which issues you think are important for the presidential candidates to discuss and debate in the 1992 campaign. As I read a list of issues, please rate each as very important, somewhat important, not too important, or not at all important:

Economy?

Very important	89%
Somewhat important	9
Not too, not at all important	2
No opinion	*

*Less than 1%

	Very impor-tant	*Some-what important*	*Not too, not at all impor-tant**
By Politics			
Republicans	87%	10%	3%
Democrats	88	9	2
Independents	91	8	1

*"No opinion" is omitted.

Education?

Very important	84%
Somewhat important	14
Not too, not at all important	2
No opinion	*

*Less than 1%

	Very impor-tant	*Some-what important*	*Not too, not at all impor-tant**
By Politics			
Republicans	79%	19%	2%
Democrats	92	8	**
Independents	80	17	3

*"No opinion" is omitted.
**Less than 1%

Federal budget deficit?

Very important 77%
Somewhat important 18
Not too, not at all important..................3
No opinion..2

	Very important	Somewhat important	Not too, not at all important*
By Politics			
Republicans	76%	21%	3%
Democrats	75	18	4
Independents	79	16	4

*"No opinion" is omitted.

Health care?

Very important 75%
Somewhat important 20
Not too, not at all important..................4
No opinion..1

	Very important	Somewhat important	Not too, not at all important*
By Politics			
Republicans	64%	29%	7%
Democrats	84	13	2
Independents	75	21	4

*"No opinion" is omitted.

Taxes?

Very important 69%
Somewhat important 25
Not too, not at all important..................5
No opinion..1

	Very important	Somewhat important	Not too, not at all important*
By Politics			
Republicans	69%	26%	4%
Democrats	73	21	4
Independents	63	30	7

*"No opinion" is omitted.

Environment?

Very important 62%
Somewhat important 32
Not too, not at all important..................5
No opinion..1

	Very important	Somewhat important	Not too, not at all important*
By Politics			
Republicans	51%	44%	4%
Democrats	70	25	3
Independents	62	30	7

*"No opinion" is omitted.

Family values?

Very important 52%
Somewhat important 28
Not too, not at all important..................19
No opinion..1

	Very important	Somewhat important	Not too, not at all important*
By Politics			
Republicans	61%	27%	12%
Democrats	50	28	20
Independents	47	28	23

*"No opinion" is omitted.

Foreign affairs?

Very important 42%
Somewhat important 42
Not too, not at all important..................14
No opinion..2

	Very important	Somewhat important	Not too, not at all important*
By Politics			
Republicans	52%	35%	12%
Democrats	40	42	15
Independents	37	47	15

*"No opinion" is omitted.

Abortion?

Very important	38%
Somewhat important	28
Not too, not at all important	31
No opinion	3

	Very important	*Somewhat important*	*Not too, not at all important**
By Politics			
Republicans	36%	25%	35%
Democrats	47	23	27
Independents	32	35	30

*"No opinion" is omitted.

Regardless of which presidential candidate you support, please tell me whether you think George Bush or Bill Clinton would better handle each of the following issues:

Health care?

Bush	27%
Clinton	62
Same; neither; no opinion	11

Environment?

Bush	30%
Clinton	58
Same; neither; no opinion	12

Federal budget deficit?

Bush	32%
Clinton	53
Same; neither; no opinion	15

Abortion?

Bush	32%
Clinton	52
Same; neither; no opinion	16

Economy?

Bush	34%
Clinton	55
Same; neither; no opinion	11

Education?

Bush	35%
Clinton	54
Same; neither; no opinion	11

Taxes?

Bush	38%
Clinton	50
Same; neither; no opinion	12

Family values?

Bush	47%
Clinton	38
Same; neither; no opinion	15

Foreign affairs?

Bush	67%
Clinton	24
Same; neither; no opinion	9

Handling of Issues as a Predictor of Vote

	Better by preferred candidate	*Better by other candidate*
Economy	83%	8%
Taxes	82	9
Education	81	11
Federal budget deficit	77	10
Health care	76	15
Family values	73	14
Environment	74	16
Abortion	69	17
Foreign affairs	62	31

Note: In a year when every measure of voter interest shows that the economy is the number one issue, the successful candidate will be the man who convinces voters that, as president, he can do something about it. Themes that fueled Ross Perot's bid for the presidency last spring now seem to be working for Bill Clinton. Voters pick Clinton by a substantial margin over Bush (55% versus 34%) as the candidate better able to handle the economy.

While Clinton is selected as the candidate better able to handle a number of key issues, his advantage on the economy is most critical. An analysis of Gallup data shows that voter perceptions of the candidates on pocketbook issues—the economy and taxes—are more closely related to candidate preference than are their perceptions of Bush and Clinton on other domestic issues and foreign policy. Eighty-three percent of those who now have a preference in the presidential race plan to vote for the candidate whom they see as better able to handle the economy. Similarly, 82% prefer their chosen candidate as better on taxes.

Issues that correlate less strongly with voting preference are the federal budget deficit, health care, family values, and the environment; roughly 75% of voters plan to choose the candidate whom they see as better able to handle each of these. The issues least predictive of voting choice are abortion and foreign affairs.

Although abortion has received the major share of attention from the media and politicians this year, education proves to be far more important to the voting public. It is rated very important as an issue for the candidates to discuss by 84% of the voters, with abortion by just 38%. And while 81% of registered voters say that they will vote for the candidate who can better handle education, only 69% plan to vote for the candidate whom they pick as better on abortion.

Despite voters' selection of Clinton as the candidate more likely to raise their taxes, he is also chosen as the candidate who would better handle taxes, with a 12-point lead over Bush on this critical issue (50% versus 38%). While only seven in ten voters (69%) say that taxes is a very important issue, there is a strong correlation between their perception of the candidates on taxes and their vote. Four out of five (82%) plan to vote for the candidate who they say would better handle taxes.

SEPTEMBER 17
MOST IMPORTANT PROBLEM

Interviewing Date: 8/28–9/2/92*
Survey #GO 322015

*Gallup survey for CNN/*USA Today*

*What do you think is the most important problem facing this country today?**

	Aug.– Sept. 1992	*March 1992*
Economic problems		
Economy in general	37%	42%
Unemployment	27	25
Federal budget deficit	9	8
Trade deficit	2	4
Cost of living; inflation	2	2
Recession	1	3
High interest rates	**	1
Other	3	3
Noneconomic problems		
Poverty; homelessness	13	15
Health care	12	12
Education	10	8
Crime	7	5
Dissatisfaction with government	7	8
Ethics, moral decline	6	5
Drugs; drug abuse	6	8
Taxes	3	6
Environment	3	3
Too much money spent overseas	3	–
Abortion	3	–
International situation	3	3
Medicare increases	2	2
Gulf War crisis	2	1
AIDS	1	3
Fear of war	1	1
Other	16	2
No opinion	3	2

*Total adds to more than 100% due to multiple replies.
**Less than 1%

Note: In a recent Gallup Poll, close to seven out of ten Americans cite the economy in general, or a specific economic concern, as the most important problem facing the country. And among noneconomic concerns, the human toll of a weak economy tops the list: poverty and homelessness is named by 13% as the nation's number one problem.

Respondents express their economic discontent slightly differently than they did in the spring. More people now cite unemployment than did so earlier (27% today versus 25% in March). Fewer people, however, now mention a recession (1% versus 3%).

Over one half of those who cite an economic concern say that the economy in general is the top problem (37%). More specific aspects mentioned include unemployment (27%), the federal budget deficit (9%), and the trade deficit (2%). In the past, when people expressed concern about the economy, they had a specific problem in mind: unemployment, inflation, the federal budget deficit. Now, most people do not focus on any specific problem but instead cite the economy as a whole. In any case, economic problems have been the major concern of Americans in every election year since 1972, when the Vietnam War topped the list.

Issues receiving greater coverage in this election year have become more salient to the public. Those citing health care as the most important problem have gone from 6% in January to 12% in March, which equals the current figure, while more modest gains have been registered since March by education (8% to 10%) and the deficit (8% to 9%).

One issue debated by the presidential candidates in 1988 has received relatively little attention this year. Mention of drugs as the top problem has actually declined somewhat. Drug abuse was mentioned by 8% of respondents in March but by only 6% in the recent poll. The issue peaked as a public concern in 1989, when President George Bush launched his "war on drugs." In November of that year, drug abuse was cited by 39% as the nation's top problem.

SEPTEMBER 19
PRESIDENTIAL TRIAL HEAT/PRESIDENTIAL CANDIDATES

Interviewing Date: 9/11–15/92*
Survey #GO 322018

Asked of registered voters: If the presidential election were being held today, would you vote for the Republican ticket of George Bush and Dan Quayle or for the Democratic ticket of Bill Clinton and Al Gore? [Those who were undecided were asked: As of today, do you lean more to Bush and Quayle, the Republicans, or to Clinton and Gore, the Democrats?]

*Gallup survey for CNN/*USA Today*

Bush-Quayle	42%
Clinton-Gore	51
Undecided; other	7

	Bush-Quayle	*Clinton-Gore*	*Undecided; other*
By Sex			
Male	46%	47%	7%
Female	38	54	8
By Ethnic Background			
White	47	46	7
Nonwhite	15	78	7
Black	11	81	8
By Education			
College Graduate	45	50	5
College Incomplete	46	46	8
No College	40	53	7
By Region			
East	40	53	7
Midwest	44	47	9
South	43	52	5
West	42	51	7
By Age			
18–29 Years	43	51	6
30–49 Years	41	53	6
50 Years and Over	43	48	9
By Household Income			
$50,000 and Over	51	43	6
$30,000–$49,999	48	46	6
$20,000–$29,999	39	55	6
Under $20,000	34	61	5
By Politics			
Republicans	85	10	5
Democrats	8	86	6
Independents	39	50	11

By Political Ideology

Liberal	17	79	4
Moderate	37	55	8
Conservative	61	34	5

Also asked of registered voters: Do you think Bill Clinton has the honesty and integrity to serve as president, or not?

Yes	62%
No	29
No opinion	9

Selected National Trend

	Yes	No	No opinion
August 21–22	70%	24%	6%
July 17–18	69	24	7
July 6–8	56	36	8

Also asked of registered voters: Do the allegations about Bill Clinton's draft status during the Vietnam War make you seriously doubt his ability to serve as commander in chief, or not?

Yes	22%
No	72
No opinion	6

Also asked of registered voters: Are you satisfied with Bill Clinton's explanation of his draft status during the Vietnam War, or not?

Yes	60%
No	30
No opinion	10

Also asked of registered voters: Regardless of which presidential candidate you support, please tell me whether you think George Bush or Bill Clinton would better handle each of the following issues:

Foreign affairs?

Bush	73%
Clinton	20
Same; neither (volunteered)	1
No opinion	6

Selected National Trend

	Bush	Clinton	Same; neither	No opinion
1992				
Aug. 31–Sept. 2	67%	24%	3%	6%
Aug. 21–22	73	19	2	6
Aug. 10–12	62	30	2	6
July 17–18	64	25	3	8
Mar. 20–22	70	22	*	8

*Less than 1%

Economy?

Bush	36%
Clinton	52
Same; neither (volunteered)	5
No opinion	7

Selected National Trend

	Bush	Clinton	Same; neither	No opinion
1992				
Aug. 31–Sept. 2	34%	55%	4%	7%
Aug. 21–22	37	52	5	6
Aug. 10–12	30	60	3	7
July 17–18	24	58	9	9
Apr. 20–22	43	36	10	11
Mar. 20–22	37	49	2	12

Taxes?

Bush	42%
Clinton	47
Same; neither (volunteered)	5
No opinion	6

Selected National Trend

	Bush	Clinton	Same; neither	No opinion
1992				
Aug. 31–Sept. 2	38%	50%	5%	7%
Aug. 21–22	43	46	4	7
July 17–18	30	49	9	12
Mar. 20–22	38	47	1	14

Also asked of registered voters: As I read some phrases, please tell me whether you think each one better describes George Bush or Bill Clinton:

Can bring about the changes this country needs?

Bush 31%
Clinton....................................51
Same (volunteered).......................2
Neither (volunteered)......................12
No opinion..................................4

Selected National Trend

	Bush	Clinton	Same; neither	No opinion
1992				
Aug. 31–Sept. 2	30%	56%	9%	5%
Aug. 21–22	36	51	8	5
Aug. 10–12	27	57	11	5

Shares your values?

Bush 44%
Clinton....................................42
Same (volunteered).......................3
Neither (volunteered)......................6
No opinion..................................5

Selected National Trend

	Bush	Clinton	Same; neither	No opinion
1992				
Aug. 31–Sept. 2	42%	45%	8%	5%
Aug. 21–22	44	43	8	5

Can be trusted?

Bush 33%
Clinton....................................41
Same (volunteered).......................3
Neither (volunteered)......................17
No opinion..................................6

Stands up to special-interest groups?

Bush 42%
Clinton....................................37
Same (volunteered).......................3
Neither (volunteered)......................8
No opinion..................................10

Note: The latest Gallup results show the Clinton-Gore ticket ahead by a margin of 51% to 42% over the Bush-Quayle ticket. Earlier this month, George Bush's lead over Bill Clinton was 15 points, 54% to 39%. However, since August, voters have become less inclined to say that the Arkansas governor has the honesty and integrity to serve as president (70% versus 62% today).

Changes in candidate support by demographic groups suggest that the controversy over Clinton's draft status during the Vietnam War may be hurting him. Voters who have shifted their support most toward Bush in the past two weeks tend to be white, male, and between the ages of 50 to 64. Moreover, the gender gap has reemerged. The race is now about even among men (47% Clinton-Gore versus 46% Bush-Quayle), while the Clinton-Gore ticket has a big lead among women (54% versus 38%).

While the draft issue may have helped Bush close the gap, the new poll suggests that Clinton may be able to avoid further damage. Six in ten voters (60%) say that they are satisfied with his explanation of this matter. Relatively few voters (22%) say that the allegations about draft evasion make them seriously doubt Clinton's ability to serve as commander in chief.

The Democratic nominee continues to hold a big edge on the key campaign issues in 1992: the economy and change. Voters prefer him over Bush on the economy by 52% to 36%, and Clinton is identified as the candidate better able to bring about needed change by a margin of 51% to 31%.

SEPTEMBER 20
PRESIDENTIAL CHALLENGERS

Interviewing Date: 9/11–15/92*
Survey #GO 322018

*Gallup survey for CNN/*USA Today*

Standing in September Polls and Election Outcome
(Ranked by Size of Challenger's Lead)

	Challenger	Incumbent	Challenger's standing, Sept.	Outcome
1976	Carter	Ford	+11	Won
1992	Clinton	Bush	+9	?
1948	Dewey	Truman	+8	Lost
1980	Reagan	Carter	±0	Won
1956	Stevenson	Eisenhower	-11	Lost
1984	Mondale	Reagan	-19	Lost
1972	McGovern	Nixon	-28	Lost
1964	Goldwater	Johnson	-30	Lost

Note: Bill Clinton is the first Democratic presidential candidate since Jimmy Carter to hold a significant lead in the Gallup Poll at this point in the race. Clinton's 9-point lead over President George Bush (51% versus 42%) is similar to the 11-point edge (51% versus 40%) that Carter enjoyed over another Republican incumbent, Gerald Ford, in September 1976.

History suggests, however, that Clinton's supporters should not be too quick to claim victory with more than six weeks of campaigning still to go. In 1976, Carter's early lead diminished as the Ford campaign, with Jim Baker at the helm, successfully raised doubts about the former Georgia governor, who was little known to most voters. Carter ended up winning the national popular vote by only 2 percentage points. If two states in which Carter eked out narrow victories—Ohio and Hawaii—had gone Republican instead, then Ford would have won an electoral majority.

The only other presidential challenger in the postwar era to lead in a September Gallup survey was Republican Thomas Dewey. Harry Truman's comeback victory over Dewey in 1948 (the most dramatic political upset in recent history) has been a source of inspiration for President Bush and his campaign this year. The Gallup Poll showed Dewey with an 8-point lead in mid-September 1948 (47% versus 39%). In that November, however, Truman captured the popular vote by 4 percentage points.

Ronald Reagan, the challenger who won by the biggest margin in a postwar presidential election, had no lead at all in September 1980. At that time he was tied, 39% to 39%, with then-incumbent Carter. Independent candidate John Anderson received 14% in that same poll, identical to the support level seen in polls today for inactive presidential candidate Ross Perot.

These three past presidential elections, in which challengers ran competitive races against incumbents, might be expected to foreshadow the outcome of this year's race, but the results of the 1980, 1976, and 1948 elections were starkly different. Thus, in assessing Clinton's chances to become the third presidential challenger of the postwar era to win the White House, one must answer the following question: Will 1992 have more in common with 1980, 1976, or 1984?

As in 1980, economic problems have fueled widespread discontent among the voters. Twelve years ago Reagan asked: "Are you better off than you were four years ago?" and voters replied with a resounding "no." Today, polls find a majority of voters taking the same view.

Analysis of historical data suggests that an incumbent's share of the vote in an election will not exceed his approval rating by more than 5 percentage points. Thus, if Bush ends up with a 40% approval rating for the year, this indicates that he will not win more than 45% of the vote in November. (Carter's approval rating averaged 41% in 1976, and he received 41% of the vote that year.) Unless Perot becomes an active candidate or makes a surprisingly strong showing as an inactive one (Anderson received close to 7% in 1980), Clinton then would be assured of at least 50% of the vote.

In 1976 voters' lack of familiarity with Carter—like Clinton, a governor of a small state with low name recognition at the beginning of the election year—gave Ford's campaign an opportunity to exploit uncertainties about turning over the White House to a newcomer. Many political observers think that if the campaign had lasted another week, Ford would have won.

This year the Bush campaign has attempted to push the issues of trust and character to the forefront. Recent polling suggests that voters' doubts about Clinton's honesty and trustworthiness have increased somewhat in the past week. While Clinton managed during the early primaries to overcome the negative publicity from charges about marital infidelity, marijuana use, and draft avoidance, many say that he remains vulnerable on this front.

Despite Clinton's vulnerabilities, it will be more difficult for the Bush campaign to close the gap by raising doubts about their opponent than it was for the Ford campaign. President Bush is significantly less popular with the public than his predecessor was in 1976. Ford's approval ratings averaged 48% in 1976; his favorability ratings equalled Carter's.

The consistency of Clinton's lead in polls since July is nonetheless no guarantee of victory in November. Dewey led Truman in every Gallup Poll taken in 1948, and his lead in mid-September was almost identical to Clinton's today. (Unfortunately, Gallup does not have sufficient data on presidential approval for that year to compare Truman's ratings then with Bush's today.)

The 1948 campaign shows that a Bush comeback is not out of the question, and the Republicans' success in recent presidential elections suggests that Clinton's current lead in the polls may not hold up. In losing five of the last six presidential elections, the vote for Democratic candidates has averaged 43%. In that period, no Democrat received more than 50% (Carter in 1976). Most recently, Michael Dukakis received close to 46% in 1988.

These figures suggest that a significant bloc of voters has habitually supported Republican candidates for president, even though the GOP remains the minority party. As the election draws closer, some of these voters now leaning to Clinton are likely to reconsider their votes. They hold the key to whether George Bush can be the Harry Truman of 1992.

SEPTEMBER 23
PRESIDENT BUSH/PRESIDENTIAL TRIAL HEAT

Interviewing Date: 9/17–20/92
Survey #GO 322019

Do you approve or disapprove of the way George Bush is handling his job as president?

Approve	36%
Disapprove	54
No opinion	10

	Approve	*Disapprove*	*No opinion*
By Sex			
Male	39%	52%	9%
Female	34	56	10
By Ethnic Background			
White	38	52	10
Nonwhite	25	66	9
Black	17	76	7
By Education			
College Graduate	42	51	7
College Incomplete	29	64	7
No College	37	52	11
By Region			
East	38	55	7
Midwest	33	56	11
South	35	53	12
West	40	52	8
By Age			
18–29 Years	29	64	7
30–49 Years	42	48	10
50 Years and Over	35	55	10
By Household Income			
$50,000 and Over	44	51	5
$30,000–$49,999	43	49	8
$20,000–$29,999	34	56	10
Under $20,000	31	58	11
By Politics			
Republicans	69	24	7
Democrats	15	79	6
Independents	26	58	16
By Political Ideology			
Liberal	21	72	7
Moderate	34	57	9
Conservative	52	41	7

Selected National Trend

	Approve	*Disapprove*	*No opinion*
1992			
September 11–15	39%	55%	6%
August 31–September 2	39	54	7

August 21–22	40	54	6
August 10–12	35	58	7
July 31–August 2	29	60	11
July 24–26	32	59	9
June 26–30	38	55	7
June 12–14	37	55	8
June 4–8	37	56	7
May 18–20	41	52	7
May 7–10	40	53	7

Asked of registered voters: If the presidential election were being held today, would you vote for the Republican ticket of George Bush and Dan Quayle or for the Democratic ticket of Bill Clinton and Al Gore? [Those who were undecided were asked: As of today, do you lean more to Bush and Quayle, the Republicans, or to Clinton and Gore, the Democrats?]

Bush-Quayle	40%
Clinton-Gore	50
Undecided; other	10

	Bush-Quayle	*Clinton-Gore*	*Undecided; other*
By Sex			
Male	42%	48%	10%
Female	38	52	10
By Ethnic Background			
White	45	44	11
Nonwhite	8	85	7
Black	5	94	1
By Education			
College Graduate	44	44	12
College Incomplete	36	57	7
No College	39	50	11
By Region			
East	39	49	12
Midwest	41	49	10
South	38	53	9
West	41	46	13
By Age			
18–29 Years	37	56	7
30–49 Years	40	49	11
50 Years and Over	40	49	11
By Household Income			
$50,000 and Over	48	45	7
$30,000–$49,999	43	43	14
$20,000–$29,999	37	58	5
Under $20,000	34	55	11
By Politics			
Republicans	81	15	4
Democrats	7	85	8
Independents	29	49	22
By Political Ideology			
Liberal	15	76	9
Moderate	38	53	9
Conservative	57	33	10

Asked of those who support George Bush or Bill Clinton: Do you support the Bush-Quayle or Clinton-Gore ticket strongly or only moderately?

	Bush-Quayle	*Clinton-Gore*
Strongly	37%	46%
Moderately	63	54

Selected National Trend
(Strength of Support in Two Previous Elections)

	Sept. 9–11, 1988	*Sept. 6–9, 1984*
Republican ticket		
Strongly	44%	57%
Moderately	56	43
Democratic ticket		
Strongly	39	44
Moderately	61	56

Asked of registered voters: Which of the following best describes your view of Bill Clinton's response to questions about his draft status during the Vietnam War—do you think Clinton has told the whole truth about his draft status, or has Clinton been mostly truthful but not told everything he knows, or has Clinton covered up the truth about his draft status?

Whole truth	14%
Mostly truthful	46

Covered up	21
No opinion	19

	Whole truth	*Mostly truthful*	*Covered up*	*No opinion*
By Sex				
Male	15%	45%	23%	17%
Female	13	47	19	21
By Ethnic Background				
White	14	46	22	18
Nonwhite	17	51	10	22
Black	19	49	10	22
By Education				
College Graduate	11	55	21	13
College Incomplete	14	50	20	16
No College	15	40	21	24
By Region				
East	10	48	19	23
Midwest	19	49	14	18
South	15	43	22	20
West	11	46	28	15
By Age				
18–29 Years	17	56	16	11
30–49 Years	12	57	16	15
50 Years and Over	15	32	27	26
By Household Income				
$50,000 and Over	12	54	26	8
$30,000–$49,999	12	51	25	12
$20,000–$29,999	19	39	19	23
Under $20,000	13	44	14	29
By Politics				
Republicans	8	44	36	12
Democrats	23	47	8	22
Independents	9	48	18	25
By Political Ideology				
Liberal	25	49	10	16
Moderate	12	51	19	18
Conservative	12	45	27	16

Also asked of registered voters: Do you think Clinton's draft status during the Vietnam War should be an important issue in the presidential campaign, or not?

Yes	26%
No	70
No opinion	4

	Yes	*No*	*No opinion*
By Sex			
Male	24%	74%	2%
Female	27	67	6
By Ethnic Background			
White	27	69	4
Nonwhite	19	79	2
Black	16	81	3
By Education			
College Graduate	25	72	3
College Incomplete	22	76	2
No College	28	66	6
By Region			
East	26	69	5
Midwest	21	73	6
South	29	67	4
West	26	74	*
By Age			
18–29 Years	30	68	2
30–49 Years	24	74	2
50 Years and Over	25	68	7
By Household Income			
$50,000 and Over	21	78	1
$30,000–$49,999	31	67	2
$20,000–$29,999	26	71	3
Under $20,000	24	70	6
By Politics			
Republicans	45	52	3
Democrats	10	87	3
Independents	22	71	7

By Political Ideology

Liberal	16	82	2
Moderate	22	75	3
Conservative	36	60	4

*Less than 1%

Note: President George Bush has failed to gain further on Bill Clinton, even though the Arkansas governor's draft record remains the focus of campaign coverage. The latest Gallup survey puts the Clinton-Gore ticket's lead at 10 points, 50% to 40%. Last week's poll showed a similar result (Clinton-Gore, 51%; Bush-Quayle, 42%).

Many voters believe that Clinton has been less than completely honest about his draft status during the Vietnam era, but few see it as a serious issue. Only 14% believe that Clinton has told the whole truth about his draft record; about one half (46%) say that he has been mostly truthful, while one in five (21%) thinks that he has covered up the truth.

Seven in ten (70%), however, say that Clinton's draft record should not be an important campaign issue. The 26% of voters who see the draft issue as relevant are a partisan group likely to vote for Bush regardless of the draft controversy.

At this point in the campaign, it is becoming more difficult for Bush to chip away at Clinton's lead. The poll shows that Clinton's support is not only broader but deeper than the president's. About one half of the Clinton-Gore ticket's current supporters (46%) say that they support it strongly. Fewer Bush-Quayle supporters (37%) strongly back their ticket.

Clinton's current edge in strength of support equals the advantage enjoyed by Bush over Michael Dukakis at this time four years ago. A September 1988 Gallup survey of the Republican and Democratic tickets showed 44% of Bush supporters and 39% of Dukakis voters in the strong, or committed, category. Clinton, however, does not have as large an advantage in support as former President Ronald Reagan enjoyed in September 1984 (57% versus 44%), en route to a landslide victory over Walter Mondale.

President Bush's approval ratings have failed to turn around. In fact, his approval in the new poll (36%) is actually 3 points lower than the 39% recorded in two polls taken earlier this month. Bush's current job performance rating mirrors Jimmy Carter's rating in a Gallup Poll conducted in September 1980 (37% approval) prior to his defeat by Reagan.

SEPTEMBER 27
PRESIDENTIAL TRIAL HEAT: THE ELECTORAL COLLEGE VOTE

Medial Analysis

If the presidential election were being held today, would you vote for the Republican ticket of George Bush and Dan Quayle or for the Democratic ticket of Bill Clinton and Al Gore? [Those who were undecided were asked: As of today, do you lean more to Bush and Quayle, the Republicans, or to Clinton and Gore, the Democrats?]

Bush-Quayle	40%
Clinton-Gore	52
Undecided; other	8

	Bush-Quayle	*Clinton-Gore*	*Undecided; other*
By Best States for Democrats in 1988			
Democratic East*	36%	56%	8%
Democratic Pacific	38	54	8
Democratic Midwest	37	53	10
Democratic Near West	44	47	9
By GOP Stronghold States			
GOP Central	42	50	8
GOP East	55	36	9
GOP Near West	36	56	8
GOP South	42	50	8
GOP Mountain West	48	44	8

*These four Democratic regions and five GOP regions are defined by states on p. 80, footnote.

Note: Can Bill Clinton win enough states to overcome the Republican party's electoral college advantage in recent presidential elections? A regional analysis of Gallup Poll data suggests that the Arkansas governor now has enough strength in the right states to translate his current lead in the popular vote into an electoral majority.

While the race may narrow in the weeks ahead, and a Ross Perot reentry could change regional support patterns, the September results outline the anatomy of a potential Clinton majority. Clinton has a comfortable lead in blocs of states that were the most fertile territory for Michael Dukakis in 1988. Voters who reside in the East, Midwest, and Pacific states which either backed Dukakis or went to George Bush by a narrow margin now favor the Democratic ticket by a wide margin.

In the South, where the Democrats were completely shut out in 1988, the Clinton-Gore ticket shows promise; the candidates' home states of Arkansas and Tennessee may not be the only southern states that move to the Democratic column in 1992. With California virtually conceded to the Democrats and with President Bush's home state of Texas still up for grabs, the Republicans seem to lack a secure geographic base in 1992. Even the Rocky Mountain states may not go solidly Republican this time around.

These conclusions are based on a special regional analysis of Gallup test election results collected over the past month. To assess how the candidates' standings in the popular vote might translate into electoral votes, the country was divided into nine regions, based on a state-by-state analysis of the 1988 presidential vote by James L. Hutter, professor of political science at Iowa State University. Professor Hutter identified three blocs of states as critical to the Democrats' chances of recapturing the White House in 1992:

Democratic East. Five of these nine states (District of Columbia, Massachusetts, New York, Rhode Island, and West Virginia) went to Dukakis in 1988, while the other four (Connecticut, Maryland, Pennsylvania, and Vermont) only narrowly supported Bush. Representing 101 electoral votes, they seem critical to Clinton's chances. After trailing Bush in the Democratic East by 37% to 52% in April, Clinton has reversed his fortunes in this region and now leads by 20 points, 56% to 36%.

Democratic Pacific. Gallup's results confirm the findings of other polls in California, the single largest electoral prize and a state that has not gone Democratic since Lyndon Johnson's landslide in 1964. Overall, Clinton leads by 16 points, 54% to 38%, in the Democratic Pacific, a region that also includes three states captured by Dukakis in 1988 (Washington, Oregon, and Hawaii).

Democratic Midwest. Six states in the upper Midwest also seem critical to Clinton's chances. The region includes three states that backed Dukakis in 1988 (Iowa, Minnesota, and Wisconsin) and three others that Bush won by close margins (Missouri, Illinois, and Michigan). Like California, Illinois has not gone Democratic in a presidential election since 1964 but favors Clinton today. Michigan is expected to be close again but is certainly within Clinton's grasp. He now leads by 16 points, 53% to 37%, in this bloc.

By sweeping these three blocs, Clinton would capture 256 electoral votes, within striking distance of the 270 votes needed to win. It is reasonable to assume, however, that one or more of these states—such as Michigan, Connecticut, or Oregon—will go into the Bush column. To win, Clinton will need to pick up electoral votes in regions of the country that lately have not been hospitable to Democratic presidential candidates:

GOP South. The South has gone solidly Republican since Jimmy Carter in 1976, but that is likely to change this year with two southerners on the Democratic ticket. Clinton leads Bush in the region as a whole by 50% to 42%. The president's home state of Texas, former President Carter's home state of Georgia, the Democratic nominees' home states of Arkansas and Tennessee, and Louisiana all seem promising for the Clinton-Gore ticket.

GOP Central. Clinton leads Bush by 50% to 42% in this region which includes Ohio, Kentucky, and Vice President Dan Quayle's home state of Indiana. An all-southern ticket may play well in this socially conservative part of the country.

It may be difficult for Clinton to win states in the Rocky Mountain region, but a surprise or two in this GOP stronghold is not out of the question. The race is statistically even in the

Democratic Near West, which includes Colorado, Montana, New Mexico, and South Dakota. And remarkably, the race is similarly tight in the *GOP Mountain West,* a bloc (Arkansas, Arizona, Idaho, Nevada, Utah, and Wyoming) that gave Bush his biggest margins four years ago.

SEPTEMBER 28
NORTH AMERICAN FREE-TRADE AGREEMENT

Interviewing Date: 9/17–20/92
(United States only)*
Survey #GO 322019

Have you read or heard anything about the recent proposal to create a so-called North American free-trade zone comprised of Canada, the United States, and Mexico?

	United States	*Mexico*	*Canada*
Yes	52%	92%	79%
No	48	6	20
No opinion	**	2	1

**Less than 1%

As you may know, Canada and the United States now share a free-trade agreement which ensures that trade between the two countries is not subject to tariffs or import quotas. It has been suggested that a wider free-trade zone could be established, consisting of Canada, the United States, and Mexico. In general, do you think a North American free-trade zone consisting of these three countries would be mostly good for [respondent's country] or mostly bad for [respondent's country]?

*Canadian interviews were conducted nationally on September 10–14; Mexican interviews were conducted in Mexico City, Guadalajara, and Monterrey on September 11–15.

	United States	*Mexico*	*Canada*
Mostly good for this country	55%	60%	27%
Mostly bad for this country	24	17	60
Neither good nor bad (volunteered)	5	13	5
No opinion	16	10	8

Which of the three countries—Canada, the United States, or Mexico—do you think would probably benefit most from a North American free-trade zone?

	United States	*Mexico*	*Canada*
Canada	11%	2%	4%
United States	19	57	53
Mexico	55	21	36
All of them equally (volunteered)	3	13	2
None of them (volunteered)	*	2	*
No opinion	12	5	5

*Less than 1%

Note: The prospect of relaxed import tariffs and the creation of new markets for U.S. goods under the proposed North American Free-Trade Agreement (NAFTA) draw significantly different reactions from the three countries involved: the United States, Canada, and Mexico. New Gallup surveys conducted in all three countries reaffirm two key findings of the 1991 polls: Americans are much less familiar with the proposed free-trade zone than their potential trading partners; and while U.S. and Mexican attitudes toward the proposal tilt positive, the Canadians' view of a regional open border is clearly negative.

U.S. awareness of NAFTA has increased since 1991, but it is still relatively low. One half of adult Americans (52%) now say that they are familiar with the proposal, compared with 32% last year. By contrast, four in five Canadians (79%) and nine in ten Mexicans (92%) surveyed are familiar with NAFTA.

The modest increase in U.S. awareness appears to be accompanied by increased skepticism about the benefits of free trade. One year ago, the vast majority of Americans (72%) thought that an agreement which ensured that trade among the three countries would not be subject to tariffs or import quotas would be mostly good for the United States. Only 15% replied that it would be mostly bad. This year, however, attitudes toward the proposal are less positive: 55% say mostly good; 24%, mostly bad.

Mexicans remain more positive toward the prospect of regional free trade. Six in ten (60%) say that the free-trade zone would be mostly good for Mexico, while only 17% say that it would be mostly bad. These figures closely mirror the Mexican findings last year (66% mostly good versus 20% mostly bad). In contrast, the Canadian view remains strongly negative. Sixty percent of all Canadians believe that a free-trade zone would be mostly bad for their country, while only 27% believe that it would be mostly good. (In 1991, 53% were negative and 28% positive.)

When asked which country is likely to benefit most from a North American free-trade zone, respondents show a strong tendency to name citizens of the other countries. A majority of Americans (55%) names Mexico as the NAFTA partner likely to benefit most. At the same time, majorities of Mexicans and Canadians believe that the United States will be the winner (57% and 53%, respectively).

OCTOBER 2
SPORTS

Interviewing Date: 9/17–20/92
Survey #GO 322017

What is your favorite sport to watch?

	Total	*Men*	*Women*
Football	38%	49%	29%
Baseball	16	14	18
Basketball	12	10	13
Tennis	5	3	7
Ice hockey	3	4	2
Golf	3	1	4
Iceskating; figure skating	2	*	4
Auto racing	2	3	*
Gymnastics	1	*	3
Soccer	1	1	1
Fishing	1	3	*
Boxing	1	1	1
Wrestling	1	1	1
Bowling	1	*	1
Swimming	*	1	*
Horse racing	*	*	*
Others	4	4	4
None; don't watch (volunteered)	8	5	11
No opinion	1	*	1

*Less than 1%

Selected National Trend

	Football	*Baseball*	*Basketball*
1990	35%	16%	15%
1981	38	16	9
1972	36	21	8
1960	21	34	9
1948	17	39	10

Overall, how interested are you in following professional and college sports such as football, baseball, and hockey—extremely interested, very interested, somewhat interested, or not at all interested?

	Sept. 1992	*Feb. 1990*
Extremely interested	11%	9%
Very interested	22	21
Somewhat interested	42	40
Not at all interested	25	30

Note: Football is the dominant spectator sport today, thus continuing a long-term downward trend in the popularity of what was formerly America's favorite pastime, baseball. A new Gallup Poll shows that almost four out of ten (38%) say that football is their favorite sport to watch, more than twice as many as name any other, including baseball, basketball, and hockey. The big impetus for this fascination with the pigskin came in the 1960s; in Gallup surveys taken in 1948 and 1960, baseball was the favorite spectator sport, with football significantly behind.

The women of America are much less interested than men in football. Their preference is not baseball, however, but a wide variety of so-called minor sports. Women are more likely than men to name such sports as tennis, golf, figure skating, and gymnastics as their favorite to watch.

For many respondents, the question is moot—they are not really interested in spectator sports at all. Despite the attention given in the media to professional and college games, two thirds (67%) say that they are only somewhat or not at all interested in following them. There is a hard-core sporting elite of one third (33%) who profess to be extremely or very interested. These fanatics are, not surprisingly, predominately male. By contrast, over three quarters of women are only somewhat or not at all interested in sports.

OCTOBER 3
PRESIDENTIAL TRIAL HEAT/H. ROSS PEROT

Interviewing Date: 9/28–30/92*
Survey #GO 322025–01(National Tracking–Phase I)

Asked of registered voters: If the presidential election were being held today, would you vote for the Republican ticket of George Bush and Dan Quayle or for the Democratic ticket of Bill Clinton and Al Gore? [Those who were undecided were asked: As of today, do you lean more to Bush and Quayle, the Republicans, or to Clinton and Gore, the Democrats?]

Bush-Quayle....................................38%
Clinton-Gore....................................54
Undecided; other.................................8

Also asked of registered voters: At the beginning of the interview you said you would probably vote for George Bush or Bill Clinton. Later, you said you might vote for Ross Perot. As of today, do you lean more to Bush or Clinton or to Perot?

*Gallup survey for CNN/*USA Today*

Bush..35%
Clinton..52
Perot...7
Undecided; other...............................6

Also asked of registered voters: Please tell me whether you have a favorable or unfavorable opinion of each of the following presidential candidates:

George Bush?

Favorable..40%
Unfavorable.....................................56
No opinion..4

Bill Clinton?

Favorable..54%
Unfavorable.....................................38
No opinion..8

Ross Perot?

Favorable..20%
Unfavorable.....................................66
No opinion.......................................14

Also asked of registered voters: Regardless of which presidential candidate you support, which candidate do you think has the best plan for improving the nation's economy—George Bush, Bill Clinton, or Ross Perot?

Bush..24%
Clinton..42
Perot..14
None of them (volunteered)...................10
All three equally; same (volunteered).......... 1
No opinion..9

Also asked of registered voters: Regardless of whether you would vote for him, would you like to see Ross Perot become an active candidate for president again, or not?

Yes..33%
No..60
No opinion..7

Note: Before Ross Perot's return to the presidential race, a new Gallup Poll showed Bill

Clinton expanding his lead over George Bush. Based on interviews conducted before Perot's announcement, the Clinton-Gore ticket led the Bush-Quayle ticket by 16 points, 54% to 38%. Polls taken in recent weeks had shown a Clinton lead of 9 to 10 points.

Some Bush supporters welcome Perot's candidacy as a means of changing the dynamics of the race. The first results of Gallup's 1992 tracking poll, however, give little indication that his presence will have a major effect on the election. Perot received only 7% in this preannouncement poll, down substantially from the high levels that he attracted in the spring, when his support peaked at 39% in a June Gallup survey. The last Gallup Poll taken before he abruptly withdrew from the race in July—conducted for *Newsweek* magazine—showed Perot at 28%.

A majority of voters (60%) does not want to see Perot return to the race. The Texas businessman's image has turned sharply negative. Only 20% of voters now say that they have a favorable opinion of Perot, while two thirds (66%) express unfavorable views of him. David Duke is the only politician who has received more negative ratings in Gallup surveys this year.

The president's favorability ratings have also slipped. More voters now view Bush unfavorably than favorably (56% versus 40%). Clinton's ratings are essentially unchanged and remain significantly more positive than those of his two opponents: 54% of voters have a favorable opinion of the Arkansas governor, while 38% see him in an unfavorable light.

OCTOBER 4
PRESIDENTIAL CANDIDATES/THE ANGRY VOTER/PRESIDENTIAL TRIAL HEAT

Interviewing Date: 9/11–15/92*
Survey #GO 322018

Are the presidential candidates talking about issues you really care about, or not?

Yes	66%
No	30
No opinion	4

	Yes	*No*	*No opinion*
By Sex			
Male	64%	34%	2%
Female	68	27	5
By Ethnic Background			
White	66	30	4
Nonwhite	68	28	4
Black	66	30	4
By Education			
College Graduate	66	31	3
College Incomplete	68	30	2
No College	66	30	4
By Region			
East	66	31	3
Midwest	66	31	3
South	68	29	3
West	65	30	5
By Age			
18–29 Years	71	26	3
30–49 Years	66	33	1
50 Years and Over	63	31	6
By Household Income			
$50,000 and Over	66	32	2
$30,000–$49,999	67	30	3
$20,000–$29,999	69	27	4
Under $20,000	65	31	4
By Politics			
Republicans	66	30	4
Democrats	71	25	4
Independents	62	35	3
By Political Ideology			
Liberal	72	27	1
Moderate	66	31	3
Conservative	66	31	3

Selected National Trend

	Yes	*No*	*No opinion*
1992			
April 20–22	53%	44%	3%

*Gallup survey for CNN/*USA Today*

	Yes	No	No opinion
February 28–March 1	53	42	5
January 6–9	60	30	10

Is there any candidate running this year that you think would make a good president, or not?

Yes	61%
No	32
No opinion	7

	Yes	No	No opinion
By Sex			
Male	62%	32%	6%
Female	59	32	9
By Ethnic Background			
White	61	32	7
Nonwhite	58	32	10
Black	60	31	9
By Education			
College Graduate	65	29	6
College Incomplete	62	34	4
No College	59	32	9
By Region			
East	61	30	9
Midwest	60	32	8
South	65	29	6
West	54	39	7
By Age			
18–29 Years	59	35	6
30–49 Years	60	36	4
50 Years and Over	62	26	12
By Household Income			
$50,000 and Over	64	32	4
$30,000–$49,999	61	34	5
$20,000–$29,999	60	31	9
Under $20,000	61	30	9
By Politics			
Republicans	66	28	6
Democrats	68	24	8
Independents	50	42	8
By Political Ideology			
Liberal	63	28	9
Moderate	60	33	7
Conservative	62	32	6

Selected National Trend

	Yes	No	No opinion
1992			
April 20–22	49%	43%	8%
January 6–9	40	41	19

Do you feel that any of the presidential candidates have come up with good ideas for solving the country's problems, or not?

Yes	50%
No	44
No opinion	6

	Yes	No	No opinion
By Sex			
Male	48%	46%	6%
Female	52	41	7
By Ethnic Background			
White	49	45	6
Nonwhite	59	34	7
Black	62	32	6
By Education			
College Graduate	55	42	3
College Incomplete	50	47	3
No College	48	43	9
By Region			
East	53	40	7
Midwest	46	49	5
South	52	42	6
West	51	42	7
By Age			
18–29 Years	55	41	4
30–49 Years	48	47	5
50 Years and Over	48	42	10
By Household Income			
$50,000 and Over	50	45	5
$30,000–$49,999	52	45	3

	Yes	No	No opinion
$20,000–$29,999	53	40	7
Under $20,000	47	45	8
By Politics			
Republicans	50	46	4
Democrats	61	34	5
Independents	41	50	9
By Political Ideology			
Liberal	57	39	4
Moderate	51	43	6
Conservative	45	49	6

Selected National Trend

	Yes	No	No opinion
1992			
April 20–22	36%	60%	4%
March 20–22	32	57	11
January 6–9	29	61	10

Does the way this year's presidential campaign is being conducted make you feel proud to be an American, or not?

Yes	49%
No	43
No opinion	8

	Yes	No	No opinion
By Sex			
Male	49%	44%	7%
Female	50	42	8
By Ethnic Background			
White	49	43	8
Nonwhite	52	38	10
Black	53	38	9
By Education			
College Graduate	39	54	7
College Incomplete	39	50	11
No College	56	37	7
By Region			
East	47	45	8
Midwest	51	39	10
South	52	40	8
West	45	49	6
By Age			
18–29 Years	43	50	7
30–49 Years	46	45	9
50 Years and Over	56	37	7
By Household Income			
$50,000 and Over	43	49	8
$30,000–$49,999	46	44	10
$20,000–$29,999	48	46	6
Under $20,000	57	39	4
By Politics			
Republicans	58	36	6
Democrats	51	43	6
Independents	42	47	11
By Political Ideology			
Liberal	38	53	9
Moderate	51	43	6
Conservative	53	39	8

Selected National Trend

	Yes	No	No opinion
1992			
April 20–22	39%	53%	8%
April 9–12	35	54	11
February 28–March 1	52	41	7
January 6–9	58	28	14

"Angry Voter" Index*

	April 1992	September 1992	Point difference
National	38%	23%	-15
By Sex			
Male	40	24	-16
Female	35	22	-13
By Ethnic Background			
White	39	24	-15
Nonwhite	29	19	-10
By Education			
College Graduate	43	24	-19
College Incomplete	44	26	-18
No College	34	21	-13
By Region			
East	40	20	-20
Midwest	41	24	-17

South	32	21	-11
West	40	28	-12
By Age			
18–29 Years	33	23	-10
30–49 Years	36	26	-10
50–64 Years	45	23	-22
65 Years and Over	38	16	-22
By Household Income			
$50,000 and Over	44	24	-20
$30,000–$49,999	45	24	-21
$20,000–$29,999	38	21	-17
Under $20,000	31	24	-7
By Politics			
Republicans	35	20	-15
Democrats	35	15	-20
Independents	49	31	-18
By Political Ideology			
Liberal	39	19	-20
Moderate	40	23	-17
Conservative	38	24	-14
By Ethnic Background/Region			
Northern White	42	23	-19
Southern White	32	23	-9
By 1988 Presidential Choice			
George Bush	39	23	-16
Michael Dukakis	44	16	-28

*"Angry voters" are defined as those who answered "no" to at least three of the four preceding questions.

Do you approve or disapprove of the way George Bush is handling his job as president?

	Total	Angry voters
Approve	39%	29%
Disapprove	55	64
No opinion	6	7

Asked of registered voters: Next, I'd like your opinion of some people in politics. As I read each name, please tell me whether you have a favorable or unfavorable opinion of this person:

George Bush?

	All voters	Angry voters
Favorable	49%	45%
Unfavorable	46	52
No opinion	5	3

Bill Clinton?

	All voters	Angry voters
Favorable	54%	39%
Unfavorable	39	55
No opinion	7	6

Also asked of registered voters: Suppose the 1992 presidential election were being held today. If George Bush were the Republican candidate and Bill Clinton were the Democratic candidate, whom would you vote for? [Those who were undecided were asked: As of today, do you lean more to Bush, the Republican, or to Clinton, the Democrat?]

	All voters	Angry voters
Bush	42%	44%
Clinton	51	47
Undecided; other	7	9

Also asked of registered voters: Please tell me whether or not you think the following political officeholder deserves to be reelected—the U.S. representative in your congressional district?

	All voters	Angry voters
Yes	54%	45%
No	25	39
No opinion	21	16

Do you think that either the Bush campaign or the Clinton campaign has been too personally negative toward the opposing candidate, or not?

	Total	Angry voters
Yes, Bush	23%	22%
Yes, Clinton	12	8
Yes, both (volunteered)	31	43

No, neither	26	23
No opinion	8	4

Note: As Ross Perot pondered reentering the presidential race this past week, he faced a far less receptive audience than he did last spring, when he first considered it. A new poll shows that voter discontent with the presidential candidates and their campaigns has abated substantially since Gallup last measured voter anger. In April nearly four in ten adults were classified by Gallup as "angry voters." Today, only one voter in four (23%) meets the same criteria.

Opinion of the caliber of the candidates and the content of the campaigns has improved significantly—a reflection of Bill Clinton's sharply improved image among the voters. Five months ago, Perot seemed an attractive choice to a large segment of the electorate who disapproved of George Bush's job performance but held vaguely negative views of the Arkansas governor. Now that many of these voters have changed their minds about Clinton, Perot has lost his natural constituency.

In the spring, as Bush's approval ratings slumped and Clinton faced a barrage of negative publicity, respondents found much to criticize about the presidential campaign. In the current poll, opinion is shifting toward the positive. Two thirds of adults (66%) now say that the candidates are addressing the issues they care about most, up from 53% in April; and six in ten (61%) believe that at least one of the candidates running would make a good president, up from 49%. One half (50%) now says that the candidates have good ideas for solving the country's problems, up from 36%. And despite growing concern about negative campaigning, those who say that the campaign makes them feel proud also has increased, from 39% to 49%.

Every major demographic and political subgroup of the population shows a significant decrease in voter anger. Some of the groups whose scores on Gallup's "Angry Voter" Index have declined most are Democrats (down 20 points), liberals (20 points), and former Dukakis voters (28 points), suggesting that a major factor behind the drop in voter anger is Clinton's increased acceptability among Democratic-oriented voters, seen since his party's national convention in early July.

In April, the typical angry voter had a college degree, was 50 to 64 years old, had an income of $30,000 or more, called himself a political independent, and lived in a midwestern state. Today, that profile is somewhat different. While their income levels and political identification have changed little, today's angry voters tend to be younger, less well educated, and more likely to live in the West. These people would appear less likely to turn out on election day than the angry voters of the spring—bad news for a Perot candidacy.

Voter anger has shifted more toward Bush and away from Clinton. While Bush approval has dropped only marginally (3 points, from 42% to 39%) among all voters since April, it has declined by 8 points (from 37% to 29%) among those classified as angry voters. Last spring six in ten angry voters (62%) expressed unfavorable views of Clinton; that percentage has dropped to 55%, about equal to the 52% of angry voters who now have unfavorable views of Bush. In their presidential candidate preferences, angry voters now divide about evenly between Clinton (47%) and Bush (44%). The April poll found them favoring Bush by a 51%-to-30% margin.

The diminished pool of angry voters is good news for congressional incumbents. Those respondents who are sharply critical of the presidential candidates and campaign continue to be more likely to say that their representative in Congress does not deserve to be reelected. Among all voters, only one quarter (25%) say that the member of Congress in their district should not be given another term. That proportion increases to four in ten (39%) among angry voters.

OCTOBER 9
ANITA HILL AND CLARENCE THOMAS/PRESIDENT BUSH

Interviewing Date: 10/1–3/92*
Survey #GO 322025–01
(National Tracking–Phase I)

I have a question about the Supreme Court confirmation hearings for Clarence

*Gallup survey for CNN/*USA Today*

Thomas held last year. During the hearings, Anita Hill charged Clarence Thomas with sexually harassing her when she worked for him in the early 1980s. Thomas denied Hill's charges. From what you remember or have heard or read since that time, whom do you believe more—Anita Hill or Clarence Thomas?

Hill	43%
Thomas	39
Neither (volunteered)	5
Both equally (volunteered)	2
No opinion	11

	Hill	*Thomas*	*Neither**
By Sex			
Male	39%	46%	7%
Female	46	36	3
By Ethnic Background			
White	43	39	5
Nonwhite	41	36	7
By Education			
College Graduate	50	36	6
College Incomplete	43	43	6
No College	40	38	4
By Region			
East	43	40	4
Midwest	45	37	4
South	38	40	5
West	46	37	6
By Age			
18–29 Years	36	48	1
30–49 Years	46	39	5
50 Years and Over	41	33	7
By Household Income			
$50,000 and Over	44	41	7
$30,000–$49,999	44	44	6
$20,000–$29,999	52	33	3
Under $20,000	40	40	4
By Politics			
Republicans	28	56	7
Democrats	57	29	4
Independents	46	35	5
By Education/Sex			
College–Male	41	44	7
College–Female	53	35	5
No College–Male	38	39	6
No College–Female	42	37	3

*"Both equally" and "no opinion" are omitted.

Do you approve or disapprove of the way George Bush is handling his job as president?

	Oct. 1–3, 1992	*Oct. 10–13, 1991*
Approve	33%	66%
Disapprove	58	28
No opinion	9	6

Note: One year ago in October, Americans sat glued to their television sets engrossed in the Senate Judiciary hearings on the confirmation of Clarence Thomas. At the time, nearly one half of them (48%) found the Supreme Court nominee's denial of sexual harassment more believable than they did Professor Anita Hill's accusations, credited by only 29%. Today, only 39% think that Justice Thomas told the truth; 43% now believe Professor Hill's charges.

This turnaround in perceptions of the truth of the matter has occurred at least to some degree in every subgroup measured. Professor Hill's biggest gains come from midwesterners, the lower-middle and high-income groups, those over age 30, and the college educated. Conversely, there have been large losses in credibility for Justice Thomas not only among these groups but also among nonwhites. One year ago, nonwhites believed the Thomas version of events by a margin of 54% to 34%. Today, they believe Professor Hill by 41% to 36%.

What caused the turnaround? First, Professor Hill has remained in the public eye as a rallying point. Politicians may have underestimated the negative reaction to the hearings, particularly among white, college-educated women. By taking advantage of the Congress-bashing mood of the electorate, record numbers of female candidates have won primaries and made Professor Hill's treatment by the Senate's "white male club" a vital issue in their election campaigns.

Second, there is Justice Thomas's position on the Pennsylvania abortion decision, whereby he aligned himself with the hard-line faction opposed by most Americans. And third, the reverse coattails effect, emanating from the sagging popularity of George Bush, cannot be ignored. At the time of the hearings, the president enjoyed the approval of two thirds of his constituents (66%); one year later, his approval rating (33%) is among the lowest in Gallup's annals.

OCTOBER 11 PRESIDENTIAL TRIAL HEAT/PRESIDENTIAL CANDIDATES

Interviewing Date: 10/6–8/92*
Survey #GO 322025–01 (National Tracking–Phase I)

Asked of registered voters: If the presidential election were being held today, would you vote for the Republican ticket of George Bush and Dan Quayle, for the Democratic ticket of Bill Clinton and Al Gore, or for the independent candidates Ross Perot and James Stockdale? [Those who were undecided were asked: As of today, do you lean more to Bush and Quayle, the Republicans; to Clinton and Gore, the Democrats; or to Perot and Stockdale, the independents?]

Bush-Quayle	34%
Clinton-Gore	49
Perot-Stockdale	10
Undecided; other	7

Also asked of registered voters: Please tell me whether you have a favorable or unfavorable opinion of each of the following presidential candidates:

George Bush?

Favorable	42%
Unfavorable	54
No opinion	4

*Gallup survey for CNN/*USA Today*

Selected National Trend

	Favorable	Unfavorable	No opinion
1992			
October 3–5	43%	51%	6%
September 28–30	40	56	4

Bill Clinton?

Favorable	56%
Unfavorable	39
No opinion	5

Selected National Trend

	Favorable	Unfavorable	No opinion
1992			
October 3–5	52%	39%	9%
September 28–30	54	38	8

Ross Perot?

Favorable	24%
Unfavorable	65
No opinion	11

Selected National Trend

	Favorable	Unfavorable	No opinion
1992			
October 3–5	22%	63%	15%
September 28–30	20	66	14

Interviewing Date: 10/5–7/92*
Survey #GO 322025–01 (National Tracking–Phase I)

Asked of registered voters: As you may know, the presidential candidates will participate in televised debates beginning next Sunday [October 11]. Who do you think is likely to do the best job in the debates—George Bush, Bill Clinton, or Ross Perot?

Bush	26%
Clinton	44
Perot	11
No opinion	19

*Gallup survey for CNN/*USA Today*

	Bush	Clinton	Perot	No opinion
By Candidate Preference				
Bush Voters...51%	21%	8%	20%	
Clinton Voters.......10	68	8	14	
Perot Voters...24	27	37	12	
Swing Voters.......25	38	16	21	

Also asked of registered voters: Do you expect the debates to make much difference in deciding your vote for president, or not?

Yes...30%
No...67
No opinion.......................................3

	Yes	No	No opinion
By Candidate Preference			
Bush Voters............	22%	73%	5%
Clinton Voters.........	29	69	2
Perot Voters............	53	45	2
Swing Voters..........	52	45	3

Note: The first presidential debate of the campaign has the potential to affect significant numbers of swing voters who have not yet made up their minds. Gallup polling shows that Democrat Bill Clinton remains the front-runner in the presidential race and is expected to win the debate. About 40% of registered voters are not firmly committed to any candidate at this point, and it is this group which is most likely to say that the debates could help them decide.

Only three out of ten (30%) claim that the debate will make much difference in their vote for president, but over one half (52%) of the voters who are not definitely committed to a candidate—swing voters—say that the debates could make a difference. Clinton supporters and voters under 50 years of age also are more likely than others to say that the debate could have an impact on their vote.

Regardless of the debate's ultimate impact on the outcome of the race, voter expectations are that Clinton will win it: 44% say that Clinton will do the best job; 26%, George Bush; and 11%, Ross Perot. Clinton supporters are the most loyal: two thirds of those whose preference is the Arkansas governor (68%) say that he will win, while only 51% of Bush voters say that their man will do the best job. One out of five Bush voters (21%) concede that, in fact, Clinton may do a better job than their own candidate. Perot voters are less optimistic about the performance of their candidate: only 37% say that Perot will do best, with the rest split about equally between Bush and Clinton.

The entry of Perot into the race so far has made no significant difference in the structure of the presidential vote. Continuous daily Gallup polling over the last two weeks has shown that Perot receives only about 10%, while Clinton continues to lead Bush by a range of 10 to 16 percentage points. The last three nights of Gallup polling [October 6–8] show the Clinton-Gore ticket with 49% of the vote, the Bush-Quayle ticket with 34%, and the Perot-Stockdale ticket with 10%.

Perot's second-time-around run for the presidency has been hampered by his extremely negative image. About two thirds of the public (65%) have an unfavorable opinion of him, while only 24% see him favorably. This is a significant turnaround from Perot's more favorable image last June, before he withdrew from the race.

Perot is not the only candidate who is hampered by a negative image, however: 54% have an unfavorable opinion of Bush, while 42% have a favorable opinion. Pacesetter Clinton is seen favorably by 56%, unfavorably by 39%.

OCTOBER 13
FIRST PRESIDENTIAL DEBATE

Interviewing Date: 10/11/92*
Survey #GO 322027 (Telephone survey)

Asked of registered voters: Regardless of which candidate you happen to support, who do you think did the best job in the debate—George Bush, Bill Clinton, or Ross Perot?

*Gallup survey for CNN/*USA Today*

	Debate viewers	Predebate preference Bush	Clinton	Perot
Bush	16%	42%	3%	12%
Clinton	30	5	49	2
Perot	47	44	42	82
None (volunteered)	5	8	3	4
No opinion	2	1	3	*

*Less than 1%

Also asked of registered voters: How has your opinion of George Bush been affected by the debate—is your opinion of Bush more favorable, less favorable, or has it not changed much?

	Debate viewers	Predebate preference Bush	Clinton	Perot
More favorable	13%	27%	5%	10%
Less favorable	24	11	31	27
Not changed much	62	61	64	63
No opinion	1	1	*	*

*Less than 1%

Also asked of registered voters: How has your opinion of Bill Clinton been affected by the debate—is your opinion of Clinton more favorable, less favorable, or has it not changed much?

	Debate viewers	Predebate preference Bush	Clinton	Perot
More favorable	29%	7%	43%	17%
Less favorable	14	27	4	23
Not changed much	57	66	52	59
No opinion	*	*	1	1

*Less than 1%

Also asked of registered voters: How has your opinion of Ross Perot been affected by the debate—is your opinion of Perot more favorable, less favorable, or has it not changed much?

	Debate viewers	Predebate preference Bush	Clinton	Perot
More favorable	62%	67%	57%	80%
Less favorable	5	5	6	*
Not changed much	33	27	37	20
No opinion	*	1	*	*

*Less than 1%

Also asked of registered voters: I'm going to read off some personal characteristics and qualities. As I read each one, tell me whether you think it applies most to George Bush, Bill Clinton, or Ross Perot:

Stands up for what he believes?

	Post-debate	Pre-debate*
Bush	21%	30%
Clinton	28	37
Perot	43	25
All the same (volunteered)	6	5
None (volunteered)	1	2
No opinion	1	1

Has a clear understanding of the issues?

	Post-debate	Pre-debate
Bush	28%	29%
Clinton	39	45
Perot	26	17
All the same (volunteered)	5	4
None (volunteered)	1	3
No opinion	1	2

Is honest and trustworthy?

	Post-debate	Pre-debate
Bush	27%	31%
Clinton	29	37
Perot	33	14

All the same (volunteered)	3	2
None (volunteered)	6	12
No opinion	2	4

*Predebate results for all three parts of this question are from tracking surveys conducted October 8–10.

Also asked of registered voters: Based on your impressions of Bill Clinton from the debate, do you have more confidence in his ability to serve as president, less confidence, or has your confidence in Clinton to be president not changed much?

	Debate viewers	Bush	Predebate preference Clinton	Perot
More confidence	32%	10%	49%	10%
Less confidence	15	31	3	34
Not changed much	51	58	47	50
Never had any confidence (volunteered)	1	1	*	4
No opinion	1	*	1	2

*Less than 1%

Also asked of registered voters: Which candidate tonight offered the best proposals for change to solve the country's problems—George Bush, Bill Clinton, or Ross Perot?

Bush	14%
Clinton	40
Perot	38
All equally (volunteered)	2
None (volunteered)	4
No opinion	2

Also asked of registered voters: George Bush tonight criticized Bill Clinton's activities when Clinton was in England, including Clinton's trip to Moscow and protests against the Vietnam War. Did these criticisms give you serious doubts about Clinton's ability to serve as commander in chief, or not?

Yes	24%
No	73
No opinion	3

Note: According to the viewing public, Ross Perot did the best job in the first presidential debate on Sunday, October 11. In a Gallup Poll of voters who watched the proceedings in St. Louis, taken as the debate ended, 47% say that they were most impressed by Perot's performance. Thirty percent think that Bill Clinton, the favorite going into the debate, did the best job, while President George Bush, who needed a clear victory to cut Clinton's lead, fell short of his goal: only 16% of voters think that Bush did best.

A majority of all debate viewers (62%), including two thirds (67%) of voters who favored Bush and six in ten (57%) who favored Clinton going into the debate, say that the exchange improved their opinion of Perot. Clinton, however, may have done what was needed to consolidate his lead. Twice as many viewers say that the debate left them with a more favorable opinion of Clinton than say that it made their opinion of him less favorable (29% versus 14%). Similarly, one third of viewers (32%) report that the debate increased their confidence in Clinton's ability to be president, while only 15% now have less confidence in him.

Perot came across as sincere, with 43% of viewers identifying him afterward as the candidate who stands up for what he believes. In polling taken before the debate, only 25% saw Perot in this light. He continues to trail behind Clinton as the candidate with the best understanding of the issues (26% versus 39%).

Polls taken in the next few days are likely to show some gains for Perot. The gap between Clinton and Bush, however, seems unlikely to close very much. The debate reaction shows Bush supporters to be at least as likely as Clinton supporters to shift toward Perot. In fact, viewers who backed Bush prior to the debate were less likely than Clinton supporters to be satisfied with their candidate's performance and more likely to be impressed with Perot.

OCTOBER 18
PRESIDENTIAL TRIAL HEAT/PRESIDENTIAL CANDIDATES/PRESIDENT BUSH

Interviewing Date: 10/13–15/92*
Survey #GO 322025–01
(National Tracking–Phase I)

Asked of registered voters: If the presidential election were being held today, would you vote for the Republican ticket of George Bush and Dan Quayle, for the Democratic ticket of Bill Clinton and Al Gore, or for the independent candidates Ross Perot and James Stockdale? [Those who were undecided were asked: As of today, do you lean more to Bush and Quayle, the Republicans; to Clinton and Gore, the Democrats; or to Perot and Stockdale, the independents?]

Bush-Quayle	34%
Clinton-Gore	47
Perot-Stockdale	13
Undecided; other	6

Asked of Perot voters: Who would be your second choice for president—George Bush or Bill Clinton?

Bush	38%
Clinton	40
No opinion	22

Asked of registered voters: Is there any chance you will vote for George Bush [or Bill Clinton or Ross Perot] in November, or is there no chance whatsoever that you will vote for him?

	Clinton voters	*Bush voters*	*Perot voters*
No chance for another candidate	63%	57%	22%
Might vote for another candidate	37	43	78

Interviewing Date: 10/12–14/92
Survey #GO 322025–01
(National Tracking–Phase I)

*Gallup survey for CNN/*USA Today*

Do you approve or disapprove of the way George Bush is handling his job as president?

Approve	33%
Disapprove	57
No opinion	10

Asked of Perot supporters: In November, if it looks like Ross Perot cannot win, will you vote for Perot, switch to George Bush, or switch to Bill Clinton?

Vote for Perot	36%
Switch to Bush	26
Switch to Clinton	30
No opinion	8

Asked of registered voters: Based on what you have learned about Ross Perot or Bill Clinton during the presidential campaign, do you think he is or is not the kind of man who would make a good president, or do you feel you don't know enough about him to say?

	Perot	*Clinton*
Yes	21%	42%
No	36	28
Don't know enough	42	28
No opinion	1	2

Also asked of registered voters: Regardless of how you might vote, who do you think is more likely to win in November—George Bush, Bill Clinton, or Ross Perot?

Bush	28%
Clinton	60
Perot	2
No opinion	10

Note: Bill Clinton continues to hold a wide lead in the Gallup tracking poll, despite Ross Perot's modest gains in support since the first presidential debate. The latest results, based on interviews completed on October 15, show the Clinton-Gore ticket with a 13-point advantage over the Bush-Quayle ticket, 47% to 34%. Perot's ticket receives 13% support, marginally above the 10% level he registered earlier this month, soon after he reentered the race.

These results do not reflect the impact of the second presidential debate, held on October 13 in Richmond, Virginia. Reaction polls taken by other organizations, however, indicate that Clinton was widely regarded as the winner of the debate by voters who watched. The final debate on October 19 in East Lansing, Michigan, may represent George Bush's last big opportunity to reverse Clinton's momentum.

Since his return to the presidential race, Perot has not played the role of spoiler. He is taking votes from both his opponents: 38% of Perot supporters say that Bush is their second choice, while 40% name Clinton. While voter opinion of the Texas billionaire has moderated, Perot has failed to be regarded as a credible candidate. Only 2% of voters predict that he will win the election; only one in five (21%) sees him as the kind of man who would make a good president (36% do not). Four in ten (42%) are withholding judgment, saying that they do not know enough to rate him. If it looks like Perot cannot win, a majority of his current supporters say that they will switch to Bush (26%) or to Clinton (30%).

During the debates, Bush so far has failed to improve voters' image of him. His latest approval rating is only 33%, comparable to Jimmy Carter's 37% at a similar point in the 1980 campaign. Carter's rating at that time foreshadowed his election defeat four years later by Ronald Reagan, whose approval stood at 58% in October 1984. Bush's approval rating today is almost identical to his support level in test elections over the past month. Since the Gallup tracking poll began in late September, Bush support has averaged 34%.

While Clinton's lead remains wide by historical standards, he has yet to "close the sale" with voters. Somewhat more than one third (37%) of his supporters say that they still might vote for either Bush or Perot. While Clinton's support is not unusually soft—in fact, his backers are more committed to their choice than are Bush and Perot supporters—he has yet to build enough core support to ensure victory.

Currently, about four in ten voters (42%) see Clinton as the kind of man who would make a good president, while 28% disagree and 28% need more information. Those voters who still are not sure about him have one more debate and two more weeks of campaigning in which to decide.

OCTOBER 21
THIRD PRESIDENTIAL DEBATE

Interviewing Date: 10/19/92*
Survey #GO 322029 (Telephone survey)

Asked of registered voters: Regardless of which candidate you happen to support, who do you think did the best job in the third debate—George Bush, Bill Clinton, or Ross Perot?

Bush	28%
Clinton	28
Perot	37
None (volunteered)	7
No opinion	**

**Less than 1%

Selected National Trend

	First debate (Oct. 11)	*Second debate (Oct. 13)*
Bush	16%	16%
Clinton	30	58
Perot	47	15
None (volunteered)	5	7
No opinion	2	4

Also asked of registered voters: How has your opinion of George Bush [or Bill Clinton or Ross Perot] been affected by the debate? Is your opinion of Bush [or Clinton or Perot] more favorable, less favorable, or has it not changed much?

	Bush	*Clinton*	*Perot*
More favorable	29%	27%	63%
Less favorable	25	22	5
Not changed much	46	50	32
No opinion	**	1	**

**Less than 1%

*Gallup survey for CNN/*USA Today*

Also asked of registered voters: Regardless of which presidential candidate you support, please tell me whether you think George Bush, Bill Clinton, or Ross Perot would best handle each of the following issues:

Economy?

	Post-debate	Predebate*
Bush	26%	26%
Clinton	34	38
Perot	39	30
No difference; no opinion	1	6

Federal budget deficit?

	Post-debate	Predebate
Bush	23%	26%
Clinton	24	30
Perot	51	35
No difference; no opinion	2	9

Taxes?

	Post-debate	Predebate
Bush	34%	–
Clinton	34	–
Perot	30	–
No difference; no opinion	2	–

*Predebate trends in the first two parts of this question are based on earlier debate viewers (interviewed October 16–18).

Also asked of registered voters: I'm going to read off some personal characteristics and qualities. As I read each one, tell me whether you think it applies most to George Bush, Bill Clinton, or Ross Perot:

Stands up for what he believes?

Bush	27%
Clinton	21
Perot	46
All the same (volunteered)	6
None (volunteered)	*
No opinion	*

*Less than 1%

Has a clear understanding of the issues?

Bush	33%
Clinton	41
Perot	18
All the same (volunteered)	5
None (volunteered)	2
No opinion	1

Is honest and trustworthy?

Bush	36%
Clinton	23
Perot	32
All the same (volunteered)	3
None (volunteered)	4
No opinion	2

Also asked of registered voters: As a result of tonight's debate, have you changed your vote from one presidential candidate to another, or not?

Yes	12%
No	86
No opinion	2

Asked of those who replied in the affirmative: Which candidate did you switch from, that is, whom were you supporting before the debate? Which candidate did you switch to, that is, whom are you supporting now?

	Votes gained	Votes lost	Net change
Bush	3%	3%	±0
Clinton	2	6	-4
Perot	7	1	+6

Asked of registered voters: Did what the candidates had to say about the Iraqi war—and the events leading up to it—make you more likely to vote for Bush, less likely to vote for him, or did it not much affect your chances of voting for him?

More likely	11%
Less likely	28
Not much effect	59
No opinion	2

Also asked of registered voters: Do you agree or disagree with the charge that Bill

Clinton has shown a pattern of trying to take both sides on controversial issues?

Agree	52%
Disagree	46
No opinion	2

Note: In the third and final presidential debate on October 19, George Bush gave his best performance, but Ross Perot scored more points with the viewing audience. A Gallup debate-reaction survey finds that over one third (37%) of voters who watched Monday night's debate live from East Lansing, Michigan, thinks that Perot did the best job. Bush and Bill Clinton tie for second place, with each seen by 28% of voters as the winner.

This is the second time in nine days that a man who never previously had sought elective office made a better impression than his major party rivals. According to a Gallup Poll taken on Sunday, October 11, 47% of voters who watched the initial debate judge Perot's performance best. Clinton finishes second in that debate with 30%, while Bush trails behind with only 16%.

The Texas entrepreneur impressed voters with his forcefulness and his economic ideas, especially his plans for reducing the deficit. Close to one half of debate viewers (46%) saw Perot as the candidate who stands up for what he believes. Prior to the debate, roughly one third (35%) identified him as the candidate best able to deal with the deficit. After Perot's performance in the final debate, that percentage increased to 51%.

Despite running mate James Stockdale's unsteady performance in the vice presidential exchange one week ago, Perot's candidacy gained momentum through the debate period. Gallup's presidential tracking poll finds Perot to be the only candidate whose support has gone up since the debates started. In surveys conducted on October 8–10, immediately prior to the first debate, Perot had 10% of the vote. Current results, which do not yet reflect the impact of the final debate, show Perot at 15%.

President Bush sorely needed to improve on his performance in the first two debates. The poll suggests that he did: nearly twice as many voters saw him the winner of debate number three (28%) as saw him winning debates one (16%) and two (16%). Similarly, three in ten voters (29%) who viewed the third debate came away with a more favorable view of the president, compared with only 13% after the first debate.

Bush's efforts to raise questions about Clinton's character and credibility have had some success. The Arkansas governor is seen as the most honest and trustworthy candidate by only 23% of voters who watched Monday night's debate, while 36% see Bush as most trustworthy. Moreover, one half of debate viewers (52%) agree with Bush's charge that Clinton has shown a pattern of trying to take both sides of controversial issues.

In this three-way race, the candidate who succeeds in damaging an opponent does not always reap the benefits. While Clinton may have lost some votes as a result of the debate, the candidate who seemed to gain was not Bush but Perot. Overall, 6% of debate viewers say that what they saw led them to switch their vote from Clinton to another candidate; another 2% did the opposite—switched their vote from another candidate to Clinton. The Arkansas governor, therefore, suffered a net loss in support of 4 percentage points. President Bush, however, did not show a net gain. As many voters say they shifted away from Bush after the debate as shifted toward him (3 percentage points each). In contrast, Perot scored a 6-point net gain, as 7% of voters moved toward him and only 1% of his original supporters defected to other candidates.

OCTOBER 25
PRESIDENTIAL TRIAL HEAT/PRESIDENTIAL CANDIDATES

Interviewing Date: 10/21–22/92*
Survey #GO 322025–02
(National Tracking–Phase II)

Asked of registered voters: If the presidential election were being held today, would you vote for the Republican ticket of George Bush and Dan Quayle, for the Democratic ticket of Bill Clinton and Al Gore, or for the independent candidates

*Gallup survey for CNN/*USA Today*

Ross Perot and James Stockdale? [Those who were undecided were asked: As of today, do you lean more to Bush and Quayle, the Republicans; to Clinton and Gore, the Democrats; or to Perot and Stockdale, the independents?]

Bush-Quayle	31%
Clinton-Gore	43
Perot-Stockdale	18
Undecided; other	8

Selected National Trend

	Bush-Quayle	*Clinton-Gore*	*Perot-Stockdale*	*Undecided; other*
1992				
Oct. 13–15	34%	47%	13%	6%
Oct. 6–8	34	49	10	7

Also asked of registered voters: Please tell me whether you have a favorable or unfavorable opinion of each of the following presidential candidates:

George Bush?

Favorable	43%
Unfavorable	50
No opinion	7

Selected National Trend

	Favorable	*Unfavorable*	*No opinion*
1992			
October 6–8	42%	54%	4%
September 28–30	40	56	4

Bill Clinton?

Favorable	53%
Unfavorable	39
No opinion	8

Selected National Trend

	Favorable	*Unfavorable*	*No opinion*
1992			
October 6–8	56%	39%	5%
September 28–30	54	38	8

Ross Perot?

Favorable	53%
Unfavorable	35
No opinion	12

Selected National Trend

	Favorable	*Unfavorable*	*No opinion*
1992			
October 6–8	24%	65%	11%
September 28–30	20	66	14

Also asked of registered voters: Do you think Bill Clinton has the honesty and integrity to serve as president, or not?

Yes	52%
No	38
No opinion	10

Selected National Trend

	Yes	*No*	*No opinion*
1992			
September 11–15	62%	29%	9%
July 6–8	56	36	8

Note: As the presidential campaign nears its final week, the third-place candidate, Ross Perot, has the momentum. In a Gallup Poll taken two weeks ago, before the first presidential debate, the Clinton-Gore ticket led with 49% of the vote, followed by the Bush-Quayle ticket with 34% and the Perot ticket with 10%. Today, after the third and final debate, the Clinton slate has slipped to 43%, the Bush slate is essentially flat at 31%, while Perot's has almost doubled to 18%.

Perot's image has improved markedly since the debates and his recent "infomercial" television spots. When he first reentered the race, as many as two thirds of voters expressed an unfavorable opinion of the Texas entrepreneur. That percentage has declined to 35%, and over one half of voters (53%) now say that they view Perot positively.

Bill Clinton's overall favorability ratings are essentially unchanged: 53% favorable versus 39% unfavorable, but George Bush's efforts to create doubts in voters' minds about the Arkansas governor's trustworthiness appear to have had some success. Only about one half of voters (52%) now says that Clinton has the honesty and integrity to serve as president, down from 62% in mid-September. Clinton has been damaged most among Republicans, baby boomers, southerners, and midwesterners.

The overall poll results might suggest that Perot's surge is coming almost exclusively at Clinton's expense, but analysis indicates otherwise. While Bush appears to be winning over some voters who had previously favored Clinton, Perot is pulling votes from both major party opponents.

OCTOBER 30
PARTY BETTER FOR PEACE AND PROSPERITY

Interviewing Date: 10/23–25/92*
Survey #GO 322025–02
(National Tracking–Phase II)

Asked of registered voters: Looking ahead for the next few years, which political party do you think would be more likely to keep the United States out of war—the Republican or the Democratic party?

Republican	36%
Democratic	40
No difference (volunteered)	11
No opinion	13

	Repub-lican	*Demo-cratic*	*No difference; no opinion*
By Sex			
Male	40%	34%	26%
Female	32	45	23
By Ethnic Background			
White	38	37	25
Nonwhite	22	61	17
By Education			
College Graduate	38	39	23
College Incomplete	35	46	19
No College	35	38	27
By Region			
East	32	42	26
Midwest	35	38	27
South	44	37	19
West	31	43	26
By Age			
18–29 Years	38	49	13
30–49 Years	40	39	21
50 Years and Over	39	36	25
By Household Income			
$50,000 and Over	41	37	22
$30,000–$49,999	39	39	22
$20,000–$29,999	41	35	24
Under $20,000	27	48	25
By Politics			
Republicans	71	11	18
Democrats	11	68	21
Independents	33	33	34

*Gallup survey for CNN/*USA Today*

Prepresidential Election Trend

	Repub-lican	*Demo-cratic**	*Party of the winner*
Oct. 1988	43%	26%	Republican
Sept. 1984	38	38	Republican
Sept. 1980	25	42	Republican
Aug. 1976	29	32	Democratic
Sept. 1972	32	28	Republican
Oct. 1968	37	24	Republican
Oct. 1964	22	45	Democratic
Oct. 1960	40	25	Democratic
Oct. 1956	46	16	Republican

*"No difference" and "no opinion" are omitted.

Also asked of registered voters: Which political party—the Republican or the Democratic—will do a better job of keeping the country prosperous?

Republican	36%
Democratic	45
No difference (volunteered)	10
No opinion	9

	Republican	Democratic	No difference; no opinion
By Sex			
Male	40%	41%	19%
Female	34	48	18
By Ethnic Background			
White	40	41	19
Nonwhite	13	69	18
By Education			
College Graduate	44	38	18
College Incomplete	37	44	19
No College	33	48	19
By Region			
East	30	54	16
Midwest	35	41	24
South	41	43	16
West	39	42	19
By Age			
18–29 Years	44	42	14
30–49 Years	38	42	20
50 Years and Over	32	48	20
By Household Income			
$50,000 and Over	41	31	28
$30,000–$49,999	43	40	17
$20,000–$29,999	38	41	21
Under $20,000	27	57	16
By Politics			
Republicans	80	10	10
Democrats	10	83	7
Independents	32	34	34

Prepresidential Election Trend

	Republican	Democratic*	Party of the winner
Oct. 1988	48%	32%	Republican
Sept. 1984	49	33	Republican
Sept. 1980	35	36	Republican
Aug. 1976	23	47	Democratic
Sept. 1972	38	35	Republican
Oct. 1968	34	37	Republican
Oct. 1964	21	53	Democratic
Oct. 1960	31	46	Democratic
Oct. 1956	39	39	Republican

*"No difference" and "no opinion" are omitted.

Note: As the general election nears, voters see the Democratic party as better able than the Republican party to keep the country prosperous, by a margin of 9 percentage points (45% to 36%)—dramatically better than its position on this measure just before the 1988 presidential election, when it trailed the GOP by 16 points, 32% to 48%. Moreover, the Democrats have improved their standing since 1988 on the prosperity question among every demographic subgroup measured by Gallup.

A political party's performance on this measure just prior to a presidential election often has been a predictor of the election's outcome. As such, the news for the Democrats is not necessarily good; their margin of 9 percentage points is considerably smaller than those of 1960, 1964, and 1976, the only years over the last eight elections when the Democrats captured the White House. In 1960 they enjoyed a margin of 15 percentage points on the prosperity measure. Just prior to Lyndon Johnson's 1964 landslide, the prosperity margin was 32 points; before Jimmy Carter's election in 1976, the Democrats led by 24 points.

There may even be some heartening news for George Bush. Unlike the Democrats, two recent Republican candidates were able to capture the White House even though their party trailed behind slightly on the prosperity measure: Richard Nixon in 1968 and Ronald Reagan in 1980.

The current poll of registered voters shows a clear difference in opinion between the sexes on the prosperity issue. Men split evenly: 41% choose the Democrats; 40%, the Republicans. Among women, 34% select the GOP and 48% the Democratic party. This gender gap also is evident on the question of which party can better keep the United States out of war, where the Democrats currently are favored by a margin of 40% to 36%. Men opt for the GOP, 40% to 34%; women choose the Democrats, 45% to 32%.

NOVEMBER 1
PRESIDENTIAL TRIAL HEAT: LIKELY VOTERS

Interviewing Date: 10/30–31/92*
Survey #GO 322025–03 (National Tracking–Phase III)

*Asked of likely voters:** If the presidential election were being held today, would you vote for the Republican candidates, George Bush and Dan Quayle; for the Democratic candidates, Bill Clinton and Al Gore; or for the independent candidates, Ross Perot and James Stockdale? [Those who were undecided were asked: As of today, do you lean more to Bush and Quayle, the Republicans; to Clinton and Gore, the Democrats; or to Perot and Stockdale, the independents?]*

Bush-Quayle	36%
Clinton-Gore	43
Perot-Stockdale	15
Undecided; other	6

**"Likely voters" were identified through seven questions about their voting history and intentions. The likely voter base assumes that 55% of the voting-age population will turn out on Tuesday, November 3, up from 1988's 50%.

Selected National Trend
(Likely Voters)

	Bush-Quayle	*Clinton-Gore*	*Perot-Stockdale*	*Undecided; other*
1992				
Oct. 28–29	40%	41%	14%	5%
Oct. 26–27	38	40	16	6
Oct. 24–25	34	43	17	6
Oct. 22–23	32	41	18	9
Oct. 20–21	35	44	15	6

Asked of those likely voters who named a candidate: Do you support the Bush-Quayle, Clinton-Gore, or Perot-Stockdale ticket strongly or only moderately?

	Bush-Quayle	*Clinton-Gore*	*Perot-Stockdale*
Strongly	57%	70%	60%
Moderately	43	30	40

*Gallup survey for CNN/*USA Today*

Bush Vote in the 1988 and 1992 Preelection Polls
(Likely Voters)

	Nov. 3–6, 1988	*Oct. 30–31, 1992*	*Point change*
By Sex			
Male	56%	36%	-20
Female	50	36	-14
By Ethnic Background			
White	57	39	-18
Black	11	7	-4
By Education			
College Graduate	57	39	-18
College Incomplete	57	30	-27
No College	47	30	-17
By Region			
East	48	34	-14
Midwest	52	32	-20
South	59	45	-14
West	52	32	-20
By Age			
18–29 Years	62	31	-31
30–49 Years	54	38	-16
50 Years and Over	50	37	-13
By Household Income*			
$50,000 and Over	65	43	-22
$30,000–$49,999	56	36	-20
$20,000–$29,999	52	39	-13
Under $20,000	41	29	-12
By Politics			
Republicans	93	76	-17
Democrats	14	7	-7
Independents	54	30	-24
By Ethnic Background/Region			
Northern Whites	54	35	-19
Southern Whites	67	50	-17

*In 1988: $15,000–$29,999; Under $15,000

Also asked of likely voters: Please tell me whether you have a favorable or unfavorable opinion of each of the following presidential candidates:

George Bush?

Favorable..45%
Unfavorable......................................51
No opinion...4

Selected National Trend
(Likely Voters)

	Favor-able	*Unfavor-able*	*No opinion*
1992			
October 28–29	49%	47%	4%
October 26–27	45	49	6

Bill Clinton?

Favorable..50%
Unfavorable......................................46
No opinion...4

Selected National Trend
(Likely Voters)

	Favor-able	*Unfavor-able*	*No opinion*
1992			
October 28–29	48%	45%	7%
October 26–27	47	47	6

Ross Perot?

Favorable..45%
Unfavorable......................................48
No opinion...7

Selected National Trend
(Likely Voters)

	Favor-able	*Unfavor-able*	*No opinion*
1992			
October 28–29	41%	47%	12%
October 26–27	44	45	11

Note: As the presidential race moves into the final weekend, Bill Clinton has regained the momentum. The results of the latest Gallup tracking poll of likely voters show Clinton's lead over George Bush expanding to 7 points, 43% to 36%. The president had surged ahead earlier in the week, moving to within 1 percentage point (40% versus 41%) of Clinton in the polling completed on October 28–29.

Ross Perot's support has declined over the past week to 15%, down from the 19% tracking poll results attained before he aired his charges of dirty tricks against the Republicans. Voter support for the Texas entrepreneur now exactly matches George Wallace's support level in Gallup's final poll in 1968, when Wallace captured 13% of the vote that year—more than any other third-party or independent presidential candidate of the postwar era.

Clinton's gains in the new poll have come from outside the South. In contrast, the president continues to gain ground in the South, where he won his largest margins of victory four years ago. Bush now has a 45%-to-36% lead in the region.

Analysis of tracking poll data from the last few weeks suggests that Perot's presence in the race is not a major factor in most of the largest states. In the industrial states of New York, Pennsylvania, Illinois, Ohio, and Michigan, and in California—the largest electoral prize—Clinton leads Bush by about the same margin in a hypothetical two-way race as he does in a three-way race with Perot.

In most states and regions where Perot does seem to affect the race, however, the front-runner benefits. Clinton's boost from Perot is most evident in the New England states, New Jersey, Texas, and the Pacific Northwest. Perot helps Bush most by taking votes away from Clinton in the West Central region, including the battleground state of Wisconsin.

Clinton's surge has occurred since new evidence suggested that Bush was not "out of the loop" on the trade of arms for hostages in the Iran-*contra* affair. The poll included no direct questions on this issue, but Clinton's gains among specific voter groups—men (up 6 percentage points), older voters (up 5), and college graduates (up 5)—are suggestive. These kinds of voters are traditionally most likely to follow political news closely.

The Arkansas governor's lead seems relatively solid, given that seven in ten of his voters (70%) are strongly committed to their choice. Clinton voters are more likely than Bush voters (57%) and Perot voters (60%) to express such a high level of commitment. If Clinton were to take all of the undecided vote in the poll, his lead would expand to 13 points, at 49% to the Bush-Quayle ticket's 36%.

The front-runner may have a further cushion in that he can expect to win the major share of the voters who remain undecided in the final days of polling. An analysis of six presidential races featuring incumbents between 1956 and 1984 shows that the incumbent president's share of the vote on election day generally does not exceed his support level in the final Gallup Poll—before any attempt is made to allocate the undecided vote among the candidates. Presidents Dwight Eisenhower, Lyndon Johnson, Richard Nixon, and Jimmy Carter all failed to improve on their poll scores on election day. President Gerald Ford gained only 1 point; President Ronald Reagan gained 2 points.

The president's 36% support in the current poll is 17 points lower than his support level of 53% in Gallup's final survey four years ago. The biggest shifts away from Bush since 1988 are seen among young voters (down 31 points among those age 18 to 29), political independents (down 24 points), and those with incomes of $50,000 or more (down 22 points). The president's support level is also down by 20 points among men and among voters in the Midwest and West.

NOVEMBER 2
PRESIDENTIAL TRIAL HEAT: FINAL SURVEY

Interviewing Date: 10/31–11/1/92*
Survey #GO 322025–03 (National Tracking–Phase III)

Asked of likely voters: If the presidential election were being held today, would you vote for the Republican candidates, George Bush and Dan Quayle; for the Democratic candidates, Bill Clinton and Al Gore; or for the independent candidates, Ross Perot and James Stockdale? [Those who were undecided were asked: As of today, do you lean more to Bush and Quayle, the Republicans; to Clinton and Gore, the Democrats; or to Perot and Stockdale, the independents?]

Bush-Quayle	36%
Clinton-Gore	44
Perot-Stockdale	14
Undecided; other	6

	Bush-Quayle	*Clinton-Gore*	*Perot-Stockdale*	*Undecided; other*
By Region				
East	32%	48%	14%	6%
Midwest	33	43	16	8
South	45	38	13	4
West	34	46	14	6

Selected National Trend
(Likely Voters)

	Bush-Quayle	*Clinton-Gore*	*Perot-Stockdale*	*Undecided; other*
1992				
Oct. 30–31	36%	43%	15%	6%
Oct. 28–29	40	41	14	5
Oct. 26–27	38	40	16	6
Oct. 24–25	34	43	17	6
Oct. 22–23	32	41	18	9
Oct. 20–21	35	44	15	6

Final Gallup 1992
Preelection Estimate*
(With "Undecided" Allocated)

Clinton-Gore	49%
Bush-Quayle	37
Perot-Stockdale	14

*The actual turnout was 55.2% of the voting-age population, the highest since 1968. Governor Clinton received 44,908,232 votes, or 43.0% of those cast; his total was 23.8% of

*Gallup survey for CNN/*USA Today*

the eligible electorate, the smallest percentage since the election of John Quincy Adams in 1824. President Bush received 39,102,282 votes, or 37.5% of those cast; Ross Perot, 19,725,433 votes, or 18.9%; and other candidates, 0.6%.

Note: A Gallup Poll conducted on October 31 and November 1 shows the Clinton-Gore ticket leading the Bush-Quayle ticket by 44% to 36% among likely voters, with the Perot slate at 14%. Bill Clinton's lead increases when the 6 percent of voters who are undecided is allocated by Gallup to the candidates: 49% for the Democratic ticket, 37% for the Republican ticket, and 14% for the independent ticket.

Clinton holds a comfortable lead over George Bush among likely voters in all regions of the country except the South. Until one week ago, southern voters, who favored Bush over Michael Dukakis by 20 points in 1988, had leaned toward the Democratic ticket in this election. Over the past week, however, the South shifted from Clinton to Bush, who now holds the edge there, 45% to 38%.

In all other regions, Clinton's margin over Bush is in the double digits: the Arkansas governor leads the president by 48% to 32% in the East, 46% to 34% in the West, and 43% to 33% in the Midwest. Ross Perot receives statistically equal levels of support in all four regions: 13% in the South, 14% each in the East and West, and 16% in the Midwest.

NOVEMBER 14
EXPECTATIONS FOR THE CLINTON ADMINISTRATION

Interviewing Date: 11/10–11/92*
Survey #GO 322032

In general, are you satisfied or dissatisfied with the way things are going in the United States at this time?

Satisfied	26%
Dissatisfied	68
No opinion	6

*Gallup survey for CNN/*USA Today*

	Satisfied	*Dis-satisfied*	*No opinion*
By Sex			
Male	30%	64%	6%
Female	22	72	6
By Ethnic Background			
White	26	68	6
Nonwhite	25	72	3
Black	26	70	4
By Education			
College Graduate	27	67	6
College Incomplete	25	69	6
High-School Graduate	22	73	5
Less Than High-School Graduate	35	57	8
By Region			
East	16	78	6
Midwest	28	65	7
South	33	61	6
West	24	71	5
By Age			
18–29 Years	33	64	3
30–49 Years	25	70	5
50 Years and Over	24	68	8
By Politics			
Republicans	35	59	6
Democrats	25	71	4
Independents	22	71	7
By Community Size			
Urban	22	74	4
Suburban	28	66	6
Rural	29	63	8
By 1992 Presidential Vote			
Bill Clinton	22	71	7
George Bush	35	61	4
Ross Perot	13	82	5
Did Not Vote	30	65	5

Selected National Trend

	Satisfied	*Dis-satisfied*	*No opinion*
1992			
June 12–14	14%	84%	2%

February 28– March 1	21	78	1
1991			
December	37	60	3
August	49	45	6
March	52	43	5

Do you think the country will be better off or worse off four years from now?

Better off....................................51%
Worse off....................................31
Same (volunteered)....................................6
No opinion....................................12

Asked of registered voters: Next, I'd like your opinion of some people in politics. As I read each name, please tell me whether you have a favorable or unfavorable opinion of this person:

Bill Clinton?

Favorable....................................60%
Unfavorable....................................34
No opinion....................................6

George Bush?

Favorable....................................47%
Unfavorable....................................51
No opinion....................................2

Al Gore?

Favorable....................................59%
Unfavorable....................................27
No opinion....................................14

Hillary Clinton?

Favorable....................................5%
Unfavorable....................................29
No opinion....................................21

Have Bill Clinton's statements and actions over the last week made you more confident or less confident in his ability to serve as president?

More confident....................................53%
Less confident....................................26
No difference (volunteered)....................................12
No opinion....................................9

Do you think Bill Clinton has the honesty and integrity to serve as president, or not?

Yes....................................69%
No....................................27
No opinion....................................4

Selected National Trend

	Yes	No	No opinion
1992			
October 20–21	52%	38%	10%
September 11–15	62	29	9
July 6–8	56	36	8

Next, I have some questions about the Clinton administration, which will take office in January. Regardless of which presidential candidate you preferred, do you think the Clinton administration will be able to do each of the following, or not:

Improve education?

Yes....................................69%
No....................................25
No opinion....................................6

Improve conditions for minorities and the poor?

Yes....................................68%
No....................................27
No opinion....................................5

Improve the quality of the environment?

Yes....................................64%
No....................................29
No opinion....................................7

Improve the health-care system?

Yes....................................64%
No....................................30
No opinion....................................6

Keep the nation out of war?

Yes....................60%
No....................27
No opinion....................13

Improve the economy?

Yes....................59%
No....................35
No opinion....................6

Reduce unemployment?

Yes....................58%
No....................37
No opinion....................5

Increase respect for the United States abroad?

Yes....................50%
No....................40
No opinion....................10

Control federal spending?

Yes....................40%
No....................54
No opinion....................6

Reduce the federal budget deficit?

Yes....................38%
No....................54
No opinion....................8

Avoid raising your taxes?

Yes....................20%
No....................74
No opinion....................6

What should be the top priority for the Clinton administration in its first hundred days: creating jobs, cutting the deficit, reforming health care, improving education, or something else?

Creating jobs....................49%
Cutting the deficit....................17
Reforming health care....................14
Improving education....................8
Something else....................10
No opinion....................2

Bill Clinton's plan to improve the economy calls for reducing the deficit, no increases in taxes on the middle class, and no cuts in spending for entitlement programs. Suppose it becomes necessary for Clinton to compromise on one of these objectives. Which one of the following should he be willing to do first—postpone reducing the deficit, raise taxes on the middle class, or cut federal spending for entitlement programs such as Social Security?

Postpone reducing the deficit....................44%
Cut entitlement programs....................24
Raise middle-class taxes....................22
All of these (volunteered)....................1
None; other....................4
No opinion....................5

Asked of registered voters: Now that Bill Clinton has been elected president, do you think he should consult with Ross Perot on economic matters, appoint Perot to a high position in his administration, do both, or do neither?

Consult Perot....................29%
Appoint Perot....................5
Both....................28
Neither....................36
No opinion....................2

From what you know about Hillary Clinton, does she come closer to your own values and life-style than previous First Ladies, or not?

Yes....................42%
No....................41
No opinion....................17

Women Only

	Yes	*No*	*No opinion*
By Ethnic Background			
White..........	40%	43%	17%
Nonwhite..........	61	27	12

By Education			
College Graduate......56	41	3	
College Incomplete...43	47	10	
No College............37	39	24	
By Region			
East......................46	37	17	
Midwest.................37	44	19	
South....................41	43	16	
West.....................46	39	15	
By Age			
18–29 Years...........49	34	17	
30–49 Years...........41	47	12	
50–64 Years...........42	39	19	
65 Years and Over.....39	36	25	
By Politics			
Republicans............17	66	17	
Democrats..............63	19	18	
Independents...........36	49	15	
By Community Size			
Urban....................50	34	16	
Suburban................35	47	18	
Rural.....................41	43	16	

Which worries you more—that Hillary Clinton won't have a large-enough role in the Clinton administration, or that she will have too large a role, or does neither worry you very much?

Not large enough..................................4%
Too large..26
Not worried..67
No opinion..3

How important is it to you that Bill Clinton increase the number of women and minorities in high administration positions—would you say it is very important, somewhat important, not too important, or not at all important?

Very important..................................32%
Somewhat important............................39
Not too important...............................18
Not at all important..............................9
No opinion..2

	Very impor-tant	*Somewhat impor-tant*	*Not too impor-tant*	*Not at all impor-tant**
By Sex				
Male............28%	39%	20%	12%
Female..........36	38	17	7
By Ethnic Background				
White...........27	42	20	10
Nonwhite......65	19	10	4

*"No opinion"—at 2% or less—is omitted.

Note: Bill Clinton has made a generally positive impression on the public during his first week as president-elect. A new postelection Gallup Poll finds a majority (53%) saying that they have more confidence in Clinton as a result of his statements and actions since the election; only about one in four (26%) has less confidence in him.

While two thirds of Americans (68%) say that they are dissatisfied with the way things are going in the country, there are signs that the change in administrations is elevating the public mood. In June, before the election, an even larger proportion (84%) expressed dissatisfaction with the direction of the country. Looking to the future, more people say that they expect the country to be better off (51%) than worse off (31%) in four years' time.

Six in ten (59%) expect the new administration to be successful in improving the economy, the top concern of the voters in this election year. Still larger majorities believe that Clinton will make progress in a variety of domestic problems, including improving education (69%), conditions for minorities and the poor (68%), the health-care system (64%), and the quality of the environment (64%).

Expectations for the new administration are lower in two areas that rated high on Ross Perot's agenda during the campaign: reducing the size of the federal budget deficit and controlling federal spending. Only 38% say that Clinton will succeed in cutting the deficit, while a similar proportion (40%) thinks that he will be able to keep federal spending in check.

The public is least confident (20%) that Clinton will be able to avoid raising their taxes. The public's skepticism, however, is nothing new. In 1988, even though George Bush promised "no new taxes," only 24% told Gallup that they thought Bush indeed would be able to avoid a tax hike.

The public seems to agree with the president-elect that improving the economy should take priority over solving the deficit problem. When asked what the Clinton administration's priority should be during its first hundred days, the public overwhelmingly chooses creating jobs (49%) over cutting the deficit (17%). Moreover, if Clinton is forced to choose among raising taxes, cutting entitlements, and putting off action on the deficit, a plurality (44%) replies that he should postpone reducing the deficit.

The response to Clinton as president-elect is more favorable than might be expected. After all, he is the first presidential candidate since Richard Nixon to reach the White House despite winning less than a majority of the popular vote (Clinton's 43% of the vote equals Nixon's total against Hubert Humphrey in 1968).

In the heat of the last days of the campaign, the Arkansas governor's favorability ratings among registered voters slumped to 51% favorable, 44% unfavorable. Since his victory, however, Clinton's ratings have improved significantly: 60% favorable versus 34% unfavorable. The voters have not been as kind to President Bush in defeat; his ratings remain negative (47% favorable versus 51% unfavorable) and are virtually unchanged from those recorded in the final days of the campaign.

Unlike her husband, Hillary Clinton has not seen her public image improve in the afterglow of the election victory. In fact, her favorability ratings have dipped slightly among registered voters. Currently, one half (50%) has a favorable opinion of her, while three in ten (29%) have an unfavorable opinion. In early September, her ratings were somewhat more positive (56% favorable versus 25% unfavorable).

Many voters may not be entirely comfortable with having a career woman with strong political views of her own in the role of First Lady. One in four (26%) is worried that Mrs. Clinton will play too large a role in the administration.

Women are evenly divided over whether the new First Lady comes closer than her predecessors to their own values and life-style (42% versus 41%). Those under 30, not women of Mrs. Clinton's own generation, are more likely to see themselves in her. One half of women under 30 (49%), compared with 41% of those age 30 to 49, feel closer to Mrs. Clinton than they do to previous First Ladies.

NOVEMBER 14
CASPAR WEINBERGER

Interviewing Date: 11/10–11/92*
Survey #GO 322032

*Do you think President Bush should give a pardon to former Defense Secretary Caspar Weinberger so that Weinberger cannot be prosecuted for his alleged involvement in the Iran-*contra *affair, or not?*

Yes	27%
No	59
No opinion	14

	Yes	*No*	*No opinion*
By Politics			
Republicans	44%	40%	16%
Democrats	16	70	14
Independents	26	61	13

Note: By a more than 2-to-1 margin, Americans say that President George Bush should not pardon former Defense Secretary Caspar Weinberger for his alleged involvement in the Iran-*contra* affair. According to a new Gallup Poll, six in ten (59%) think that Weinberger should not be pardoned, while 27% believe that he should.

*Gallup survey for CNN/*USA Today*

In 1988, when President Ronald Reagan was under similar pressure to pardon National Security Adviser John Poindexter and Colonel Oliver North for their respective roles in the clandestine arms-for-hostages deal, the public was more supportive: 49% favored pardoning Poindexter and North, while 41% were opposed.

President Gerald Ford's pardon of Richard Nixon for Watergate misdeeds was not supported by the public, however. More than one half of respondents (55%) thought that Ford made the wrong decision in granting the pardon, while only 35% said that he did the right thing.

NOVEMBER 21
CLINTON'S MANDATE FOR CHANGE

Interviewing Date: 11/10–11/92*
Survey #GO 322032

I'm going to read to you some proposals that are now being discussed nationally. As I read each one, please tell me whether you generally favor or oppose:

Raising federal income taxes on those making over $200,000?

Favor	80%
Oppose	17
No opinion	3

	Favor	*Oppose*	*No opinion*
By 1992 Vote			
Clinton Voters	93%	5%	2%
Bush Voters	72	26	2
Perot Voters	82	15	3

Requiring companies to allow employees up to twelve weeks' unpaid leave if they had a new baby, or if there were a serious illness in the immediate family?

Favor	75%
Oppose	23
No opinion	2

*Gallup survey for CNN/*USA Today*

	Favor	*Oppose*	*No opinion*
By 1992 Vote			
Clinton Voters	83%	15%	2%
Bush Voters	66	30	4
Perot Voters	71	27	2

Allowing doctors and health-care workers at federally funded clinics to discuss abortion with their patients as a family-planning option?

Favor	65%
Oppose	33
No opinion	2

	Favor	*Oppose*	*No opinion*
By 1992 Vote			
Clinton Voters	73%	25%	2%
Bush Voters	55	42	3
Perot Voters	66	34	*

*Less than 1%

Allowing women in the military into combat jobs?

Favor	55%
Oppose	42
No opinion	3

	Favor	*Oppose*	*No opinion*
By 1992 Vote			
Clinton Voters	59%	37%	4%
Bush Voters	46	51	3
Perot Voters	58	40	2

Allowing gays to serve in the military?

Favor	49%
Oppose	45
No opinion	6

	Favor	*Oppose*	*No opinion*
By 1992 Vote			
Clinton Voters	69%	27%	4%

Bush Voters	34	61	5
Perot Voters	41	54	5

Banning companies from hiring permanent replacement workers during strikes?

Favor	36%
Oppose	57
No opinion	7

	Favor	Oppose	No opinion
By 1992 Vote			
Clinton Voters	37%	56%	7%
Bush Voters	34	56	10
Perot Voters	35	60	5

Note: President-elect Bill Clinton soon will be able to test the "mandate for change" that his election has been said to represent. The Arkansas governor campaigned on a number of domestic issues against the policies of the Bush administration and promised quick action to reverse those policies, if elected. To achieve this, Clinton is hoping that the majority of Americans who voted against George Bush will support his agenda for change.

According to a new Gallup Poll, there appears to be little political cost to Clinton for raising taxes on the rich, mandating family leave, or removing abortion counseling restrictions at federally funded clinics. An overwhelming majority (80%) supports raising federal income taxes on those making over $200,000; only 17% oppose the idea. This is nearly as true among Bush voters (72% favor such a tax hike) as among Clinton voters (93%) and is supported by 82% of Perot voters.

Moreover, three quarters (75%) favor requiring companies to allow employees up to twelve weeks' unpaid leave for a new baby or for a serious family illness. And a clear majority (65%) favors allowing doctors and health-care workers at federally funded clinics to discuss abortion as an option with their patients. Perot voters and independents are somewhat closer to Clinton's position on this question than are those who voted for Bush.

Clinton has promised change in areas which appeal to Democratic constituencies such as labor unions, feminists, and homosexuals. While these groups provided strong financial and political backing to Clinton's candidacy, satisfying their agendas may be a difficult task. Only a slight majority supports women in military combat (55% favor versus 42% oppose), while a slim plurality favors allowing gays to serve in the military (49% versus 45%). Allowing women to serve in combat is favored by nearly six in ten Clinton and Perot voters (59% and 58%). Another seven in ten (69%) who backed Clinton in the election favor allowing gays to serve in the military, but only 41% of Perot voters favor the proposal. Least popular on Clinton's list for change is his proposal to ban companies from hiring permanent replacement workers during strikes (only 36% favor it).

NOVEMBER 26
SUPERMAN AND SUPERHEROES

Interviewing Date: 11/20–22/92
Survey #GO 322034

Did you ever read superhero comics as a child or as a teenager?

Yes	52%
No	47
No opinion	1

	Yes	No	No opinion
By Age			
18–29 Years	51%	49%	*
30–49 Years	56	44	*
50 Years and Over	51	49	*

*Less than 1%

Do you now, or did you ever in the past, read superhero comics as an adult?

Yes, now	6%
Yes, in the past	11
No	83

	Yes, now	Yes, in the past	No
By Age			
18–29 Years	12%	13%	75%

30–49 Years	7	12	81
50 Years and Over	3	9	88

Regardless of whether you have ever read superhero comics, who would you say is your favorite superhero?

Superman	44%
Batman	8
Spiderman	5
Others	14
None; no opinion	29

	Superman	*Batman*	*Spiderman*	*Others**
By Age				
18–29 Years	41%	14%	12%	20%
30–49 Years	55	9	6	12
50 Years and Over	35	3	1	13

*"None; no opinion" is omitted.

Thinking about the DC Comics character Superman, do you happen to know the name of his home planet?

Yes, Krypton	39%
Yes, incorrect; no	59
No opinion	2

	Yes, Krypton	*Incorrect; no*	*No opinion*
By Age			
18–29 Years	51%	47%	2%
30–49 Years	51	45	4
50 Years and Over	22	77	1

Do you happen to know the name of Superman's girlfriend?

Yes, Lois Lane	66%
Yes, incorrect; no	33
No opinion	1

	Yes, Lois Lane	*Incorrect; no*	*No opinion*
By Age			
18–29 Years	70%	29%	1%
30–49 Years	81	18	1
50 Years and Over	49	50	1

As you may know, Superman dies in the most recent issue of his DC comic book. Do you think DC Comics should find a way to bring Superman back to life in a future issue, or do you think his time has passed and he shouldn't be brought back?

Bring Superman back	60%
His time has passed	25
Don't care	12
No opinion	3

	Bring Superman back	*His time has passed*	*Don't care*	*No opinion*
By Age				
18–29 Years	64%	30%	5%	1%
30–49 Years	70	19	9	2
50 Years and Over	48	30	17	5

Note: In the public's view, Superman should not join such heroes as Captain Marvel and Flash Gordon in permanent retirement from the comic pages. According to a new Gallup Poll, a majority of adults hopes that the Man of Steel's exploits will continue, despite his death in the current issue of Superman comics: 60% want to see the slain Kryptonian brought back to life, while only one quarter (25%) views him as a faded superhero whose time has passed.

Superman made his debut in 1938, during the Great Depression, but the character holds the most sentimental appeal for the baby-boom generation. As youths in the 1950s and 1960s, they helped make Superman comics the top seller of the time. Today, as adults in the 30 to 49 years group, they overwhelmingly vote to see their hero resurrected: 70% say that he should be brought back to life, while only 19% think that his time is over. Both younger and older people are half again as likely as baby boomers to say that Superman's time has passed.

Today, Superman's publisher, DC Comics, is a distant second in sales to industry leader Marvel, home of Spiderman, the Incredible Hulk, and the X-Men. Superman, however, still rates as the favorite comic-book superhero of U.S. adults: 44% of those polled say that the Man of Steel is their personal favorite. Yet the growing competition from other costumed crime fighters is evident in the response of different age groups. Among those over 30, there is more mention of Superman than all other superheroes combined (45% versus 22%). Among those under 30, however, as many name someone else—Batman (14%), Spiderman (12%), and others (20%)—as name Superman (41%).

Featured in a 1940s radio serial, a 1950s television series (currently rerunning on cable's Nickelodeon network), and four movies starring Christopher Reeve, Superman has become an American icon. The public evidently knows more about him than it does about American history. For example, four in ten adults polled (39%), and fully one half (51%) of those under age 50, can correctly identify Superman's home planet as Krypton. By comparison, in a Gallup Poll last year only 13% of adults could identify Delaware as the first state. Two thirds of those polled this year (66%) name Lois Lane as the Man of Steel's girlfriend; however, in last year's poll, only one third (34%) could identify John Adams as our second president.

The audience for superhero comics used to be limited almost exclusively to teenagers and children. Today, nearly one in six (17%) say that they have read superhero comics as adults, including 6% who are current readers of the genre. A generational difference is apparent. Adults under age 30 are no more likely than those over 50 to say that they read superhero comics in their youth (51% each), but these same young people are twice as likely as those over 50 to say that they have read superhero comics as adults (25% versus 12%).

DECEMBER 5
GAMBLING: LEGALIZATION

Interviewing Date: 11/20–22/92
Survey #GO 322034

As you may know, some states legalize betting so that the state can raise revenues. Please tell me whether you would approve or disapprove of legalizing each of the following types of betting in your state to help raise revenues. [Those who replied "already legal" were then asked: Do you approve or disapprove of its being legal?]

Bingo for cash prizes?

Approve..........72%
Disapprove..........25
No opinion..........3

Selected National Trend

	Approve
1989	75%
1982	74
1975	68

Casino gambling at resort areas?

Approve..........51%
Disapprove..........47
No opinion..........2

Selected National Trend

	Approve
1989	55%
1982	51
1975	40

Casino gambling in a major city?

Approve..........40%
Disapprove..........57
No opinion..........3

Lotteries for cash prizes?

Approve..........75%
Disapprove..........24
No opinion..........1

Selected National Trend

	Approve
1989	78%
1982	72
1975	61

Offtrack betting on horse races?

Approve..........49%
Disapprove..........47
No opinion..........4

Selected National Trend

	Approve
1989	54%
1982	54

Betting on professional sports such as baseball, basketball, or football?

Approve....................................33%
Disapprove....................................65
No opinion....................................2

Selected National Trend

	Approve
1989	42%
1982	51
1975	31

Casino gambling on Indian reservations?

Approve....................................42%
Disapprove....................................51
No opinion....................................7

Casino gambling on so-called riverboats?

Approve....................................60%
Disapprove....................................38
No opinion....................................2

I'd like to know whether you agree or disagree with each of the following arguments in favor of legalized state-sponsored gambling:

It provides much-needed revenue for education and programs for senior citizens?

Agree....................................57%
Disagree....................................41
No opinion....................................2

If the state sponsors gambling, organized crime can be kept out?

Agree....................................37%
Disagree....................................59
No opinion....................................4

It creates jobs and helps stimulate the local economy?

Agree....................................64%
Disagree....................................33
No opinion....................................3

People will gamble anyhow, so the state might as well make it legal and get some of the revenue?

Agree....................................61%
Disagree....................................38
No opinion....................................1

Now, I'd like to know whether you agree or disagree with each of the following arguments against legalized state-sponsored gambling:

It encourages people who can least afford it to squander their money?

Agree....................................64%
Disagree....................................34
No opinion....................................2

It is immoral?

Agree....................................32%
Disagree....................................65
No opinion....................................3

It can make compulsive gamblers out of people who would never participate in illegal gambling?

Agree....................................58%
Disagree....................................40
No opinion....................................2

It opens the door for organized crime?

Agree....................................62%
Disagree....................................33
No opinion....................................5

What is your opinion of legalized betting on professional sports such as NFL football games and NBA basketball games—do you think it should be banned altogether, limited to a few states (as it is now), or allowed to expand into other states?

Banned altogether....................................48%
Limited....................................15

Expanded....................................33
No opinion....................................4

If additional states permit legalized betting on professional sports, do you think this would seriously affect the integrity and honesty of pro sports events, or not?

Yes....................................64%
No....................................31
No opinion....................................5

Note: The public's enthusiasm for expanding state-sponsored forms of gambling, strong in the 1980s, now shows signs of waning. A recent Gallup Poll finds a big decline in approval of legal betting on sports and marginal declines in approval of various games of chance—even the popular state lotteries. Support remains high for several forms of legalized gambling, but not without concern about the negative aspects.

The most acceptable forms of gambling, when offered by states as revenue raisers, are lotteries and bingo for cash prizes. Three quarters (75%) approve of state lotteries (down from 78% in 1989), and 72% support bingo (down from 75% in 1989). Least acceptable is betting on professional sports such as baseball, basketball, or football; indeed, approval of sports betting has fallen more sharply than any other game of chance.

The public divides about evenly on casino gambling and offtrack betting. Casino gambling on so-called riverboats, recently introduced in a few states along the Mississippi, rates as the most acceptable form (60% approve). Support for gambling at resort sites such as Las Vegas and Atlantic City, the traditional locale for casinos, is down slightly to 51%, from 55% in 1989. Recent proposals to institute casinos in urban centers such as Chicago, Providence, and Bridgeport are likely to meet significant public resistance: 40% approve, but 57% disapprove. Another 42% approve of casino gambling on Indian reservations (now legal in twenty states), while 51% disapprove.

A large majority agrees that state-sponsored gambling provides a financial boost to government coffers and regional economies. Sixty-four percent support the contention that legalized gambling creates jobs and helps stimulate the local economy, while 57% agree that it provides much-needed revenue for education and programs for senior citizens.

Practical reasons also make sense: 61% agree that people will gamble anyhow, so the state might as well take some of the revenue. What does not make sense to the public is the argument that legalized gambling will keep organized crime out of the business; only 37% agree with this justification, while 59% disagree.

By a nearly 2-to-1 margin, Americans think that legalized gambling encourages people who can least afford it to squander their money (64% agree versus 34% disagree). Similar percentages contend that it opens the door for organized crime (62%) and can make compulsive gamblers out of people who otherwise would never participate in illegal gambling (58%). And while immorality may once have been the traditional reason for opposing gambling, only one third (32%) takes this view today.

Moreover, only one third (33%) now approves of legalized betting on professional sports, down 9 percentage points from 1989 (42%). Nearly one half (48%) says that betting on NFL football and NBA basketball games should be banned altogether. At the other extreme, one third (33%) would like to see legal sports betting extended to other states, while only 15% think that it should be limited to just a few states, as it is now. More than six in ten (64%) believe that expanding sports betting to other states would seriously affect the integrity and honesty of pro sports events.

DECEMBER 11
SOMALIA

Interviewing Date: 12/4–6/92*
Survey #GO 322036

Do you approve or disapprove of the decision to send U.S. armed forces into the African nation of Somalia as part of a

*Gallup survey for CNN/*USA Today*

United Nations effort to deliver relief supplies there?

Approve	74%
Disapprove	21
No opinion	5

Do you think the role of U.S. troops in Somalia should be limited to delivering relief supplies there, or should they also attempt to bring a permanent end to the fighting in Somalia?

Should be limited	59%
Also attempt to end fighting	31
Neither (volunteered)	3
Other (volunteered)	2
No opinion	5

Regarding the situation in Somalia, how confident are you that each of the following will happen—very confident, somewhat confident, not too confident, or not at all confident:

The United States will be able to accomplish its goals with very few or no American casualties?

Very confident	27%
Somewhat confident	37
Not too confident	22
Not at all confident	10
No opinion	4

U.S. troops will be able to withdraw within a few months, as planned?

Very confident	18%
Somewhat confident	34
Not too confident	29
Not at all confident	14
No opinion	5

The U.S. effort will succeed in ending the widespread famine?

Very confident	14%
Somewhat confident	35
Not too confident	28
Not at all confident	18
No opinion	5

Other countries will do their fair share in supporting the UN effort?

Very confident	10%
Somewhat confident	33
Not too confident	34
Not at all confident	19
No opinion	4

Note: The recent announcement that U.S. armed forces were being sent to Somalia on a humanitarian mission is met with widespread approval by the American public. In the context of a United Nations effort to deliver relief supplies to the African country, three quarters (74%) surveyed in a new Gallup Poll approve of the decision to send U.S. troops.

Public opinion is split, however, on whether the mission will eventually succeed in ending the widespread famine in Somalia. One half (49%) is very or somewhat confident that our troops can bring an end to the famine, while 46% are not too or not at all confident that it can be accomplished.

Support for U.S. involvement is underscored by public perceptions that the military risks in Somalia are relatively slight. Nearly two thirds (64%) express at least some confidence that the United States will be able to accomplish its goals with very few or no American casualties. Optimism on this score is highest among young people.

A majority (52%) is very or somewhat confident that U.S. troops will be able to withdraw from the country within a few months, as planned. And according to a recent Gallup/*Newsweek* Poll, only 15% expect the operation to last one year or more.

Respondents are not strongly supportive of expanding the mission to achieve political goals. By a nearly 2-to-1 margin (59% versus 31%), they favor limiting the U.S. role to delivering relief supplies in Somalia, rather than attempting to bring a permanent end to the fighting there. Further inhibiting their willingness to commit U.S. forces to a more political and thus more dangerous role is the fact that a majority (53%) has little or no confidence that other countries will do their fair share in supporting the UN effort against the famine.

DECEMBER 16
GAMBLING: PARTICIPATION

Interviewing Date: 11/20–22/92
Survey #GO 322034

Please tell me whether or not you have done any of the following in the past twelve months:

Played bingo for money?

	Yes
National	9%

Selected National Trend

	Yes
1989	13%
1982	9
1950	12

Visited a casino?

	Yes
National	21%

Selected National Trend

	Yes
1989	20%
1984	18
1982	12

Bet on a horse race?

	Yes
National	12%

Selected National Trend

	Yes
1989	14%
1984	11
1982	9
1950	4
1938	10

Bought a state lottery ticket?

	Yes
National	56%

Selected National Trend

	Yes
1989	54%
1982	18

Bet on a professional sports event such as baseball, basketball, or football?

	Yes
National	12%

Selected National Trend

	Yes
1989	22%
1984	17
1982	15

Bet on a college sports event such as basketball or football?

	Yes
National	6%

Bet on a boxing match?

	Yes
National	6%

Participated in an office pool on the World Series, Superbowl, or other game?

	Yes
National	22%

Asked of those who purchased a state lottery ticket within the past twelve months: How much money do you usually spend each month on lottery tickets?

	1992	*1989*
$30 or more	9%	12%
$20–$29	11	11
$10–$19	19	18
$5–$9	17	24
$1–$4	28	22
Less than $1	14	11
No opinion	2	2
Mean	$28	$53
Median	5	5

Asked of those who gambled within the past twelve months: How often—once a week or more often, two to three times a month, once a month, once every few months, or less often—do you:

Visit a casino?

	1992	1989
Weekly or more	1%	1%
Monthly	2	1
Less often	19	18
No opinion	*	*
	22%	20%

*Less than 1%

Bet on a horse race?

	1992	1989
Weekly or more	1%	1%
Monthly	2	3
Less often	8	10
No opinion	1	*
	12%	14%

*Less than 1%

Buy a state lottery ticket?

	1992	1989
Weekly or more	19%	23%
Monthly	20	16
Less often	16	14
No opinion	1	1
	56%	54%

Bet on pro football during the season?

	1992	1989
Weekly or more	5%	6%
Monthly	3	5
Less often	4	11
No opinion	*	*
	12%	22%

*Less than 1%

Asked of those who gamble: How much do you, yourself, enjoy making bets—a lot, a little, not too much, or not at all?

	1992	1989
A lot	7%	7%
A little	22	27
Not too much	26	27
Not at all	45	38
No opinion	*	1

*Less than 1%

Also asked of those who gamble: Do you sometimes gamble more than you think you should?

	1992	1989
Yes	9%	10%
No	91	90
No opinion	*	*

*Less than 1%

Also asked of those who gamble: Has gambling ever been a source of problems within your family?

	1992	1989
Yes	5%	4%
No	95	96
No opinion	*	*

*Less than 1%

Note: Americans' mounting reservations about state-sponsored gambling, reported in a recent Gallup Poll, are reflected in their behavior. In five of seven activities tracked over time, there are at least modest declines from a 1989 Gallup survey in the number of people who report that they have gambled within the past twelve months. And the two areas that show slight gains—buying lottery tickets and visiting a casino—can be accounted for by the increased number of states where these gambling options are available: thirty-five states now have lotteries, and twenty-seven offer some form of casino gambling.

The parallel between levels of approval and participation seems most evident in the area of betting on professional sports. As previously reported, approval declined sharply from 1989 (42%) to 1992 (33%), statistically identical to the reported drop in actual gambling on pro sports: from more than one in five in 1989

(22%) to barely more than one in ten (12%) in the current survey.

The profusion of state lotteries is becoming counterproductive, especially in the context of recent hard economic times. In 1989, Americans reported an average of $53 per month spent on lottery tickets. Although the median amount ($5) has remained the same, in 1992 the average amount (or mean) spent has dropped to $28 per month. In addition to the monetary decline, the frequency of purchase has fallen off over the past three years. In 1989 at least 23% bought tickets weekly or more often; in 1992 only 19% do.

Pro football traditionally has attracted the most betting action, but it too reflects the general decline in sports wagering. Although the number of weekly bettors (5%) is about the same as in 1989 (6%), there has been a significant decline among more casual bettors, from 16% in 1989 to 7% today.

The joys of gambling are of limited appeal. While 29% enjoy betting at least somewhat, nearly one half (45%) do not enjoy it at all; an additional 26% derive not too much pleasure. Seven percent enjoy betting a lot, identical to the 1989 survey; however, the percentage of those who find at least some joy in betting has shrunk from 27% to 22%, and those who say that they take no pleasure whatsoever is up 7 points (45%) from 1989's 38%. In addition, 9% admit to gambling sometimes more than they should, but only 5% say that gambling has ever caused family problems.

DECEMBER 19
MOST ADMIRED MAN

Interviewing Date: 12/4–6/92*
Survey #GO 322036

What man whom you have heard or read about, living today in any part of the world, do you admire most? And who is your second choice?

*Gallup survey for CNN/*USA Today*

The following are listed in order of frequency of mention, with first and second choices combined.

George Bush
Bill Clinton
Ross Perot
Norman Schwarzkopf
Billy Graham
Pope John Paul II
Ronald Reagan
Colin Powell
Michael Jordan
Boris Yeltsin

Note: Despite the election returns, President George Bush wins top billing for the second consecutive year as Americans' "most admired" man. His most serious competition on Gallup's 1992 list comes from his election opponents: Bill Clinton ranks a close second, and Ross Perot comes in third.

This is not the first time that respondents have ranked an outgoing president as "most admired" above the president-elect. In 1988, Ronald Reagan topped the list, while Bush ranked third. In 1980 defeated President Jimmy Carter ranked second to Pope John Paul II but ahead of President-elect Reagan, who came in fifth.

Timing also can affect the results. Last year, former hostage Terry Anderson, just released by his captors, appeared in second place on the list. This year, Anderson does not receive a single mention. And 1991's newsmaker, Nelson Mandela, does not make the 1992 top ten.

The Gulf War seems to have created at least one hero with staying power. General Norman Schwarzkopf ranks near the top of the list for the second year in a row—in fourth place behind the presidential candidates. General Colin Powell, who did not make the top ten last year, appears in eighth place this year.

Perennial favorites include Billy Graham, Pope John Paul II, and Reagan. Meanwhile, Mikhail Gorbachev and Earvin "Magic" Johnson have dropped off the list, while Russian President Boris Yeltsin debuts in tenth place. The only active sports figure making the list this year is Michael Jordan, ranking ninth, who tied in tenth place last year with Jesse Jackson.

DECEMBER 19
MOST ADMIRED WOMAN

Interviewing Date: 12/4–6/92*
Survey #GO 322036

What woman whom you have heard or read about, living today in any part of the world, do you admire most? And who is your second choice?

The following are listed in order of frequency of mention, with first and second choices combined.

Barbara Bush
Mother Teresa of Calcutta
Margaret Thatcher
Hillary Clinton
Queen Elizabeth II
Oprah Winfrey
Katharine Hepburn
Jacqueline Kennedy Onassis
Diana, Princess of Wales
Elizabeth Taylor

Note: At the top of this year's list of "most admired" women are five world-class nominees: Barbara Bush, Mother Teresa, Margaret Thatcher, Hillary Clinton, and Queen Elizabeth. Completing the first ten are five preeminent celebrities: Oprah Winfrey; Diana, Princess of Wales; and three American icons: Katharine Hepburn, Jacqueline Kennedy Onassis, and Elizabeth Taylor.

While U.S. presidents frequently have headed Gallup's "most admired" lists over the years, very few First Couples have received double billing at the top. In fact, in addition to George and Barbara Bush in 1991 and 1992, only one other presidential couple has headed the list more than once: Ronald and Nancy Reagan in 1985 and 1987. Mrs. Reagan does not appear among the 1992 top ten, nor do two others from the 1991 list: Betty Ford and Sandra Day O'Connor.

*Gallup survey for CNN/*USA Today*

DECEMBER 23
PRESIDENT-ELECT CLINTON IN TRANSITION

Interviewing Date: 12/18–20/92*
Survey #GO 322037

Do you approve or disapprove of the way George Bush is handling his job as president?

Approve....................................49%
Disapprove....................................41
No opinion....................................10

Selected National Trend

	Approve	*Dis-approve*	*No opinion*
1992			
December 4–6	49%	7%	4%
November 20–22	43	46	11

Do you approve or disapprove of the way Bill Clinton is handling his presidential transition?

Approve....................................67%
Disapprove....................................15
No opinion....................................18

How would you rate the appointments that President-elect Bill Clinton has made so far to cabinet-level positions—would you say his choices have been outstanding, above average, average, below average, or poor?

Outstanding....................................8%
Above average....................................24
Average....................................43
Below average....................................5
Poor....................................4
No opinion....................................16

How would you rate the cabinet-level appointments that George Bush made during his years in office—would you say

*Gallup survey for CNN/*USA Today*

his choices were outstanding, above average, average, below average, or poor?

Outstanding 4%
Above average 19
Average 49
Below average 14
Poor...9
No opinion...5

Do you have a clear idea of what actions Bill Clinton plans to take to improve the economy when he takes office, or not?

Yes...33%
No...64
No opinion...3

As you may know, President-elect Clinton held a conference in Little Rock, Arkansas, this week where people from business, labor, and government came together to discuss the nation's economy. How closely did you happen to follow the news coverage of this economic conference—very closely, somewhat closely, not too closely, or not at all?

Very closely.......................................9%
Somewhat closely..............................26
Not too closely..................................36
Not at all..29
No opinion...*

*Less than 1%

	Very closely	*Somewhat closely*	*Not too closely*	*Not at all**
By Politics				
Clinton Voters	12%	36%	34%	18%
Bush Voters	9	28	37	26
Perot voters	4	28	33	35
Did Not Vote	6	11	38	44

*"No opinion"—at 1% or less—is omitted.

Asked of those who followed the conference very or somewhat closely: Do you think those who spoke at the conference represented many different political views, or did they generally share the same political views?

Represented different views..................49%
Shared same views 40
No opinion...11

Also asked of those who followed the conference very or somewhat closely: Do you think the conference participants found solutions to the economic problems facing the nation, or did they mostly talk about problems but come up with little in the way of solutions?

Found solutions 18%
Mostly talk.......................................72
No opinion...10

Also asked of those who followed the conference very or somewhat closely: Do you think Bill Clinton offers new and different ideas for improving the nation's economy, or does he represent the same approach you've heard from the Democrats in the past?

Offers new ideas 73%
Same approach..................................24
No opinion...3

Also asked of those who followed the conference very or somewhat closely: Did the economic conference give you more confidence in Bill Clinton's ability to handle the economy, less confidence, or did it not change your opinion much either way?

More confidence................................44%
Less confidence.................................6
Not change much...............................48
No opinion...2

Next, I'm going to read some proposals that have been made to reduce the federal budget deficit. For each one, please tell me whether you generally favor or oppose it:

Increasing the gasoline tax by 25 cents per gallon?

Favor 28%
Oppose...69
No opinion...3

Requiring employees to pay taxes on the health insurance provided by their employers?

Favor	28%
Oppose	66
No opinion	6

Raising taxes on Social Security benefits for people with incomes over $50,000?

Favor	62%
Oppose	35
No opinion	3

Which do you think should be more important for the new Clinton administration—reducing the deficit, even if it might slow down economic recovery; or stimulating economic recovery, even if it might mean less deficit reduction?

	Dec. 18–20	*Nov. 19–20*
Reduce deficit	33%	35%
Stimulate economy	57	53
Neither (volunteered)	2	2
No opinion	8	10

Note: One month before Inauguration Day, the public has good feelings about the incoming Clinton administration. According to a new Gallup Poll, two thirds (67%) now approve of the way that Bill Clinton is handling his presidential transition—a larger percentage (62%) than did so one month ago. So far, the public rates Clinton's appointments to cabinet-level positions more favorably than the appointments made by President George Bush. And while last week's economic conference in Little Rock did not capture the attention of the public at large, those who are aware of the event were generally left with a more positive impression of Clinton.

In regard to the cabinet, close to one third (32%) rates Clinton's choices as outstanding or above average; in contrast, only 9% characterize his choices as below average or poor. The public is far less charitable in its retrospective evaluations of Bush's cabinet-level appointments: as many rate the president's choices below average or poor (23%) as call them outstanding or above average (23%).

The economic conference in Little Rock was not a major news event to the great majority of Americans. Only one third (35%) say that they followed it very or somewhat closely. If one of Clinton's primary objectives for holding the conference was to impress Perot voters, he had only limited success. Most likely to have followed conference coverage at least somewhat closely were Clinton voters (48%), followed by Bush voters (37%), and then by Perot voters (32%).

Close to three fourths of those who followed the conference (72%) say that the event consisted mostly of talk about economic problems, with little in the way of solutions. The attentive public is divided on whether the speakers at the conference represented a true diversity of political viewpoints (49%) or essentially shared the same views (40%).

Despite its relatively small audience and the somewhat skeptical response from those who were attentive, on balance the economic conference was a political plus for Clinton. Among those who followed the conference coverage, 44% say that it improved their confidence in Clinton's ability to handle the economy, while only 6% say that it made them less confident in the president-elect. Seventy-three percent believe that Clinton offers new and different ideas for improving the economy, rather than more of the traditional Democratic solutions of the past (24%).

The public continues to believe that Clinton's top economic priority should be stimulating economic recovery (57%), rather than reducing the federal deficit (33%). Finding ways to finance his economic plan will be politically difficult for the incoming president. For example, increasing the gasoline tax by 25 cents per gallon is endorsed by only 28% of the public, while support for taxing employer-provided health-care benefits is no more popular (28% favor). While these broad-based taxes are widely opposed, respondents would support a more targeted tax increase: six in ten (62%) favor raising taxes on Social Security benefits for people with incomes over $50,000.

DECEMBER 25
LENO VERSUS LETTERMAN

Interviewing Date: 12/18–20/92*
Survey #GO 322037

Would you prefer to watch a late-night talk show hosted by Jay Leno or one hosted by David Letterman if they were both on television at the same time?

Leno	26%
Letterman	39
No difference (volunteered)	9
No opinion	26

	Leno	*Letter-man*	*No difference*	*No opinion*
By Age				
18–49 Years				
Men	26%	52%	9%	13%
Women	34	40	7	19
50 Years and Over				
Men	17	27	14	42
Women	22	26	10	42
By Late-Night Viewers				
Would Watch	35	47	11	7
Would Not Watch	16	29	7	48

Note: David Letterman beats "Tonight Show" host Jay Leno as America's choice for late-night talk show viewing. A new Gallup Poll shows that respondents favor Letterman over Leno by a 39%-to-26% margin; and among that smaller group who regularly watches talk shows after the week-night late news, his margin is even greater: 47% to 35%.

Letterman recently received a lucrative offer from CBS to defect from NBC and compete against Leno in the "Tonight Show" time slot. The relative popularity of the two late-night hosts has become a critical issue for NBC, which faces a choice of dropping Leno in favor of Letterman for the "Tonight Show" or putting its dominance of the late-night talk show franchise at risk.

The new Gallup Poll shows that Letterman's strength over Leno holds solid across most demographic groups but is particularly strong among younger (18 to 49) viewers most coveted by advertisers, and among men. Leno does better among older viewers and women.

*Gallup survey for CNN/*USA Today*

DECEMBER 30
CHARLES AND DIANA

Interviewing Date: 12/18–20/92*
Survey #GO 322037

There has been a lot of news lately from England about Prince Charles and Princess Diana. Please tell me whether you have a favorable or unfavorable opinion of:

Prince Charles?

Favorable	25%
Unfavorable	44
No opinion	31

Princess Diana?

Favorable	56%
Unfavorable	18
No opinion	26

As you may know, Charles and Diana have decided to separate. Who do you think is personally more responsible for what has happened—Prince Charles or Princess Diana?

	United States	*United Kingdom***
Charles	46%	44%
Diana	11	12
Both equally (volunteered)	17	34
Neither (volunteered)	5	†
No opinion	21	10

**Survey conducted December 11–13 by Social Surveys, Ltd. (Gallup UK/*Daily Telegraph*)
†Less than 1%

*Gallup survey for CNN/*USA Today*

In view of all that has happened, do you now think the British monarchy should be abolished, or not?

	United States	*United Kingdom**
Yes	31%	24%
No	45	69
No opinion	24	7

*Survey conducted December 11–13 by Social Surveys, Ltd. (Gallup UK/*Daily Telegraph*)

Note: Royals watchers on both sides of the Atlantic agree: Prince Charles is a spoilsport, while Princess Diana is charming. In a recent Gallup Poll, 46% of Americans pin the blame on Charles for the breakup of the fairy-tale marriage; only 11% blame Diana. A similar survey conducted in Great Britain earlier in the month shows nearly identical results, with 44% of the British blaming Charles and 12% Diana. In the United States, Diana's popularity far exceeds her husband's. More than one half of Americans (56%) has a favorable view of the princess of Wales; only 25% have a favorable view of her husband.

The recent spate of royal scandals may have the House of Windsor in turmoil, but support for the British monarchy as an institution persists. Forty-five percent of Americans—and 69% of Britons—think that the monarchy should carry on. Thirty-one percent of Americans and 24% of Britons think that it should be abolished.

DECEMBER 31
CASPAR WEINBERGER

Interviewing Date: 12/28/92*
Survey #GO 322038

*How closely have you followed news coverage of President Bush's pardoning of former Defense Secretary Caspar Weinberger and others linked to the Iran-*contra *affair—very closely, somewhat closely, not too closely, or not at all?*

Very closely	10%
Somewhat closely	33
Not too closely	32
Not at all	25
No opinion	*

*Less than 1%

*Asked of those who replied "very" or "somewhat closely": Do you approve or disapprove of President Bush's decision to issue a pardon so that Caspar Weinberger cannot be prosecuted for his alleged involvement in the Iran-*contra *affair?*

Approve	27%
Disapprove	54
No opinion	19

	Approve	*Dis-approve*	*No opinion*
By Politics			
Republicans	42%	39%	19%
Democrats	19	65	16
Independents	26	52	22

*Also asked of those who replied "very" or "somewhat closely": Which one of the following do you think is the main reason Bush decided to pardon Weinberger and the other Iran-*contra *defendants:*

To protect people he felt acted honorably and patriotically from unfair prosecution?	15%
To put the Iran-*contra* affair in the country's past?	21
To get back at Iran-*contra* prosecutor Lawrence Walsh for bringing charges against Weinberger right before the election?	2
To protect himself from legal difficulties or embarrassment resulting from his own role in the Iran-*contra* affair?	49

*Gallup survey for CNN/*USA Today*

Other (volunteered) 2
No opinion....................................... 11

	Protect people	Put in past	Get back at Walsh	Protect himself*
By Pardon Approval				
Those Who Approve......	34%	33%	2%	22%
Those Who Disapprove....	7	15	2	71

*"Other" and "no opinion"—at 6% or less—are omitted.

Note: President George Bush's Christmas Eve pardons of Caspar Weinberger and five other Iran-*contra* defendants are not playing well with the American people. Only one quarter (27%) of those who took part in a recent Gallup Poll approve of the Weinberger pardon, while over one half (54%) expresses disapproval. The timing of Bush's actions, however, appears to have dampened the public outcry. With the holiday season in full swing, less than one half (43%) reports having followed this news story closely.

The negative response was expected, given that six in ten adults (59%) polled by Gallup in November opposed clemency for the former secretary of defense. The level of public opposition to the Weinberger pardon seen today (54%) is comparable to that seen for the Nixon pardon in June 1976. At that time, 55% said that President Gerald Ford made the wrong decision in pardoning Richard Nixon for his Watergate misdeeds.

Respondents suspect that Bush, in pardoning the six Iran-*contra* figures, was motivated by self-interest rather than by compassion for the men involved. Overall, one half (49%) of adults believes that the president acted primarily to protect himself from legal difficulties or embarrassment resulting from his own role in the Iran-*contra* affair. Fewer than four in ten say that he acted to protect the defendants from unfair prosecution (15%) or to put the Iran-*contra* affair in the past (21%).

Those who disapprove of the pardons solidly believe that Bush was motivated by self-preservation (71%). On the other hand, those who approve are about equally likely to see compassion for the defendants (34%) and a desire to put the Iran-*contra* affair in the past (33%) as the major motivation.

INDEX

D

G

H

I

J

K

O

P

Q

R

S

T

Y